AF576760

Religious Liberty: Essays on First Amendment Law

The principle aim of the establishment and free exercise clauses of the First Amendment was to preclude congressional imposition of a national church. A balance was sought between states' rights and the rights of individuals to exercise their religious conscience. While the founding fathers were debating such issues, the potential for serious conflict was confined chiefly to variations among the dominant Christian sects. Today, issues of marriage, child bearing, cultural diversity, and corporate personhood, among others, suffuse constitutional jurisprudence, raising difficult questions regarding the nature of beliefs that qualify as "religious" and the reach of law into the realm in which those beliefs are held.

The essays collected in this volume explore in a selective and instructive way the intellectual and philosophical roots of religious liberty and contemporary confrontations between this liberty and the authority of secular law.

DANIEL N. ROBINSON is Fellow of the Faculty of Philosophy, University of Oxford. He has published in a wide variety of subjects, including moral philosophy, the philosophy of psychology, legal philosophy, the philosophy of the mind, intellectual history, legal history, and the history of psychology. He is a Senior Fellow of Brigham Young University's Wheatley Institution. In 2011 he received the Gittler Award from the American Psychological Association for significant contributions to the philosophical foundations of Psychology.

RICHARD N. WILLIAMS is Professor of Psychology and founding Director of the Wheatley Institution at Brigham Young University. Most recently, he has co-edited with Daniel N. Robinson, *The American Founding: Its Intellectual and Moral Framework, Continuum*, and *Scientism: The New Orthodoxy*, Bloomsbury. He has published four other co-authored or co-edited books and more than seventy professional papers on a variety of topics dealing with psychology, and issues of human agency, morality, and religion.

Religious Liberty

Essays on First Amendment Law

Edited by

DANIEL N. ROBINSON AND
RICHARD N. WILLIAMS

CAMBRIDGE
UNIVERSITY PRESS

CAMBRIDGE
UNIVERSITY PRESS

University Printing House, Cambridge CB2 8BS, United Kingdom

Cambridge University Press is part of the University of Cambridge.

It furthers the University's mission by disseminating knowledge in the pursuit of education, learning and research at the highest international levels of excellence.

www.cambridge.org
Information on this title: www.cambridge.org/9781107147607

First published 2016

A catalogue record for this publication is available from the British Library

Library of Congress Cataloging-in-Publication data
Names: Robinson, Daniel N., 1937– editor. | Williams, Richard N., 1950– editor.
Title: Religious liberty : essays on First Amendment law /
Daniel N. Robinson and Richard Williams, eds.
Description: New York : Cambridge University Press, 2016. |
Includes bibliographical references and index.
Identifiers: LCCN 2016021101 | ISBN 9781107147607 (hardback)
Subjects: LCSH: Freedom of religion–United States. |
Liberty of conscience–United States.
Classification: LCC KF4783.R436 2016 | DDC 342.7308/52–dc23
LC record available at https://lccn.loc.gov/2016021101

ISBN 978-1-107-14760-7 Hardback

Contents

Contributors

AKHIL REED AMAR was formerly the Southmayd Professor of Law at Yale Law School, and was named Sterling Professor of Law in 2008. A *Legal Affairs* poll placed Amar among the top twenty contemporary US legal thinkers. He was elected a Fellow of the American Academy of Arts and Sciences in 2007.

HADLEY ARKES is Edward N. Ney Professor of Jurisprudence and American Institutions at Amherst College, where he has taught since 1966. His works draw on political philosophers from Aristotle through the US Founding Fathers, Lincoln, and contemporary authors and jurists. Arkes serves on the advisory board and writes for *First Things*, an ecumenical journal that focuses on encouraging a "religiously informed public philosophy for the ordering of society."

GERARD V. BRADLEY is a professor of law at the University of Notre Dame, where he teaches legal ethics and constitutional law. At Notre Dame, he directs (with John Finnis) the Natural Law Institute and co-edits *The American Journal of Jurisprudence*, an international forum for legal philosophy. His most recent books are an edited collection of essays titled, *Challenges to Religious Liberty in the Twenty-First Century* (Cambridge University Press in 2012), *Essays on Law, Religion, and Morality* and *Unquiet Americans: U.S. Catholics and the Common Good.*

THOMAS GRIFFITH is a federal judge on the United States Court of Appeals for the District of Columbia Circuit. Before his appointment to the bench he was Senate Legal Counsel, the chief legal officer of the United States Senate. In November of 2011, Griffith was included on *The New Republic*'s list of Washington's most powerful, but least famous, people.

MICHAEL P. MORELAND is Professor of Law and Vice Dean of the Villanova faculty. He received his B.A. in philosophy from the University of Notre Dame, his M.A. and Ph.D. in theological ethics from Boston College, and his J.D. from the University of Michigan Law School. Before coming to Villanova, he served as Associate Director for Domestic Policy at the White House under President George W. Bush.

DANIEL N. ROBINSON is a Distinguished Professor, Emeritus of Philosophy at Georgetown University and a Fellow of the Faculty of Philosophy at Oxford University. He is on the Board of Consulting Scholars of Princeton University's James Madison Program in American Ideals and Institutions, and is a Senior Fellow of BYU's Wheatley Institution. In 2011, he received the Joseph B. Gittler Award from the American Psychological Association for significant contributions to the philosophical foundations of psychology.

BRETT G. SCHARFFS is Francis R. Kirkham Professor of Law and associate dean for Research and Academic Affairs at the J. Reuben Clark Law School of Brigham Young University (BYU), where he is also associate director of the International Center for Law and Religion Studies. Scharffs has largely focused on international law and religious law issues. He has served as chair of the law and religion section of the Association of American Law Schools.

ROGER SCRUTON is an English philosopher and barrister. He specializes in aesthetics. He has written over thirty books, including *Art and Imagination* (1974), *The Meaning of Conservatism* (1980), *Sexual Desire* (1986), *The Philosopher on Dover Beach* (1990), *The Aesthetics of Music* (1997), *Beauty* (2009), *How to Think Seriously About the Planet: The Case for an Environmental Conservatism* (2012), *Our Church* (2012), and *How to be a Conservative* (2014).

Foreword

It is an ancient question at least as old as Aeschylus and Sophocles: What role should religion play in public life? The Framers of the American republic thought the matter of such importance that they addressed the issue in the Bill of Rights to the Constitution: "Congress shall make no law respecting an establishment of religion, or prohibiting the free exercise thereof."[1] Beyond the importance of the Religion Clauses, however, there has been little agreement about their meaning since ratification. As my former colleague on the US Court of Appeals Michael McConnell points out:

> The religion provision is unique among the rights-protecting provisions of the Constitution in that it has a dual aspect: It forbids both laws 'respecting an establishment of religion' and laws 'prohibiting the free exercise thereof.' What is the relationship between these clauses? Surprisingly, more than 200 years after those 16 words were added to the Constitution, that basic question remains contested.[2]

But is it really surprising? After all, the meanings of the Religion Clauses don't seem obvious. What is meant by "an establishment of religion?" Is it clear when government is "prohibiting the free exercise" of religion? Madison originally proposed protection for "the full and equal rights of conscience."[3] Was that simply another way to say "the free exercise of religion," or did the ratified language mean something narrower? Further complicating the matter, any effort to understand the meaning of the Religion Clauses must look at two periods of time: the initial ratification of the First Amendment, which was a limitation on what Congress could do regarding religion, and the ratification

[1] U.S. Const., amend. 1.

[2] Michael W. McConnell, John H. Garvey, and Thomas C. Berg, *Religion and the Constitution*, 3rd Edition (New York: Aspen Publishers, 2011), p. 3.

[3] *Annals of Congress*, 1789, 434.

of the Fourteenth Amendment, which arguably applied the First Amendment to the states at a time when the view of state government and its relationship to religion had changed.[4]

Even the most casual study of American history shows that the meaning of the Religion Clauses has vexed judges, scholars, politicians, opinion leaders, and citizens for decades. Debates over their history, purpose, and philosophical underpinnings have been regular features of public life of the United States. But these debates have taken on a new urgency as religious life in American society undergoes dramatic change. Although some diversity of religious views was present at the founding and no doubt informed the original purposes of the Religion Clauses, the mainstream Protestantism that played such a dominant role in American life and the founding occupies more narrow ground in an American citizenry of the twenty-first century that is increasingly characterized by pluralism. In fact, the fastest growing group is those not affiliated with a religion or who reject belief in the divine altogether. The percentage of those reporting no religious preference more than tripled from 5–7% of adults who reached adulthood before 1960 to 20–30% among those who reached adulthood in the 1990s and 2000s.[5] In 2012, one-third of adults under thirty identified as religiously unaffiliated.[6] This increased religious pluralism in American society is thus set against the backdrop of an even more dramatic change two centuries in the making: a secular age. As described by Charles Taylor, we have moved "from a society where belief in God is unchallenged ... to one in which it is understood to be one option among others, and frequently not the easiest to embrace." This "change ... takes us from a society in which it was virtually impossible not to believe in God, to one in which faith, even for the staunchest believer, is one human possibility among others ... Belief in God is no longer axiomatic."[7]

Shifts in political ideals also contribute to changing views as to the place of religion in society. As McConnell explains, where once "[e]quality under the law meant that our rights as citizens did not depend on belonging to the right religion ... [t]oday there is a widespread sense not only that the government should be neutral, tolerant, and egalitarian, but so should all of us, and so should our private associations."[8] In a society where open-mindedness is glorified, faith and conviction in religious tradition are more often depreciated

4 Akhil Reed Amar, *The Bill of Rights: Creation and Reconstruction* (New Haven: Yale University Press, 1998), p. 42

5 Robert D. Putnam and David E. Campbell, *American Grace: How Religion Divides and Unites Us* (New York: Simon & Schuster, 2010), pp. 122–25

6 Pew Research and Public Life Project, "'Nones' on the Rise," Pew Research Center, October 9, 2012, accessed January 2, 2015, www.pewforum.org/2012/10/09/nones-on-the-rise/.

7 Charles Taylor, *A Secular Age* (Cambridge: Belknap Press, 2007), p. 3.

8 Michael W. McConnell, "Why is Religious Liberty 'The First Freedom?'," *Cardozo L. Rev.* 21, (2000), 1243, 1259.

and undervalued. Replacing a pluralistic understanding of neutrality is a search for a common denominator, where space is made for a multitude of different views and practices, where religion is set aside as "particularistic" and thus non-neutral.[9]

Into this fray over the role of religion in American life today, the Wheatley Institution at Brigham Young University offers this collection of essays by scholars who push back against the efforts of secularists to devalue religion and deny its benefits to society at large. They ask us to think seriously about what religious liberty should look like today. These essays are noteworthy not only for their distinguished authors, but for the breadth of their analysis, which draws upon case law, intellectual history, and philosophical analysis to make the argument that religious liberty is a distinctive freedom that remains vital to the well-being of the Republic constructed by the Framers of the Religion Clauses.

These authors reject the notion (that finds some support in recent decisions of the Supreme Court) that religious expression is but a subset of a larger category of freedom of expression that lacks any separate ground to justify its encouragement or protection. They also take on the more ominous suggestion advanced by some respected academics that there is nothing about religion that merits any protection at all.[10] In this regard, these essays are of a piece with these words from Barack Obama:

> [S]ecularists are wrong when they ask believers to leave their religion at the door before entering into the public square. Frederick Douglass, Abraham Lincoln, William Jennings Bryan, Dorothy Day, Martin Luther King – indeed, the majority of great reformers in American history – were not only motivated by faith, but repeatedly used religious language to argue for their cause. So to say that men and women should not inject their 'personal morality' into public policy debates is a practical absurdity. Our law is by definition a codification of morality, much of it grounded in the Judeo-Christian tradition.[11]

As President Obama notes, religious expression and the religious life from which it springs have been part of the warp and woof of the fabric of the American experience. The Religion Clauses of the First Amendment not only recognize the important role that religion has played in the nation's public life, but they seek to guarantee space for a continuation of that role even as the religious landscape of the country continues to change. These essays explore the basis for that understanding, arguing against those who assert that the Clauses have outlived their usefulness.

[9] *Ibid.* at 1262.

[10] See, *e.g.*, Brian Leiter, *Why Tolerate Religion?* (Princeton: Princeton University Press, 2012); Micah Schwartzman, "What If Religion Is Not Special?," *University of Chicago Law Review*. 79 (2012), 1351–1427.

[11] Barack Obama, Call to Renewal Keynote Address (June 28, 2006), available at http://obamaspeeches.com/081-Call-to-Renewal-Keynote-Address-Obama-Speech.htm.

The timing of this publication is timely as fewer of today's Americans understand the first principles of religious belief and practice and their place in the constitutional structure. This volume is a significant contribution to improve understanding of the reasons for religious liberty and its importance to the well-being of the Republic and assuring its future vitality.

Thomas Griffith

Introduction

Daniel N. Robinson

> *I contemplate with sovereign reverence that act of the whole American people which declared that their legislature should 'make no law respecting an establishment of religion, or prohibiting the free exercise thereof,' thus building a wall of separation between church and State.* (Thomas Jefferson, Letter to the Danbury Baptist Association, 1802)

On June 14, 2015, a number of conferences and special programs were held to celebrate the 800th anniversary of Magna Carta, signed at Runnymeade, and marking a significant chapter in the history of political liberty. The charter itself would bear the seal of King John – *bad* King John – but, alas, not his fidelity, for the very terms of the document were systematically violated from the first. Nonetheless, the document itself was a successful challenge to the presumption of absolute rule. Credit duly noted, it was not born full blown from the collective brow of self-interested barons.

The history leading to Runnymeade is complex and far beyond the aims of this introduction. It is sufficient to look back to the celebrated conflict between Thomas Becket (1118–1170), Archbishop of Canterbury, and the widely resented King, Henry II. A major source of the conflict was the arrogation by the King of the right to prosecute clergy in secular courts. Becket claimed that the clergy stood apart from the reach of secular powers, and that only the Church could judge them for crimes. Henry's counter relied on willingness of the previous archbishop, Theobald of Bec, who had admitted that the English custom was for secular courts to try clerks accused of crimes. Henry II's *Constitution of Clarendon* (1164) challenged the independence of the clergy and required an allegiance to the Crown, even in defiance of Rome. Becket would have none of it and, at the hands of four Knights, would lose his head and his life in Canterbury Cathedral. Henry's youngest son, King John, carried on the family tradition of royal overreach only to face formidable baronial power at Runnymeade.

Magna Carta contains sixty-three provisions, many of them of merely local and of dated consequence, covering such momentous issues as fishing rights in the Thames ("23. All fish weirs (kidelli) on the Thames and the Medway and throughout England are to be entirely dismantled, save on the sea coast"). Clearly, the document was the work of a successor to the Archbishop of Canterbury, Stephen Langton. Among its diverse contents, it is the very first provision that summons attention here:

> In the first place we have granted to God, and by this our present charter confirmed for us and our heirs forever that the English Church shall be free, and shall have her rights entire, and her liberties inviolate; and we will that it be thus observed; which is apparent from this that the freedom of elections, which is reckoned most important and very essential to the English Church, we, of our pure and unconstrained will, did grant, and did by our charter confirm and did obtain the ratification of the same from our lord, Pope Innocent III, before the quarrel arose between us and our barons: and this we will observe, and our will is that it be observed in good faith by our heirs forever. We have also granted to all freemen of our kingdom, for us and our heirs forever, all the underwritten liberties, to be had and held by them and their heirs, of us and our heirs forever.

We see here in 1215 that Magna Carta begins with an acknowledged wall of separation between church and state, this some six centuries before Jefferson's reassuring letter to the Baptists of Connecticut. As has been observed often, the provision grew out of attempts by both Church and Crown to gain controlling power over valued assets: land, taxing authority, rank, and standing. Less noted, however, are the doctrinal foundations on which men such as Becket relied. No less an authority than Jesus Christ had stipulated that Caesar be given his due, but that what is owed to God is different – and the two must never be confused (Mark 12:17). Also, in Romans 13, the Apostle Paul requires obedience to secular authority, for it was God's creation and warrants fidelity within its proper sphere.

As Magna Carta begins with the immunity of religion to secular intrusions, so does the First Amendment of the U.S. Constitution forbid secular authority from imposing religious orthodoxy. This, by today's understanding, illustrates one of the "rights" comprising that "Bill of Rights" required if all the colonies were to ratify the new Constitution. It was on August 15, 1789, that the House of Representatives struggled further with the need for and the contents of a "Bill of Rights."

Who, after all, would oppose the clear statement of such rights? As it happens, there had been a number of principled grounds on which to question the enumeration of basic rights. Might the very act suggest that the rights in question are (merely) political? Might it be assumed that they are somehow granted as opposed to being endowed, as stated in the *Declaration*? Also, might the delineation of rights be extended to absurdity? On this point, one member of the house during the deliberations, Mr. Sedgwick, argued that the very statement of something as obvious as freedom of speech would lead to viewing rights as trifling. To him, the effort was all too labored. Once freedom of speech is guaranteed, freedom of assembly is logically entailed. In reply, Mr. Benson contended that the wording was more or less a reminder that the Government not overstep its authorized bounds. Sedgwick's rejoinder remains a classic:

> Mr. Sedgwick replied, that if the committee were governed by that general principle, they might have gone into a very lengthy enumeration of rights; they might have declared that a man should have a right to wear his hat if he pleased; that he might get up when he pleased, and go to bed when he thought proper; but he would ask the gentleman whether he thought it necessary to enter these trifles in a declaration of rights, in a Government where none of them were intended to be infringed.

The rest, as the expression goes, is history: the troubled, often elegant, frequently confusing history of First Amendment jurisprudence.

Over and against these reservations were challenges from the Anti-Federalists, so convinced that the Constitution left far too much room for a power-seeking executive in charge of an unopposable national government. At first tepid, but then strongly encouraged by Jefferson and others, James Madison took it upon himself to draft a large number of amending clauses. After due consideration by State houses, the House of Representatives now would address a more economical collection of amendments. Thus did the House grapple with the promise that, "The freedom of speech and of the press, and the right of the people peaceably to assemble and consult for their common good, and to apply to the Government for redress of grievances, shall not be infringed."

There was a robust history behind these considerations. From the earliest colonial period, settlers in the new world had made provision for the public support of religion. Of the thirteen charters establishing the original colonies – the earliest being Virginia (1606) and the latest New Jersey (1702) – a number identified a specific form of religious worship to be supported. Virginia, New York, Maryland, North Carolina, and South Carolina were officially Anglican. Massachusetts, Connecticut, and New Hampshire were Congregational. Article XXXVIII of the Charter of South Carolina (1663) proclaims "That all persons and religious societies who acknowledge that there is one God, and a future state of rewards and punishments, and that God is publicly to be worshipped, shall be freely tolerated. The Christian Protestant religion shall be deemed, and is hereby constituted and declared to be, the established religion of this State." Several colonies that adopted a specific confession were nonetheless at pains to spare those of a different persuasion any civic or financial burden. Thus, North Carolina:

> Article XXXIV. That there shall be no establishment of any one religious church or denomination in this State, in preference to any other; neither shall any person, on any presence whatsoever, be compelled to attend any place of worship contrary to his own faith or judgment, nor be obliged to pay, for the purchase of any glebe, or the building of any house of worship, or for the maintenance of any minister or ministry, contrary

to what he believes right, or has voluntarily and personally engaged to perform; but all persons shall be at liberty to exercise their own mode of worship (1663).

New Hampshire records its respect for the unalienable right of conscience, but then sets the qualification for public office quite narrowly:

Article V. Every individual has a natural and unalienable right to worship GOD according to the dictates of his own conscience and reason; and no person shall be hurt, molested, or restrained in his person, liberty, or estate for worshipping God in the manner most agreeable to the dictates of his own conscience, or for his religious profession, sentiments, or persuasion; provided he doth not disturb the public peace or disturb others in their religious worship.

Senate. Provided, nevertheless, That no person shall be capable of being elected a senator who is not of the Protestant religion ... House of Representatives. Every member of the house of representatives ... shall be of the Protestant religion ... (1639)

The Founding generation did indeed face sectarian issues, but such internecine conflicts among Episcopal, Presbyterian, and Congregationalist were of a nature that rendered the guidance and constraints of the Federal Constitution fairly transparent. The point of the First Amendment was to preclude the imposition of a national church. It remained for the constituent states to sort out the details judged to be right for their residents. The rejection of England's "Test acts" and the long and often bloody history of religious intolerance had hardened the resolve of the Founding generation against intrusion by the national government into this vital and combustible sphere of private and civic life. Much closer to home, James Madison had witnessed the intolerance permitted under the banner of Virginia's quasi-official religion. In a letter to William Bradford (January 24, 1774), he writes:

I want again to breathe your free Air. I expect it will mend my Constitution & confirm my principles. I have indeed as good an Atmosphere at home as the Climate will allow: but have nothing to brag of as to the State and Liberty of my Country ... There are at this [time?] in the adjacent County not less than 5 or 6 well-meaning men in close [Gaol] for publishing their religious Sentiments which in the main are very orthodox. I have neither patience to hear talk or think of anything relative to this matter, for I have squabbled and scolded abused and ridiculed so long about it, [to so lit]tle purpose that I am without common patience. So I [leave you] to pity me and pray for Liberty of Conscience [to revive among us].

Perhaps the most influential commentator of the age was the redoubtable Thomas Paine, his best-seller, *Common Sense*, appearing in 1776. On religious liberty, Paine could not be clearer:

As to religion, I hold it to be the indispensable duty of every government, to protect all conscientious professors thereof, and I know of no other business which government hath to do therewith ... Suspicion is the companion of mean souls, and the bane of all good society. For myself, I fully and conscientiously believe, that it is the will of the Almighty, that there should be a diversity of religious opinions among us: it affords a larger field for our Christian kindness. Were we all of one way of thinking, our religious dispositions would want matter for probation; and on this liberal principle, I look on the various denominations among us, to be like children of the same family, differing only, in what is called, their Christian names.

Think of it: Various denominations differing solely in their Christian names, as might brothers and sisters in the same family. The current situation in the United States is so utterly different. Issues of marriage, child bearing, cultural diversity, corporate personhood – the list is long – have leaked into every joint of our constitutional jurisprudence and have raised the most vexing questions regarding the nature of beliefs that qualify as "religious," and the reach of law into the realm in which those beliefs are held. Might Madison's judgment be different in light of such diversity and complexity? Actually, there is remarkable stability in his position over a period of decades. The Madison of 1774 reappears unchanged on this matter in 1789. We find him once again in the much altered United States of 1832, just four years before his death at age 85, displaying consistency and resolve. Writing to Rev. Adams, he says:

It may not be easy, in every possible case, to trace the line of separation between the rights of religion and the Civil authority with such distinctness as to avoid collisions & doubts on unessential points. The tendency to a usurpation on one side or the other, or to a corrupting coalition or alliance between them, will be best guarded agst. by an entire abstinance of the Govt. from interference in any way whatever, beyond the necessity of preserving public order, & protecting each sect agst. trespasses on its legal rights by others.

For all this resolve to oppose interference in any way whatever, Madison's protective barrier, as with Jefferson's wall of separation, proved to be rather porous. The pores would then become veritable channels with the ratification of the Fourteenth Amendment 1868. Thus amended, the Constitution orders that, "No State shall make or enforce any law which shall abridge the privileges or immunities of citizens of the United States; nor shall any State deprive any person of life, liberty, or property, without due process of law; nor deny to any person within its jurisdiction the equal protection of the laws."

The principal and intended effect of the Amendment was to eradicate those laws of local enclaves (including entire states) that would restrict or deny rights conferred or protected by the Federal Constitution. It was to secure for a now freed slave population protections that would reach them wherever they lived, including and especially in the recalcitrant south. "States' Rights," so jealously guarded at the time of the Founding, proved to be impediments to those aspirations over which a civil war had been waged. Initially conceived as a remedy for the lingering effects of slavery, the Fourteenth Amendment was progressively stretched to identify and prevent any and every official form of selective treatment. As for religion – either writ large or religion in the narrowest sectarian sense – it could not elude the reach of the Amendment. The extent of that reach was and remains uncertain.

The Constitution was a century old before the First Amendment was applied to religious liberty. The case was *Reynolds* v. *United States* (98 U.S. 145, 1878) and the question pertained to polygamy. Reynolds, a member of the Mormon faith and a resident of the Utah Territory, was charged with the crime of polygamy. He understood Mormon teachings not only as permitting but as encouraging polygamy and argued that it was clearly covered by the anti-establishment clause of the First Amendment. Speaking for a unanimous court, Chief Justice Waite ruled that,

> ... The statute immediately under consideration is within the legislative power of Congress. It is constitutional and valid as prescribing a rule of action for all those residing in the Territories, and in places over which the United States have exclusive control. This being so, the only question which remains is, whether those who make polygamy a part of their religion are excepted from the operation of the statute. If they are, then those who do not make polygamy a part of their religious belief may be found guilty and punished, while those who do, must be acquitted and go free. This would be introducing a new element into criminal law. Laws are made for the government of actions, and while they cannot interfere with mere religious belief and opinions, they may with practices ... Can a man excuse his practices to the contrary because of his religious belief? To permit this would be to make the professed doctrines of religious belief superior to the law of the land, and in effect to permit every citizen to become a law unto himself. Government could exist only in name under such circumstances ...

The distinction between a "mere" religious belief and those actions compelled by sincere belief must raise fundamental questions as to what constitutes the establishment of norms favoring one religion over another. However, for the full century from the founding to *Reynolds* (1878), the Establishment Clause had not reached the Supreme Court bar. Then, between *Reynolds* and *Cantwell* v. *Connecticut* (310 U.S. 296, 1940), a span of sixty more years was marked by comparable silence. In *Cantwell*, Jesse Cantwell and his son, both Jehovah's Witnesses, had distributed religious materials door-to-door in a predominantly Roman Catholic neighborhood. Angry targets of the Cantwells' religious appeal complained, and the Cantwells were charged with a breach of the peace. The Supreme Court ruled unanimously that the charge violated the First Amendment. Although they acknowledged that maintaining public order is a valid state interest, the Court determined that the aims of public order cannot restrict the free communication of views, including religious views. Apparently knocking on the doors of private residences and distributing literature – though going beyond a "mere" belief – was understood to be protected.

Uncertainties prevail when complexities multiply. In *Everson v. Board of Education of the Township of Ewing* (330 U.S. 1, 1947), we find a public school system compensating families for the cost of transporting their children to a local Catholic school, which provided supplementary instruction. Delivering the opinion of the Court, Justice Black summarizes the gravamen of the issues and the test New Jersey had to pass for the actions on which the lawsuit was initially based:

A New Jersey statute authorizes its local school districts to make rules and contracts for the transportation of children to and from schools. The appellee, a township board of education, acting pursuant to this statute, authorized reimbursement to parents of money expended by them for the bus transportation of their children on regular busses operated by the public transportation system. Part of this money was for the payment of transportation of some children in the community to Catholic parochial schools ... The structure of our government has, for the preservation of civil liberty, rescued the temporal institutions from religious interference. On the other hand, it has secured religious liberty from the invasion of the civil authority. The "establishment of religion" clause of the First Amendment means at least this: neither a state nor the Federal Government can set up a church. Neither can pass laws which aid one religion, aid all religions, or prefer one religion over another. Neither can force nor influence a person to go to or to remain away from church against his will or force him to profess a belief or disbelief in any religion ... The First Amendment has erected a wall between church and state. That wall must be kept high and impregnable. We could not approve the slightest breach. New Jersey has not breached it here.

Over the years, a number of litmus tests have been fashioned by the Court to impose rhyme, if not always reason, on its findings. One of these, the *Lemon test*, was first articulated in the 1971 case of *Lemon* v. *Kurtzman* (403 U.S. 602). The syllabus in *Lemon* summarizes the main points:

Rhode Island's 1969 Salary Supplement Act provides for a 15% salary supplement to be paid to teachers in nonpublic schools at which the average per-pupil expenditure on secular education is below the average in public schools. Eligible teachers must teach only courses offered in the public schools, using only materials used in the public schools, and must agree not to teach courses in religion. A three-judge court found that about 25% of the State's elementary students attended nonpublic schools, about 95% of whom attended Roman Catholic affiliated schools, and that to date about 250 teachers at Roman Catholic schools are the sole beneficiaries under the Act. The court found that the parochial school system was "an integral part of the religious mission of the Catholic Church," and held that the Act fostered "excessive entanglement" between government and religion, thus violating the Establishment Clause.

The *Lemon* test raises three challenges: Does a law or practice have a bona fide secular purpose? Is its principal effect one of promoting or restricting religion? Does the law or practice measurably entangle religion and government? In *Lemon*, the practice under scrutiny called for the payment for instruction given to public school students by faculty drawn from a neighboring Roman Catholic school. The course material was entirely secular and there was no evidence of actual or implied religious content. Nevertheless, Chief Justice Burger, speaking for the Court, noted that:

The language of the Religion Clauses of the First Amendment is, at best, opaque, particularly when compared with other portions of the Amendment. Its authors did not simply prohibit the establishment of a state church or a state religion, an area history shows they regarded as very important and fraught with great dangers. Instead, they commanded that there should be "no law respecting an establishment of religion." A law may be one "respecting" the forbidden objective while falling short of its total realization. A law "respecting" the proscribed result, that is, the establishment of religion, is not always easily identifiable as one violative of the Clause. A given law might not establish a state religion, but nevertheless be one "respecting" that end in the sense of being a step that could lead to such establishment, and hence offend the First Amendment.

Constitutions are at a minimum words: sometimes written on a page, at other times created by judges as *lex dicta* and then stabilized by a deference to precedent. Accordingly, constitutions not only allow but unavoidably confront the vagaries of interpretation as novel cases and claims make their seasonal appearance. On some accounts, this establishes that the original constitutive principles were "organic" from the outset, such that what might have been decisive in 1800 may be impracticable – even unintelligible – in 2000. On other accounts, the constitutive principles are abiding, the task at law now requiring careful and apolitical judgment based on a competent grasp of what the principle covers alone. The criterion of "original intent" in this understanding calls not for the mind reader but for a jurist capable of identifying the intent of the principle, whatever might have been in the mind of the one who framed it. "Congress shall make no law ..." means what it says, full stop. But then how is the "establishment" of a specific religious precept to be understood? Suppose Congress authorized per capita subsidies for every member of every identifiable religious denomination, showing no favoritism toward any, while making similar amounts available to atheists and agnostics. Would this breach the wall? Is even-handedness ("fairness") a necessary or sufficient rite of passage for the civic authority to enter the religious realm?

For there to be an attempt to establish or favor religion, there must be an agreement on what qualifies as a religion. Taking history and cultural anthropology as guides, there is little firm ground on which to rule out any community of shared convictions regarding powers, entities, or figures regarded as divine. Even the qualification of "community" raises questions about conditioning a right on the size of a group that claims it. And is there a test to assess the degree of "sharing" in order to enjoy the benefits accorded to a "community"?

One recalls in this connection the first of the public lectures John Ruskin gave on ancient Greek mythology. The lectures would be published in 1893 under the title *Queen of the Air*, treating a Victorian audience to the subtle and pervasive influence the gods of Olympus had on the very character of the Hellenic age. Ruskin begins his address with a disarming passage:

> We cannot justly interpret the religion of any people, unless we are prepared to admit that we ourselves, as well as they, are liable to error in matters of faith; and that the convictions of others, however singular, may in some points have been well founded, while

our own, however reasonable, may be in some particulars mistaken. You must forgive me, therefore, for not always distinctively calling the creeds of the past "superstition," and the creeds of the present day "religion"; as well as for assuming that a faith now confessed may sometimes be superficial, and that a faith long forgotten may once have been sincere.

A version of this perspective is apparent in the recent decision of the Supreme Court in *Burwell* v. *Hobby Lobby Stores*. Delivering the majority opinion, Justice Alito underscored the complex relationship between the moral and legal precepts at work, as well as the Court's self-imposed silence on the credibility or rational grounding of religious convictions. The plaintiffs, he notes, raise,

> ... a difficult and important question of religion and moral philosophy, namely, the circumstances under which it is immoral for a person to perform an act that is innocent in itself but that has the effect of enabling or facilitating the commission of an immoral act by another. It is not for the Court to say that the religious beliefs of the plaintiffs are mistaken or unreasonable ... The Court's "narrow function ... is to determine" whether the plaintiffs' asserted religious belief reflects "an honest conviction."

Would such a narrow function be adopted in applying First Amendment jurisprudence to cases of honor killings, slavery, female genital mutilation, polygamy, animal sacrifice? These and scores of other practices fall far from a cultural domain shaped either by Hellenism or by Judeo-Christian teaching. Nonetheless, they form part of the bedrock of contemporary religious communities, some extremely populous and even present in the United States, and all claiming to reflect "an honest conviction." Rereading the Madison of 1832 in this light, one asks what points he might take to be "unessential" when he says that, "It may not be easy, in every possible case, to trace the line of separation between the rights of religion and the Civil authority with such distinctness as to avoid collisions & doubts on unessential points."

Where is the line to be drawn when the points at issue are taken to be essential by both religion and the civil authority? Moreover, does Justice Alito's reference to acts judged to be "immoral" implicitly endorse the view that it is solely or chiefly by way of religious convictions that moral ascriptions come to deserve special consideration? Surely there are non-religious grounds on which to assess the moral quality of an act.

These and related matters highlight the vexing questions that guided the choice of topics and authors featured here. The original plan called for a series of public lectures by the contributors, which later expanded to full chapters. Complete and ungrudging financial support by the Wheatley Institution of Brigham Young University made the entire project possible. The contributors, whether drawn from law, intellectual history, political science, or religion have all achieved standing for their scholarly contributions. Each arrived, if not with a firmly settled position on the issues addressed, then surely with a position on what the reasonable options are. By way of their words, readers are not told what to think, but are guided as to what to think *about* when considering how First Amendment jurisprudence helps or hinders the more noble and hopeful aspirations of the founding generation.

We thank several anonymous reviewers for their excellent suggestions. Our editor at the Press, Robert Dreesen, was supportive at every stage of the work. Laura Macy's careful and constructive editing of the text was invaluable.

1

Two concepts of liberty … and conscience

Robert P. George

One of the dubious achievements of the Obama administration has been to put the issue of religious freedom and the rights of conscience back on the agenda in American politics. Most notoriously, the administration sought to impose upon private employers, including religious people and even religious institutions, a requirement to provide health insurance coverage that includes abortion-inducing drugs, sterilizations, and contraceptives, even if the employer cannot, as a matter of conscience, comply. The administration's mandates were challenged on under the Religious Freedom Restoration Act (RFRA) by employers seeking exemptions for themselves and others who conscientiously object, and the Supreme Court in *Burwell* v. *Hobby Lobby Stores, Inc.* and *Conestoga Wood Specialties Corp.* v. *Burwell* required the administration to grant the exemptions.

Of course, the administration contended and continues to contend that its mandates do not violate religious freedom or the rights of conscience, properly understood. Indeed, its defenders argue that the mandates – which contain only the narrowest of exemptions – are necessary to protect the freedom and rights of conscience of women who wish to use contraceptives and abortifacient drugs such as "Ella" (some of which they deny are actually abortion-inducing), or to avail themselves of sterilization procedures. So we find people on both sides in the debate claiming to be the defenders of liberty and conscience. It would be well for us, then, to pause to reflect in a philosophically rigorous way on the moral foundations of competing concepts of liberty and conscience. To that end, we might consider the ideas of two of modern intellectual history's most distinguished thinkers – John Stuart Mill and John Henry Newman.

Mill and Newman were the greatest English intellectuals of the nineteenth century. They were men of deep and wide learning and formidable intelligence. Both wrote powerful defenses of freedom. Mill's was in the form of an essay entitled simply "On Liberty" (1859). There he defended what he described as "one very simple principle [that is] entitled to govern absolutely the dealings of society with the individual in the way of compulsion and control, whether the means used be physical force in the form of legal penalties, or the moral coercion of public opinion." That principle has been dubbed Mill's "harm principle:"

> The only purpose for which power can be rightfully exercised over any member of a civilized community, against his will, is to prevent harm to others. His own good, either physical or moral, is not a sufficient warrant. He cannot rightfully be compelled to do or forbear because it will be better for him to do so, because it will make him happier, because, in the opinions of others, to do so would be wise, or even right.[1]

Mill's principle is frequently invoked in cocktail party conversations and in freshman class discussions. It has, however, been sharply criticized even by philosophers of a generally liberal persuasion, such as the late H. L. A. Hart of Oxford University, who argue that it is too sweeping in ruling out paternalistic reasons for limiting certain forms of liberty.[2] More conservative philosophers, I myself among them, have been even more skeptical and critical. For present purposes, though, I am less interested in the scope or breadth of Mill's principle, or with its content, than with its *ground*. What, for Mill, provides the moral basis for respecting people's liberty? What is the basis of the obligation?

Mill doesn't hide the ball:

> It is proper to state that I forego any advantage which could be derived to my argument from the idea of abstract right, as a thing independent of utility. I regard utility as the ultimate appeal on all ethical questions; but it must be utility in the largest sense, grounded on the permanent interests of man as a progressive being.[3]

Mill grounds his principle of liberty and the obligation to respect it in the belief that respect for liberty will, in its consequences, be net beneficial to ... well, to whom? Or to what?

To the community? Which community? Local? National? Imperial? International? Mill doesn't exactly say. As we've seen, he does, however, say that the concept of utility that must govern as the criterion of morality in our choosing, and as the ground of moral obligation, including the obligation to respect and protect liberty, must be utility "in the largest sense, as grounded on the permanent interests of man as a progressive being."

So note two things about Mill's defense of liberty, whether it is freedom of speech, which is a freedom Mill treats as quite central, or freedom of religion, which interests him less, or any other freedom. First, the ultimate basis of the moral claims of freedom is social benefit: "utility." It is not "abstract right." Second, Mill's view of humanity is imbued with nineteenth-century optimism

[1] John Stuart Mill, *On Liberty and Other Essays* (Oxford: Oxford University Press, 1991), pp. 13–14.

[2] Herbert L. A. Hart, *Law, Liberty, and Morality* (Oxford: Oxford University Press, 1963).

[3] Mill, *On Liberty*, p. 15.

and belief in progress. Man is naturally good – a "progressive being." He therefore will, in his cultural and personal maturity, do well by himself and others if only he is left free of paternalistic and moralistic constraints to engage in experiments in living from which he, corporately and individually, will learn what conduces to happiness and what does not. Freed from the old moralisms and religious and other superstitions – liberated to be the progressive being that, by nature, he is – he will flourish. Those old moralisms and superstitions – far from preventing him from descending into vice and degradation, or even assisting him in that project – tie him down and wound his spirit. They profoundly impede (and have impeded) his full flourishing and self-realization. Free to do as they please, free to do what they want to do so long as they do not harm others, mature persons in mature cultures will, on the whole, want to do good and productive – i.e., utility enhancing – things. (And there is no danger of regression to the former condition of things in barbarian societies and in small threatened communities, in both of which cases Mill's defense of liberty did not, he thought, hold good.)

I began my academic career by writing several articles and a book[4] that were severely critical of the concept and defense of liberty that readers are offered by Mill. I see no reason today to alter any of those criticisms. But Mill was by no means completely wrong. The naïve optimism and progressivism – they were wrong, to be sure. And the utilitarianism, that was wrong too. The Christian philosophical anthropology Mill regarded as a relic of superstitious ages has proved to be far more plausible and reliable than the alternative that Mill, quite uncritically, accepted. And utilitarian and other forms of consequentialism in ethics are in the end unworkable and even incoherent. They presuppose a kind of commensurability of human values and their particular instantiations that simply does not square either with reality or with conditions of deliberation and choice. The basic aspects of human well-being and fulfillment that, together, constitute the ideal of integral human flourishing are reducible neither to each other not to some common substance or factor they share. These basic human goods, though they all provide more-than-merely-instrumental reasons for action and are partially constitutive of our all-round well-being (which is how and why they constitute more-than-merely-instrumental reasons – they are intrinsic, rather than merely instrumental, goods), are good not in a univocal sense, as if they were constituted by the same substance but merely manifested it differently, but only in an analogical sense. They differ substantially as distinct dimensions of our flourishing and fulfillments of our capacities as human persons (rational animals); they are, as such, incommensurable in a way that renders hopeless the utilitarian project of identifying an option for choice – or even a rule for choosing – that promises "the greatest happiness of the greatest number," or the production of the net best proportion of benefit to harm overall and in the long run.[5]

4 *Making Men Moral: Civil Liberties and Public Morality* (Oxford: Clarendon Press, 1993).

5 See John Finnis, *Fundamentals of Ethics* (Oxford: Oxford University Press, 1983), ch. 3.

So where was Mill right? He was right, in my opinion, in forgoing an appeal to "abstract right" and looking for the moral ground of liberty in a consideration of the well-being and fulfillment – in a word, the flourishing – of human beings (what he calls in Chapter Three, paragraph 2 "the end of man" and characterizes in paragraph 10 as "bringing human beings themselves closer to the best they can be"). People have rights, including rights to liberties, because there are basic human goods, i.e., ends or purposes that not only conduce to, but *constitute*, their flourishing. The full defense of any particular liberty, including the freedom of religion, requires the identification and defense of those human goods, those basic aspects of human well-being and fulfillment, that the liberty secures, protects, or advances.

In a recent paper,[6] I offered a detailed account and defense of religious freedom as necessary for the protection of the human good of *religion*, considered as the active quest for spiritual truth and the conscientious effort to live with integrity and authenticity in line with one's best judgments regarding the ultimate sources of meaning and value, and to fulfill one's obligations in spiritual and moral matters in both the public and private dimensions of one's life.

Now, John Stuart Mill, as I mentioned earlier, wasn't greatly interested in religious freedom, though he did not, so far as I can tell, disdain it. The trouble was, I think that he had something of a tin ear for religion, at least in its traditional manifestations. His "harm principle" would, of course, extend to religious activity and practices, but I doubt that he viewed those as having much real value. They would, I suspect he believed, soon wither away in an age of freedom (since man is a "progressive being," and freedom brings "enlightenment").

By contrast, John Henry Newman did not have a tin ear for religion. He was a religious genius. And his understanding of religion enabled him to produce an account of freedom – in particular the freedom of conscience – that was profoundly superior to Mill's, and from which we today have much to learn. Like Mill, Newman does not appeal to "abstract right" as the ground of liberty, but instead locates the foundation of honorable freedoms in a concern for human excellence and human flourishing. Newman has the immense advantage over Mill of believing in human fallenness (what Christian faith knows as original sin), and so is spared naïve optimism and faith in human progress. Moreover, as a serious Christian, a utilitarian approach to moral decision-making (and all that it presupposes and entails) has no appeal whatsoever to Newman. So he is spared that, too. He is cognizant of both the need for *restraints* on freedom, lest men descend into vice and self-degradation, and on the supreme importance of central freedoms as conditions for the realization of values that truly are constitutive of the integral flourishing of men and women as free and rational

[6] "Religious Liberty and the Human Good," *International Journal of Religious Freedom* 5 (2012), 35–44.

creatures – creatures whose freedom and rationality reflects their having been made in the very image and likeness of God.

Newman's dedication to the rights of conscience is well-known. Even long after his conversion from Anglicanism to Catholicism, he famously toasted "the Pope, yes, but conscience first," as he put it in his *Letter to the Duke of Norfolk* (1875). Our obligation to follow conscience was, he insisted, in a profound sense primary and even overriding. Is there a duty to follow the teachings of the Pope? Yes, to be sure. As a Catholic, he would affirm that with all his heart. If, however, a conflict were to arise, such that conscience (formed as best one could form it) forbade one's following the Pope, well, it is the obligation of conscience that must prevail.

Of course, many a contemporary dissenting Catholic would be tempted right there to shout "Right on, Brother Newman!" But that's only if they didn't know the rest of the story. For Newman, though the most powerful defender of freedom of conscience, held a view of conscience and of freedom that could not be more deeply at odds with the liberal ideology that is dominant (even, dare one say, orthodox?) in the contemporary secular intellectual culture, and in those sectors of religious culture that have fallen under its influence. Let's permit Newman to speak for himself, for he had already identified in the nineteenth century the tendency of thought about rights, liberty, and conscience that would become the secular liberal orthodoxy in the late twentieth:

> Conscience has rights because it has duties; but in this age, with a large portion of the public, it is the very right and freedom of conscience to dispense with conscience. Conscience is a stern monitor, but in this century it has been superseded by a counterfeit, which the eighteen centuries prior to it never heard of, and could not have mistaken for it if they had. It is the right of self-will.[7]

Conscience, as Newman understood it, is the very opposite of "autonomy" in the modern liberal sense. It is not a writer of permission slips. It is not in the business of licensing us to do as we please or conferring on us "the right to define one's own concept of existence, of meaning, of the universe, and of the mystery of human life."[8] Rather, conscience is one's last best judgment specifying the bearing of moral principles one grasps, yet in no way makes up for oneself, on concrete proposals for action. Conscience identifies one's *duties* under the moral law. It speaks of what one must do and what one must not do. Understood in this way, conscience is, indeed, what Newman said it is: a stern monitor.

Contrast this understanding of conscience with what Newman condemns as its counterfeit. Conscience as "self-will" is a matter of feeling or emotion, not reason. It is concerned not so much with the identification of what one has a

[7] John Henry Newman, *Certain Difficulties Felt by Anglicans Considered ... A Letter Addressed to the Duke of Norfolk* (London: Longmans, Green, 1897), p. 250.

[8] *Planned Parenthood* v. *Casey* 505 U.S. 833 (1992) (plurality opinion by Justices Sandra Day O'Connor, Anthony Kennedy, and David Souter).

duty to do or not do, one's feelings and desires to the contrary notwithstanding, but rather, and precisely, with sorting out one's feelings. Conscience as self-will identifies permissions, not obligations. It licenses behavior by establishing that one doesn't feel bad about doing it, or, at least, one doesn't feel so bad about doing it that one prefers the alternative of not doing it.

I'm with Newman. His key distinction is between conscience, authentically understood, and self-will – conscience as the permissions department. His core insight is that conscience has rights *because it has duties*. The right to follow one's conscience, and the obligation to respect conscience – especially in matters of faith, where the right of conscience takes the form of religious liberty of individuals and communities of faith – obtain not because people as autonomous agents should be able to do as they please; they obtain, and are stringent and sometimes overriding, because people have duties and the obligation to fulfill them. The duty to follow conscience is a duty to do things or refrain from doing things not because one wants to follow one's duty, *but even if one strongly does not want to follow it*. The right of conscience is a right to do what one judges oneself to be under an obligation to do, whether one welcomes the obligation or must overcome strong aversion in order to fulfill it. If there is a form of words that sums up the antithesis of Newman's view of conscience as a stern monitor, it is the imbecilic slogan that will forever stand as a verbal monument to the "Me-generation": "If it feels good, do it."

Of course, properly understood, and even toasted ahead of the Pope, there are limits to the rights of conscience, even in the fulfillment of perceived vocational obligations, institutional apostolates, and other religious duties. As I have observed elsewhere, gross evils – even grave injustices – can be committed by people sincerely acting for the sake of religion. Unspeakable wrongs can be done by people seeking sincerely to get right with God or the gods or their conception of ultimate reality, whatever it is. The presumption in favor of respecting liberty must, for the sake of the human good and the dignity of human persons as free and rational creatures – creatures who, according to Judaism and Christianity, are made in the very image and likeness of God[9] – be powerful and broad. But it is not unlimited. Even the great end of getting right with God cannot justify a morally bad means, even for the sincere believer. I don't doubt the sincerity of the Aztecs in practicing human sacrifice, or the sincerity of those in the history of various traditions of faith who used coercion and even torture in the cause of what they believed was religiously required. But these things are deeply wrong, and need not (and should not) be tolerated in the name of religious freedom. To suppose otherwise is to back oneself into the awkward position of supposing that violations of religious freedom (and other injustices of equal gravity) must be respected for the sake of religious freedom.

[9] Genesis 1:26–27.

Still, to overcome the powerful and broad presumption in favor of religious liberty, to be justified in requiring the believer to do something contrary to his faith or forbidding the believer to do something his faith requires, political authority must meet a heavy burden. The legal test in the United States under the Religious Freedom Restoration Act is one way of capturing the presumption and burden: to justify a law that bears negatively on religious freedom, even a neutral law of general applicability must be supported by a compelling state interest and represent the least restrictive or intrusive means of protecting or serving that interest. We can debate, as a matter of American constitutional law or as a matter of policy, whether it is, or should be, up to courts or legislators to decide when exemptions to general, neutral laws should be granted for the sake of religious freedom, or to determine when the presumption in favor of religious freedom has been overcome; but the substantive matter of what religious freedom demands from those who exercise the levers of state power should be something on which reasonable people of goodwill across the religious and political spectrums can broadly (though perhaps not perfectly) agree.

Let me conclude with a few words about the centrality and one might even say *priority* of religious freedom among the basic civil liberties. Observed from a certain perspective, any basic liberty might be assigned a kind of priority: Free speech, for example, which is so essential to the enterprise of republican government (and, in truth, good government of any kind); or freedom of association and assembly; or the right of self-defense and defense of one's family and community. One might note in the case of any of these rights that its collapse would place all the others in jeopardy.

There is certainly truth in the idea that civil liberty is a sort of seamless garment. Basic civil liberties support each other and, in certain ways, even depend on each other. Tyrannical regimes may begin by dishonoring one or a few basic liberties, but the get round in the end to dishonoring them all as the perceived interests of the rulers or dominant classes incentivize them to do so. Still, there is a special sense in which freedom of religion has priority or at least a sort of pride of place. Religious liberty played a foundational historical role in the establishment of the conditions of free institutions. Even more importantly, it protects an aspect of our flourishing as human persons which is architectonic to the way we lead our lives. Religion concerns ultimate things. In the focal cases, it represents our efforts to bring ourselves into a relationship of friendship with transcendent sources of meaning and value. Our religious questioning, understanding, judging, and practicing, shapes what we do not only in the specifically "religious" aspects of our lives (prayer, liturgy, fellowship, and so forth) but in every aspect of our lives. It helps us to view our lives as a whole and to direct our choices and activities in ways that have *integrity* – both in the moral sense of that term and in the broader sense of having a life that hangs together, than makes sense.

Religion is not the only basic human good; nor are the other basic human goods mere means to the fuller realization of the good of religion. But religion *is* an intrinsic and constitutive aspect of our integral flourishing as human persons, *and also* a good that plays a shaping and integrating role with respect to all the other intrinsic and constitutive aspects of human well-being and fulfillment.[10]

Finally, there is the critical role of religion, and thus of religious freedom, in civil society in the carrying out of essential health, education, and welfare functions, and thus limiting the scope of government and checking the power of the state. Religion provides authority structures and, where it flourishes and is healthy, is among the key institutions of civil society providing a buffer between the individual and the state. This is a vital way in which religion and religious institutions, when they respect the legitimate autonomy of the secular sphere and avoid illiberalism, time-serving subservience to the state, and theocracy, serve the common good. In the face of tyrannical regimes, they can, if they avoid corruption and cooptation, serve the common good even more dramatically by doing, for example, what the Catholic Church did in the face of communist tyranny in Poland.[11]

Religion can, in other words, contribute both to the theory and practice of resistance – but only where it is basically healthy (that is, uncorrupted) and capable of providing, or providing resources for, prophetic witness. This is one more reason to cherish religious freedom and to push back hard against forces that threaten to erode or diminish it – especially when the threats come from overreaching governments.

[10] See John Finnis, *Natural Law and Natural Rights*, 2nd edition (Oxford: Clarendon Press, 2011), pp. 89–90.

[11] See George Weigel, *Witness to Hope: The Biography of Pope John Paul II* (New York: Harper Collins, 1999).

2

Religious liberty: The first freedom?

Daniel N. Robinson

> And then there is Arthur, a young man who sustained a terrible head injury in an automobile crash and soon afterward claimed that his father and mother had been replaced by duplicates who looked exactly like his real parents. He recognized their faces but they seemed odd, unfamiliar. The only way Arthur could make any sense out of the situation was to assume that his parents were impostors.

This is a brief passage from *Phantoms in the Brain: Probing the Mysteries of the Human Mind* by V. S. Ramachandran and Sandra Blakeslee.[1] Described here is the rare condition known as Capgras syndrome first described by Capgras and Reboul-Lachaux in 1923.[2] The patient has the unshakeable conviction that persons and relatives well known to them have been replaced by copies or clones. The condition is sometimes associated with severe psychiatric disturbances but is also the consequence of brain lesions in otherwise normal persons. There are comparably startling instances of pathological beliefs. Instances of the so-called *Fregoli* delusion finds the patient convinced that different persons are actually a single person donning various disguises. Those suffering from the *Cotard* delusion believe themselves to be dead.

There are still other beliefs, held as firmly and comparably lacking in direct empirical support; these beliefs are widely shared across vast stretches of time and among cultures that might have little else in common. Some of these are taken to be moral beliefs; others as religious, others as political; still others as aesthetic. Many persons have an unwavering belief in certain principles of fairness, even while lacking any direct measure of fairness or proof that the principles are reliably redeemed at a pragmatic level. No one would seriously

[1] New York: William Morrow, 1999, p. 2.

[2] J. Capgras, and J. Reboul-Lachaux, "Illusion des 'sosies' dans un délire systématisé chronique," *Bulletin de la Société Clinique de Médicine Mentale* 2 (1923), 6–16.

argue that the "Happy Birthday" song is of greater aesthetic merit than, say, Mozart's *Cosi fan Tutte*, though, in the realm of taste, standards are elusive and arguable.

From the perspective of psychology, beliefs are recognized as a ubiquitous feature of daily life, often of greater significance than knowledge itself, and sometimes so at variance with standards of common sense and ordinary perception as to be of clinical concern. From the perspective of philosophy, belief is the veritable grounding of knowledge. As treatises in epistemology insist, "Knowledge" is a justified true belief for which we have rational warrants. Pathologies aside, beliefs ground not only knowledge but life; life in its various projects and plans, in its values and judgments.

Religious liberty, the topic of this essay, is at once a liberty of conscience but even more foundationally a liberty of belief. By way of clarifying how I would have this essay understood, I note that it is not intended to be contentious, nor is the use of the interrogative voice a veiled assertion. The main proposition is that religious liberty, understood in a certain light, is, as it were, the first freedom and foundational for the rest. The argument for this begins with presuppositions, some factual, some stipulative. To wit: Nature – as in Jefferson's "Nature's God" – renders the objects of creation recognizable in terms of certain inherent properties. With marginal nurturance and in the absence of such tragic defects as those cited above, human beings are recognizable as rational creatures with the power of acting and withholding action on the basis of reasons. As social animals, inclined to live in the company of others, their reasons for action or restraint are typically framed in social and political terms. Bound up with their reasons for acting are beliefs regarding likely consequences to themselves and others. Finally, and on the whole, the lives of such creatures are organized in ways designed to secure safety and happiness.

Integral to such plans are *beliefs*, for planning envisages a future that cannot be known with certainty. It is an imagined future. Summing up, rational creatures base innumerable and significant action-plans on the basis of beliefs in imagined possibilities. I take this to be an inherent and profoundly significant feature of a human life. As such, opposition to the expression and implementation of such powers must inevitably face either direct resistance or a demand for justification. Such grounds of opposition and demands for justification are expressed politically in the language of *rights*.

In so far as religious belief is a species of belief, it draws upon the limitless resources of the imagination. In this, however, religious belief is the most profound of all beliefs, for it seeks to identify both the originating causes and the ultimate purposes of – everything. To this extent, it serves as the framework for any number of subsidiary beliefs. In this connection, consider that most general belief that has long guided the scientific enterprise itself; namely, that the basic laws unearthed today, under these limited conditions, may well be instances of a universal law operative throughout time and cosmic space; operative over a range that only the imagination can embrace. Jefferson's reference to "nature and nature's God" is exemplary of that never fully successful attempt to imagine what stands behind the order and lawfulness of uncorrupted nature.

We seem naturally inclined to look for the causes of things. We believe that recurring events are moved by recurring and similar antecedent events. The powers of the imagination are generative of such beliefs, some of which courageously even if tentatively come to be invested in what is taken to be divine. This, then, is the sense I would have you attach to the notion of religious liberty being "the first freedom," a freedom to employ sense, reason, and imagination in an attempt to know oneself and one's place in the larger scheme of things. Put another way, we believe that the diversity and complexity of natural events is a kind of surface "noise" and that the revealing "signal" becomes audible by way of an imaginative reconstruction of reality – a reconstruction that moves us to the first and to the final points in the arc of reality itself. There is religion here, even when the gods are nameless.

Note again that I do not refer to freedom of the imagination for, by its very nature, it is not subject to external authority. This greatest voyage of inquiry needs no vehicle and seeks no license. It is constrained, when it is constrained, by reason and experience. Actually, "constrained" is the wrong word. Experience and rational reflection work to redirect the imagination to yet other and more promising or truth-bearing possibilities more worthy of belief. Reason and experience redirect by pointing, not by commanding. One can be punished for a belief but not commanded to surrender it. In a somewhat mysterious way, we seem to have little say in the matter of what we believe. Oppressive regimes hold on by confining the imagination through censorship, bread and circus, but sooner or later the hostage breaks loose.

Typically, regimes of every sort claim an authority of divine origin, for without this fear is the only means of social control. Hammurabi's laws were followed by those who believed them to be divinely inspired by no less than Marduk, just as the Mosaic Law claimed a comparable pedigree. Rome's laws were obeyed not merely out of fear of punishment but in the belief that one's own safety and good fortune were tied to allegiance to a State protected by divinities.

Such beliefs are sustained by an active and productive imagination liberated from the welter of current facts. One imagines what a world without law would be like, or what God might do to those who steal or give false witness. The point I'm pressing is that even the most practical affairs of daily life are conducted on the basis of beliefs that enjoy neither strict logical warrants nor unfailing validation in experience. That form of life we recognize as human unfolds within a framework of such beliefs. The most profound and productive of these are religious. Whatever would suppress them must finally install an ironclad orthodoxy likely to be hostile to thought itself.

In less abstract terms, we tend to think of religious liberty as a modern development, reaching back to such rich sources as Milton's *Areopagitica*, Locke's *A Letter Concerning Toleration* (1689) and then to full development in the revolutionary literature of the Enlightenment which would culminate in the *Declaration of Independence* and the US Constitution. We recall with admiration Locke's claim that, "The toleration of those that differ from others in matters of religion is so agreeable to the Gospel of Jesus Christ, and to the genuine reason of mankind, that it seems monstrous for men to be so blind as not to perceive the necessity and advantage of it in so clear a light." Liberty understood this way arises from a duty to tolerate difference, to respect what is often referred to as a liberty of conscience tied to a set of rights possessed by each person individually. Although Locke understood any religion to be a society of persons whose membership is voluntary, there is nothing in his *Letter* that sets a minimum number. Moreover, the requirement that membership be voluntary installs the individual person as the beneficiary of toleration. Locke's thesis leaves room for as many religions as there are individual persons; even more on the assumption that no one is limited as to the number and variety of doctrines laying claim to one's conscience. There is but one exception: There is no room in this for the toleration of religious *intolerance*! Note, then, that once we press on beyond the stage of broad generalizations, we come to grips with real difficulties surrounding the concepts of "religious" and "liberties" and the nature of those claims that conscience must be free to satisfy.

Locke seeks toleration for differences. But for there to be differences in matters of religion, parties to the dispute will base their positions on what they take to be authoritative. In developed and literate societies, such authority is typically vested in texts, teachings, and recorded doctrines. Where this is so, liberty of conscience is itself dependent on liberty of inquiry. It is not a mere coincidence that the First Amendment insulates both the press and religion against infringements by the national government. The Founding generation was ever mindful of the blood that was shed in the name of religion during years of turmoil in Britain and on the Continent. Nor were they unmindful of the still heated sectarian animosities at work in the new world.

A half-century before Locke composed his *Letter*, John Milton's *Areopagitica* (1644) offered an impassioned plea for and defense of freedom of the press, addressed to Parliament and directly opposing laws that had been put in place by Queen Mary and rendered ever more constraining by Elizabeth I. As early as 1559, the Crown had issued *Injunctions Concerning Religion*. No work in any language could be printed except with a license issued either by the Queen or her Privy Council, or by the Chancellor either of Oxford or Cambridge, or by the Archbishop of Canterbury, York, or London. The more oppressive of the *Injunctions* is captured by the following:

> LI. Item, because there is a great abuse in the printers of books, which for covetousness chiefly regard not what they print, so they may have gain, whereby ariseth great disorder by publication of unfruitful, vain, and infamous books and papers; the queen's majesty straitly charges and commands, that no manner of person shall print any manner of book or paper, of what sort, nature, or in what language soever it be, except the same be first licensed by her majesty by express words in writing, or by six of her privy

council; or be perused and licensed by the archbishops of Canterbury and York, the Bishop of London, the chancellors of both universities, the bishop being ordinary, and the archdeacon also of the place, where any such shall be printed, or by two of them, whereof the ordinary of the place to be always one. And that the names of such as shall allow the same to be added in the end of every such work, for a testimony of the allowance thereof. And because many pamphlets, plays, and ballads be oftentimes printed, wherein regard would be had that nothing therein should be either heretical, seditious, or unseemly for Christian ears; her majesty likewise commands that no manner of person shall enterprise to print any such, except the same be to him licensed by such her majesty's commissioners, or three of them, as be appointed in the city of London to hear and determine divers causes ecclesiastical, tending to the execution of certain statutes made the last Parliament for uniformity of order in religion. And if any shall sell or utter any manner of books or papers, being not licensed as is above-said, that the same party shall be punished by order of the said commissioners, as to the quality of the fault shall be thought meet. And touching all other books of matters of religion, or policy, or governance that have been printed, either on this side the seas or on the other side, because the diversity of them is great, and that there needs good consideration to be had of the particularities thereof, her majesty refers the prohibition or permission thereof to the order which her said commissioners within the city of London shall take and notify. According to the which her majesty straitly commands all manner her subjects, and especially the wardens and company of Stationers, to be obedient.[3]

The aim here could not be clearer: All this was *for uniformity of order in religion*. In 1556 this order was ratified by a decree of the infamous Star-Chamber which would add ever tighter restrictions over a period of years.

These developments had a strange and momentous history of their own. The often painful ironies of history are vividly featured in events that would lead Milton, Locke, and others to record their pleas for liberty. Pope Leo X in 1521 declared Henry VIII to be *Fidei Defensor*, a title earned by Henry when he declared Martin Luther a heretic! Thirteen years later, this "defender of the faith" would sign the first *Act of Supremacy* by which,

... the king, our sovereign lord, his heirs and successors, kings of this realm, shall be taken, accepted, and reputed the only supreme head in earth of the Church of England, called Anglicans Ecclesia ... and that our said sovereign lord, his heirs and successors, kings of this realm, shall have full power and authority from time to time to visit, repress, redress, record, order, correct, restrain, and amend all such errors, heresies, abuses, offenses, contempts and enormities, whatsoever they be ...[4]

Not only was the pleasure of Almighty God the aim of this legislation but the added benefits included nothing less than "... the increase of virtue in Christ's religion, and ... the conservation of the peace, unity, and tranquility of this realm." Under such controls, any government is able to manage – or, as

3 "The Injunctions of 1559," accessed August 18, 2015, https://history.hanover.edu/texts/engref/er78.html.

4 "Henry VIII's Act of Supremeacy (1534)," accessed August 18, 2015, www.britainexpress.com/History/tudor/supremacy-henry-text.htm.

one might say today, micro-manage – that part of thought and critical reflection otherwise enlarged and deepened by multiple and conflicting perspectives. In saying, then, that one should be free to embrace the tenets of a religion and discharge the duties imposed by them, one must suppose that the beneficiary of the freedom has enjoyed the associated freedoms that render this one credible. Thus understood, religious liberty, if it is to rise higher than a slogan, is dependent on liberty of thought and liberty of that inquiry and intellectual engagement that moves feelings toward the plane of understanding. In his *Areopagitica*, Milton puts it this way: "I cannot praise a fugitive and cloistered virtue unexercised and unbreathed, that never sallies out and seeks her adversary, but slinks out of the race, where that immortal garland is to be run for, not without dust and heat. Assuredly we bring not innocence into the world, we bring impurity much rather; that which purifies us is trial, and trial is by what is contrary."[5] With all this as background, I now move on to the "new world," that heralded *Novus Ordo Saeclorum.* "We hold these truths to be self-evident ..." With these words the world is introduced to a veritable creation – the creation of a new political entity awaiting the outcome of a war and a Constitution if the idea itself was to move from a political entity to a political reality. These seven words are then followed by claims that have fired the tools of cynics and romantics alike, claims to the effect that in some unspecified respect each person is the equal of another, each possessing certain rights which, unlike others, are *unalienable.*

Even after many drafts shaped by many hands, the *Declaration* is Jefferson's, through and through. It is the product of a first-rate mind, cultivated in an age of critical inquiry and further refined by an education that was, indeed, "higher" in all relevant respects. Of that education, Jefferson's own recollections are informing. Writing in 1815 to Louis Girardin, a French emigre teaching at William & Mary, Jefferson recalls his own student days at the College. Of his major teacher, Dr. William Small, Jefferson says he was, "... to me as a father. To his enlightened and affectionate guidance of my studies while at college, I am indebted for everything ... At [his] dinners I have heard more good sense, more rational and philosophical conversations, than in all my life besides."[6]

William Small was a native Scot, a graduate of Marichal College, Aberdeen, and one of those illustrious sons of the Scottish Enlightenment. Thus did he reach William & Mary with a rich and developed philosophical tradition; the very tradition that, more than any other, would influence major figures of the American Founding: Jefferson, Madison, James Wilson, Benjamin Rush, John

[5] "Areopagitica," accessed August 18, 2015, www.columbia.edu/itc/journalism/j6075/edit/readings/areopagitica_milton.html.

[6] "The Writings of Thomas Jefferson," accessed August 18, 2015, www.yamaguchy.com/library/jefferson/1815.html.

Witherspoon – the list is long. This is all a well-told tale, even if now routinely neglected in our own centers of allegedly "higher" education.

Just as the fact is neglected, so too are the very texts that supported the claims and aspirations at the foundation of the new nation. As with many of his Scottish colleagues, Small was fully instructed in the moral teaching of Francis Hutcheson (1694–1746). He was perhaps the most influential of the Scots moralists at the time of Jefferson's studies.[7] His influence was broad and reached William Small with special power and focus. There is good evidence supporting the claim that the principles and actual wording of Jefferson's *Declaration of Independence* were directly indebted to Hutcheson.

In the present context it is sufficient to cite just two of his influential contributions, that contrasting rights that are *alienable* and those that are *unalienable*, and a theory of moral sentiments in which benevolence has pride of place. He develops this in *An Inquiry into the Original of Our Ideas of Beauty and Virtue* (1726),[8] which went through many editions and was a staple in the intellectual life of colonial America. Toward the end of the Second Treatise, Hutcheson examines the difference between alienable and unalienable rights. He frames the distinction this way:

> VII ... To determine what Rights are alienable, and what not, we must take these two Marks: 1st. If the Alienation be within our natural Power, so that it be possible for us in Fact to transfer our Right; and if it be so, then, 2dly. It must appear, that such Rights may serve some valuable Purpose. By the first Mark it appears, "That the Right of private Judgment, or of our inward Sentiments, is unalienable;" since we cannot command ourselves to think what either we our selves, or any other Person pleases ... By the second Mark it appears, "That our Right of serving God, in the manner which we think acceptable, is not alienable ...[9]

The inner resources of consequence here manifest themselves as *sentiments*, more particularly, as *moral sentiments*. Hutcheson takes these to be part of the very constitution of human nature and thus effectively universal within the human family. These sentiments are not to be confused with selfish motives or narrow desires shaped by pleasure and pain:

> That the Perceptions of moral Good and Evil, are perfectly different from those of natural Good, or Advantage, every one must convince himself, by reflecting upon the different Manner in which he finds himself affected when these Objects occur to him. Had we no Sense of Good distinct from the Advantage or Interest arising from the

[7] For a general introduction to this part of American intellectual history, Garry Wills's *Inventing America* is a worthy effort. Wills speaks of Jefferson's introduction to the works of Francis Hutcheson and the influence such works had on the precepts advanced in the Declaration of Independence. Garry Wills, *Inventing America* (New York: Mariner Press, 2002).

[8] Francis Hutcheson, *An Inquiry into the Original of Our Ideas of Beauty and Virtue*, accessed August 18, 2015, http://oll.libertyfund.org/titles/2462.

[9] Hutcheson, *Inquiry*, Treatise II, Section 7, VII, accessed August 18, 2015, http://oll.libertyfund.org/titles/2462#n1135_ref.

external Senses, and the Perceptions of Beauty and Harmony; our Admiration and Love toward a fruitful Field, or commodious Habitation, would be much the same with what we have toward a generous Friend, or any noble Character; for both are, or may be advantageous to us: And we should no more admire any Action, or love any Person in a distant Country, or Age, whose Influence could not extend to us, than we love the Mountains of Peru, while we are unconcern'd in the Spanish Trade. We should have the same Sentiments and Affections toward inanimate Beings, which we have toward rational Agents; which yet every one knows to be false.[10]

The claims of conscience are actually *felt* and, though entirely compatible with rational appraisals of right and wrong courses of action, have the power to excite and inhibit action in ways that mere logic cannot achieve. Unlike inert matter and the balance of the animal kingdom, rational agents,

... study our Interest, and delight in our Happiness, and are Benevolent toward us. We are all then conscious of the Difference between that Love and Esteem, or Perception of moral Excellence, which Benevolence excites toward the Person in whom we observe it, and that Opinion of natural Goodness, which only raises Desire of Possession toward the good Object ... [Whereas] we have a distinct Perception of Beauty, or Excellence in the kind Affections of rational Agents; whence we are determin'd to admire and love such Characters and Persons."[11]

It is benevolence that binds a people in friendship and creates the possibility for ordered liberty and self-governance. The right to think, to believe, to identify an entity worthy of worship – this all proceeds from innate sentiments over which even we do not have the power of alienation. Governments indeed might "visit, repress, redress, record, order, correct, restrain, and amend all such errors, heresies, abuses, offenses, contempts and enormities," but the inner resources by which one is drawn to beauty, virtue, and fellow-feeling remain fully shielded even when silenced. Indeed, the very authority claimed by any rule of law depends on these very same resources. Were rational beings solely impelled by selfish motives, grudging in their dealings with others and indifferent to the general welfare, the rule of law would be reduced to a whip and a chair. To assume that the moral dimensions of life are drawn within the constricted circle of self-interest is to fly in the face of human nature itself. Later, John Witherspoon (1723–1794), in the first of his *Lectures on Moral Philosophy*, expressed the point with characteristic clarity:

The noble and eminent improvements in natural philosophy, which have been made since the end of the last century, have been far from hurting the interest of religion; on the contrary, they have greatly promoted it. Why should it not be the same with moral philosophy, which is indeed nothing else, but the knowledge of human nature? It is true, that infidels do commonly proceed upon pretended principles of reason. But as it is

[10] Hutcheson, *Inquiry*, Treatise II, Sec. 1, I, accessed April 10, 2016 http://oll.libertyfund.org/titles/2462#lf1458_label_182.

[11] *Ibid.*

impossible to hinder them from reasoning on this subject, the best way is to meet them upon their own ground, and to show from reason itself, the fallacy of their principles. I do not know any thing that serves more for the support of religion than to see, from the different and opposite systems of philosophers, that there is nothing certain in their schemes, but what is coincident with the word of God.[12]

Acts of Supremacy might be powerless over the claims of conscience but not over the public consequences of the moral sentiments. Thus must a heavy price be paid just in case personal conviction rises to the level of public display. Accordingly, the Acts of Supremacy were followed by additional impositions. The *Test Acts* made religious orthodoxy a precondition for holding any public office whatever. The *Act of James I* provided that all who were "naturalized or restored in blood" should receive the sacrament of the Lord's Supper. In 1661, under the reign of Charles II, the Corporation Act was passed, requiring both an Oath of Supremacy and receiving the sacrament of Communion according to the Anglican rite. This was followed by the Test Act of 1673, requiring the denial of transubstantiation. Roman Catholics and dissenters were barred from public office as well as from student or faculty status at Oxford and Cambridge. These obstacles remained in place until 1828. In the face of a powerful and committed authority, there may well be an unalienable right to believe, but one might be otherwise denied access to all settings in which one's beliefs might be refined, constructively challenged or put in the service of others.

None of this was new, of course, and ancient examples abound. Historical starting points must be arbitrary. Hammurabi's famous Code (1772 BC), he tells us, was composed under the direction of the god Marduk and thereby removed from the realm of argument and critical appraisal. We know much more about religion in the world of ancient Greece, though we must follow the caution of Walter Burkert: "Greek religion has to some extent always remained familiar, but is far from easy to know and understand ... It is unique and unrepeatable."[13]

Ancient Athens, itself unique and unrepeatable, was the first and most ardent defender of the democratic process. Religion was polytheistic but not static. Victory over Persia altered the relative position of the dozen Olympians, just as defeat at the hands of Sparta had the deck shuffled once again. Over time, Athenian religion made room for new gods, even as other gods fell from favor. It is in the *quid pro quo* character of polytheism that the real and practical consequences of worship generate degrees of favor and of fervor.[14]

[12] John Witherspoon, *Lectures on Moral Philosophy*, ed. Varnum Lansing Collins (Princeton: Princeton University Press, 1912), 2, accessed August 18, 2015, http://archive.org/stream/lecturesonmoralpoowithrich#page/n9/mode/2up.

[13] Walter Burkert, *Greek Religion: Archaic and Classical* (Oxford: Blackwell, 1985), p. 1.

[14] For a discussion of the processes involved in installing deities in the official pantheon, see Robert Garland, *Introducing New Gods: The Politics of Athenian Religion* (Ithaca, Cornell University Press, 1992).

As the very grounds of worship are inextricably tied to fortune and misfortune, it follows that, impelled by self-interest, the faithful will choose their divinities accordingly. The liberty of choosing, however, was not unbounded. In Athens, entire assemblies and courts had to recognize a sect and authorize the installation of its divinities. Many factors were considered but the necessary and originating factor was the number of petitioners. It was not the conscience of the individual or a claimed epiphany that summoned the respect or indulgence of the community. Athenian democracy was the gift of democracy itself. A woeful fate awaited anyone who would elevate his own interests, let alone his own religion, above the interests of the πολις. The gods of ancient Rome were drawn from the Greek pantheon and other Indo-European sources. The Romans were readily inclined to appropriate divinities and include them among those featured in their little residential altars (*Lararia*). But there was nonetheless a *state* religion, presided over by the *Pontifex Maximus* and a group of colleges – *collegia* – composed of eminent Romans with life-tenure. Again, diversity of worship was tolerated, but within limits politically established. Rome's addiction to bureaucracy is evident in the rules attached to the office of Jupiter's high priest, the *Flamen Dialis*: He could not appear in public with his hat off or on a horse, nor could a slave give him a haircut.[15]

The once outcast religion of the Christians was officially acknowledged by Constantine and made official in the Roman Empire by Theodosius in 380 AD. It is interesting to compare the restrictions he imposed with those that proceeded from Britain's *Acts of Supremacy* twelve centuries later. Under Theodosius decrees were issued that removed non-Nicene Christians from church office, eliminated all public displays of Roman religion, converted religious holidays to workdays, banned blood sacrifices, closed the Roman temples, and disbanded the Vestal Virgins.[16] The Supreme Court could do no better!

The emergence of Christianity and its hegemony in the West gave new meaning to the concept of heresy. The ancient Greek noun, 'αιρεσις connotes no more than an act of choosing. Where a moral choice is involved, the ancient philosophers would generally use προαιρεσις. In the Greek of the New Testament, 'αιρεσις refers non-judgmentally to a sect, as Judaism classified the Sadduces and Pharisees. However, as early as the close of the second century the same word now designated adherence to sacrilegious doctrine. The Church did distinguish between the innocent and the merely ignorant who held false beliefs.

Doctrine and orthodoxy are the unintended consequence of diversity. The world or empire bequeathed by Rome included large geographically dispersed populations differing in culture, custom, language, and religion. Rome's own polytheism was pliant enough to absorb some of the differences and ignore

[15] Jörg Rüpke, *The Religion of the Romans* (Cambridge: Polity Press, 2007).

[16] Charles Freeman, *A.D. 381: Heretics, Pagans, and the Christian State* (London: Penguin Press, 2010), p. 116.

some of the others. What mattered was that tribute be paid, peace preserved and the gods of Rome given pride of place. The movement of Christianity into and through this world was impelled less by political and military ambition and more by an unstinting commitment to convert, to bring glad tidings, at the expense of ancient superstition and ignorance. Challenges were mounted equally by village shamans and educated Greek philosophers.

Thus was doctrine refined, hardened, rendered ever more orthodox and formulaic. By the close of the sixteenth century the boundaries identifying European peoples simultaneously identified Christianity's multiple *isms*. In England, Elizabeth I set out to suppress factionalism through the *Act of Uniformity*, passed by Parliament in 1559. The terms of the Act were insufferable to most Catholics and Presbyterian non-conformists, a number of whom fled to Amsterdam. In time, the harsh conditions and poverty of a life lived in a tolerant but foreign country led a desperate band back to England in their little wreckage of a ship, the *Speedwell*. There in 1620 they joined another band of forsaken emigres in possession of a worthier craft, the *Mayflower*.

The new world was settled by persons with long and punishing experience at the hands of secular authority presuming to dictate the relationship of God to man. A century and a half later, the great John Witherspoon would ask his new countrymen in this new world to understand just why their British kin fail to see what is so evident, even self-evident. Witherspoon left a world in which many of those judged to be leading lights tended to be rather casual in the matter of scripture, and perhaps more than eager to enjoy the benefits of worldly celebrity. They were well schooled in the amusing productions of the Salons of Paris and comfortable with the political stability made possible by monarchy. That same world was the home of multitudes who had never paid close attention to a political world that had obtained since times beyond memory. As America moved toward the decisive split, Witherspoon observed that, "It is natural for the multitude in Britain, who have been from their infancy taught to look upon an act of parliament as supreme and irresistible, and to consider the liberty of their country itself as consisting in the dominion of the house of commons, to be surprised and astonished at any society or body of men, calling in question the authority of parliament, and denying its power over them."[17]

I noted earlier the influence of such luminous figures as John Milton and John Locke. This is something of a standard acknowledgement, nearly a required citation. It is important, however, to qualify the Founders' debts to the past. Locke, for example, was aide and faithful friend to Anthony Ashley Cooper, First Earl of Shaftesbury and founder of the Whig Party. He was, by the standards of the day, a liberal thinker, strongly behind penal reforms and generous in his attitude toward the non-conformists. But he was also an ardent

[17] "On Conducting the American Controversy," in *The Works of John Witherspoon*, Vol. IX (Edinburgh: Parliament Square, 1815), 85. Available at http://archive.org/download/worksofjohnwithe09with/worksofjohnwithe09with.pdf.

defender of the Test Acts and saw to it that no Roman Catholic would have a seat in Parliament.

Locke, of course, stood four-square behind popular sovereignty, arguing that a tyranny effectively dissolves the bonds between the people and the government. It was James Wilson, one of the leading architects of American constitutional jurisprudence, who underscored the difference between the sovereignty of the people and the sovereignty of the person.[18] Wilson fully endorsed what has come to be called popular sovereignty, but he understood it as derived from the standing of the person. Moreover, Wilson required no hypothetical "state of nature" to establish this. The collective is but an assembly of individual persons whose standing is not dependent on any government they might from time to time bring about with like-minded others. In recording his opposition to having all this spelled out in a Bill of Rights, Wilson noted that, "... for it would have been superfluous and absurd to have stipulated with a federal body of our own creation, that we should enjoy those privileges of which we are not divested, either by the intention or the act that has brought the body into existence."[19]

His wry reflections are worth more than a moment's consideration: The people have declared independence from the mother land. They have secured it through a long, costly, and painful war. They now will establish a government they regard as compatible with the unique powers and aims of a rational and moral being. Why on earth would they set about to stipulate protection of the very rights fully expressed in the formation of the government itself? On this understanding, religious liberty is not somehow brought about, either by law or fiat or custom. It is implicit in the active and imaginative powers of the person. It is implicit in the very logic of the case that theocratic tyranny stands on no higher ground than any other version of the *genre*. If the Founders were unalterably opposed to the Crown's *Test Act* or *Act of Supremacy*, no leap of the imagination is necessary to establish how, for example, *Shariah*, would fare, or any other doctrine that would presume to dictate revealed truth to a rational being. It is instructive here to return again to Francis Hutcheson, the question now being the relationship between the moral sense and love of country. Hutcheson says:

Here we may transiently remark the Foundation of what we call national Love, or Love of one's native Country. Whatever place we have liv'd in for any considerable time, there we have most distinctly remark'd the various Affections of human Nature; we have known many lovely Characters; we remember the Associations, Friendships,

[18] I discuss this at length in Daniel N. Robinson, "Do the People of the United States Form a Nation? James Wilson's Theory of Rights," *International Journal of Constitutional Law* 8 (2010), 287–97.

[19] James Wilson, "State House Yard Speech October 6, 1787," in *Collected Works of James Wilson* edited by Kermit L. Hall and Mark David Hall (Indianapolis: Liberty Fund Inc., 2007), accessed April 4, 2016, http://oll.libertyfund.org/titles/2072#lf4140_head_084.

Familys, natural Affections, and other human Sentiments: our moral Sense determines us to approve these lovely Dispositions where we have most distinctly observ'd them; and our Benevolence concerns us in the Interests of the Persons possess'd of them. When we come to observe the like as distinctly in another Country, we begin to acquire a national Love toward it also; nor has our own Country any other preference in our Idea, unless it be by an Association of the pleasant Ideas of our Youth, with the Buildings, Fields, and Woods where we receiv'd them. This may let us see, how Tyranny, Faction, a Neglect of Justice, a Corruption of Manners, and any thing which occasions the Misery of the Subjects, destroys this national Love, and the dear Idea of a Country.[20]

The account developed here leads to an important conclusion, even as it leaves a number of significant issues unaddressed. The conclusion is that, unlike life, liberty, and the pursuit of happiness – each of which has been readily and even eagerly abandoned, if only episodically and in behalf of a putative higher cause – the summons of moral conscience actually is *unalienable*. Indeed, it is owing to this that the status of those celebrated rights of the *Declaration of Independence* rise to the level of *self-evident* truths. Saints and heroes have routinely sacrificed their lives and their liberties, not to mention what most would regard as the grounds of happiness. That they have done so with the full power of agency, the power to answer the summons of conscience, reaches something in their nature that could not be surrendered without contradiction. To surrender it would indicate a still higher calling of conscience, a still higher duty on the scale of duties.

I refer to conscience but would be reluctant to analyze it. There may be, in Hutcheson's sense, a moral sentiment – even a sentiment of benevolence – universally distributed among human beings. However, no sentiment as such can establish whether an action or motive is "moral." Witherspoon, for example, in his *Lectures on Moral Philosophy*, grants benevolence an important place in the pantheon of virtues, but is careful to distinguish one sense of moral duty from any aim exhausted by benevolence. It is enough to say that there are various theories of morality on offer, each with assets and defects and none standing as the last word on the matter.[21] Moreover, on any of the developed moral theories, the right course of action or reason for acting need not proceed from devotion to a specific set of religious tenets or even any set of propositions patently religious. What it does entail, however, is allegiance to a principle of action whose validity is not settled by convention or statute or the shifting enthusiasms of a neighborhood or an epoch. Less the gift of religious belief, it is its bedrock, as it is the bedrock of conviction itself.

On this point, Witherspoon's teaching is instructive, especially in light of his influence on the Founding generation. He grants that, "The love of our country

[20] Hutcheson, Hutcheson, *Inquiry*, "Treatise II," Sec. II, X, accessed April 10, 2016, http://oll.libertyfund.org/titles/2462#lf1458_label_227.

[21] For a critical appraisal, see Daniel N. Robinson, *Praise and Blame: Moral Realism and Its Application*. (Princeton: Princeton University Press, 2002).

to be sure, is a noble and enlarged affection, and those who have sacrificed private ease and family relations to it, have become illustrious, yet the love of mankind is still greatly superior."[22] He turns next to the question of duties and rights – "the rights or claims that one man has upon another," and concludes that, "Right in general may be reduced, as to its source, to the supreme law of moral duty; for whatever men are in duty obliged to do, that they have a claim to, and other men are considered as under an obligation to permit them."[23]

Witherspoon here adopts what by now is the conventional view according to which, if Smith has a basic duty, Jones is obliged not to prevent Smith from discharging it. In this sense, Smith's "right" reflects a species of protection against interference. A skeptic regarding anything proposed as "the supreme law of moral duty" would find nothing in Witherspoon's account that would ground either rights or duties. Nor does the conventional account explain the sense in which entities might be robust in "rights," though devoid of duties. At both a common sense and fundamental ontological level, "rights" – if they refer to anything observable – would seem to arise from specific *vulnerabilities* suffered by the bearers of rights. Duties, on the other hand, reach what falls under the agentic *powers* possessed by those who might exploit or enlarge such vulnerabilities. It is in just these respects that law defends the vulnerable by controlling the powerful.

It is not every or just any vulnerability that can claim the protection of law. Nor are the powers possessed by persons somehow and without qualification subject to the law's constraints. Thus, one must be cautious about conferring immunity (protection) on any or every action arising from a sincere religious belief or, as it were, even the moral sentiment of benevolence itself. In ways peculiar and often difficult to comprehend, the US Supreme Court has tended to confer such immunity in judging actions that surely violate the sentiments of many, while refusing to protect still other actions prompted by religious belief.

The difficulties here began nearly a century after the ratification of the US Constitution when polygamous marriages were permissible in the territory of Utah (See *Reynolds* v. *United States* 98 U.S. 145 (1878)). As early as *Reynolds* one finds points of conflict and tension between the Establishment clause and the civic reach of government into the complex world of religious belief and conviction. The Court in *Reynolds* recognizes this. In the opinion given by Chief Justice Waite, the central question raised by the plaintiff is, "Whether religious belief can be accepted as a justification of an overt act made criminal by the law of the land. The inquiry is not as to the power of Congress to prescribe criminal laws for the Territories, but as to the guilt of one who knowingly violates a law which has been properly enacted if he entertains a religious belief that the law is wrong." Noting that religious freedom is guaranteed throughout the United States, Waite is nonetheless at pains to acknowledge that "The word

[22] Witherspoon, *Lectures*, 54

[23] *Ibid.*

'religion' is not defined in the Constitution. We must go elsewhere, therefore, to ascertain its meaning, and nowhere more appropriately, we think, than to the history of the times in the midst of which the provision was adopted. The precise point of the inquiry is what is the religious freedom which has been guaranteed."

Seeking originalist grounds for the Court's ruling, Waite recurs to a time when colonists lived under locally established religions and were taxed to support religions that were not their own. Failure to attend public worship was subject to punishment, as were heretical opinions. Attempts in Virginia to solidify these practices led Madison to compose his famous *Memorial and Remonstrance*, extricating one's duty to the Creator from the reach of civil government. At the time, Waite notes, Jefferson was in France but, seeing a draft of the Constitution, he expressed disappointment that freedom of religion was not explicitly guaranteed. Later, in his celebrated letter to the Connecticut Baptists, Jefferson contemplated, "... with sovereign reverence that act of the whole American people which declared that their legislature should 'make no law respecting an establishment of religion or prohibiting the free exercise thereof,' thus building a wall of separation between church and State."

However encouraging the opinion might have seemed to Reynolds to this point, Waite's next few lines were dispositive (italics added): "Coming as this does from an acknowledged leader of the advocates of the measure, it may be accepted almost as an authoritative declaration of the scope and effect of the amendment thus secured. Congress was deprived of all legislative power over mere opinion, *but was left free to reach actions which were in violation of social duties or subversive of good order*." The core issues remain, settled somewhat differently by the application of somewhat different principles. As one example, there is *Church of Lukumi Babalu Aye* v. *City of Hialeah*.[24] In this action, Cuban exiles, followers of the religion of Santeria, were denied the right to engage in animal sacrifices in Hialeah, Florida. The jurisdiction rested its ban on considerations of animal cruelty and public health. A unanimous Court found for the Church, noting that Hialeah failed,

> ... to prohibit nonreligious conduct that endangers these interests in a similar or greater degree than Santeria sacrifice does ... Many types of animal deaths or kills for nonreligious reasons are either not prohibited or approved by express provision. For example, fishing ... Extermination of mice and rats within a home is also permitted ... The city ... asserts, however, that animal sacrifice is "different" from the animal killings that are permitted by law. According to the city, it is "self-evident" that killing animals for food is "important"; the eradication of insects and pests is "obviously justified"; and the euthanasia of excess animals "makes sense."

In light of these activities, the Court finds that the city of Hialeah has offered no compelling reason for religion alone having to bear the burden of the ordinances, "... when

[24] *Church of Lukumi Babalu Aye* v. *City of Hialeah* 508 U.S. 520 (1993).

many of these secular killings fall within the city's interest in preventing the cruel treatment of animals."[25]

The reasoning of the Court was perhaps too linear. Surely a jurisdiction, with no animus toward any religion, might have good and even compelling reasons to allow fishing, even while barring the torture of the fish on the line. It might also have good reason to permit the culling of herds but not their public butchery. And it might permit members of Santeria the practice of private exsanguination while barring a public display that many others would find offensive, even if ridiculous. To reason from the fact that only devotees of Santeria face legal impediments may be no more than to recover the fact that only they are engaged in the practice.

Moving from the troubling to the macabre, without suggesting even the slightest degree of moral equivalence, one might consider the invocation of this same rationale in the matter of female mutilation or "honor killing" within the framework of Islamic fundamentalism. The point must be emphasized that this is offered as a hypothetical, not as kindredly related to, e.g., Santeria. It is a fact that governments send military personnel on missions in which mutilation and death are likely. Yet other jurisdictions reserve the death penalty. Euthanasia is permitted in Oregon. Such examples of the lawful termination of human life are numerous. These were taken by the Court to support the claim that, "Many types of ... deaths or kills for nonreligious reasons are either not prohibited or approved by express provision." Why, then, must Islamic law alone bear the burden of restrictive ordinances? Again, the point of the question is to underscore the inevitable tensions between the claims of conscience and the very possibility of ordered liberty and decent forms of civic life. It would seem to be a consequence of one's sense that one is answerable to one's own conscience that one moves from this (if haltingly) to the belief that conscience arises from sources supersensuous and assuredly apolitical.

How collisions between one's moral and civic standing are to be averted or softened is a question resistant to easy answers. Historically, statutes such as *Acts of Supremacy* and forced religious conformity tend to rise no higher than impertinence in principle and thuggishness in practice. In these respects, it matters little whether the attempt to command or control comes from a tyrant, a king, an Imam, or even a Supreme Court. Opposing such commands seems to be based on something broader than the particulars of a given faith. Oppressive measures presume to command assent while defeating the very powers in virtue of which assent itself is possible. Rational beings able to imagine possibilities, frame plans of action, consider myriad options and the consequences plausibly contained in each are not merely worthy of the law's respect but serve as the ultimate ground of the law's own authority. In very large numbers over much of recorded history, such beings have been moved by

[25] Justice Kennedy, for the unanimous Court.

a sense of the transcendent, a reverence for an unseen power behind the order of nature itself. Out of this would emerge idealized conceptions of civic life, cooperative and trusting associations, strongly sensed duties to oneself and to others. The unopposable freedom to imagine – and to believe in the prospects made evident by the imagination – would seem to be that first freedom rendering liberty itself intelligible.

3

The creation and reconstruction of the First Amendment

Akhil Reed Amar*

We inhabit a world whose constitutional terrain is dominated by landmark Supreme Court cases invalidating state laws and administrative practices in the name of individual constitutional rights. Living in the shadow of *Brown* v. *Board of Education* and the second Reconstruction of the 1960s, many lawyers embrace a tradition that views state governments as the quintessential threat to individual and minority rights, and federal officials – especially federal courts – as the special guardians of those rights.

This nationalist tradition has deep roots. Over the course of two centuries, the Supreme Court has struck down state action with far more regularity than it has invalidated acts of coordinate national branches. In the early twentieth century, Justice Holmes declared, "I do not think the United States would come to an end if we lost our power to declare an Act of Congress void. I do think the Union would be imperiled if we could not make that declaration as to the laws of the several States."[1] Professor Thayer's famous 1893 essay on judicial review also embraced an expansive role for federal courts in reviewing state legislation, even as Thayer preached judicial deference to congressional acts of doubtful constitutionality.[2] Holmes and Thayer had reached maturity during the Civil War era, and they understood from firsthand experience that

* Sterling Professor of Law and Political Science, Yale University. This essay borrows liberally from Akhil Reed Amar, *The Bill of Rights: Creation and Reconstruction* (New Haven: Yale University Press, 1998), which in turn is built upon Akhil Reed Amar, "The Bill of Rights as a Constitution," *YALE L.J.* 100 (1991), 1131 and Akhil Reed Amar, "The Bill of Rights and the Fourteenth Amendment," *YALE L.J* 101 (1992), 1191. Readers seeking more details and more citations for the claims made here are warmly invited to consult these earlier works.

1 Oliver Wendell Holmes, *Collected Legal Papers* (New York: Harcourt, Brace and Howe, 1920), pp. 295–96.

2 James Thayer, "The Origin and Scope of the American Doctrine of Constitutional Law," *HARV. L. REV.* 7 (1893), 129.

the constitutional amendments adopted following the war – particularly the Fourteenth Amendment – evinced a similar suspicion of state governments.

In fact, the nationalist tradition is far older than Reconstruction; its deepest roots lie in Philadelphia, not Appomattox. One of the Federalists' most important goals was to forge a strong set of federally enforceable rights against abusive state governments, a goal dramatized by the catalog of rights in Article I, section 10 – the Federalist forebear of the Fourteenth Amendment. Indeed, the very effort to create a strong central government stemmed in part from the Federalists' dissatisfaction with small-scale politics and their belief that an "enlargement" of the government's geographic "sphere" would improve the caliber of public decision making. The classic statement of this view is Madison's Federalist No. 10.

Alongside this nationalist tradition, however, lay a states' rights tradition – also championed by Madison – extolling the ability of local governments to protect citizens against abuses by central authorities. Classic statements of this view include Madison's Federalist No. 46, his Virginia Resolutions of 1798, and his Report of 1800. Heavy traces of these ideas appear even in the work of the strong centralizer Alexander Hamilton (See, e.g., Hamilton's Federalist No. 28).

The foundations of this states' rights tradition are even older than those of the nationalist tradition – indeed, older than the Union itself. During the fateful years between the end of the French and Indian War and the beginning of the Revolutionary one, it was colonial governments that took the lead in protecting Americans from perceived parliamentary abuses. Colonial legislatures kept a close eye on the central government, sounded public alarms whenever they saw oppression in the works, and organized political, economic, and (ultimately) military opposition to perceived British abuses. The rallying cry of the Revolution nicely illustrates how states' rights and citizens' rights were seen as complementary, rather than conflicting: "No taxation without representation" sounds in terms of both federalism and the rights of Englishmen.

The complementary character of states' rights and personal rights was dramatized yet again by the Virginia and Kentucky Resolutions of 1798–1800. Self-consciously echoing their colonial forebears, legislators in these two states sounded the alarm when they saw the central government taking actions that they deemed dangerous and unconstitutional.[3] Like its 1776 predecessor, the

[3] Eight years earlier, the Virginia legislature had adopted resolutions denouncing as unconstitutional the federal government's assumption of state war debts. See Virginia Resolutions on the Assumption of State Debts, in Henry Steele Commager, *Documents of American History* (Upper Saddle River: Prentice Hall, 1975), pp. 155–56 (describing state legislators as "guardians ... of the rights and interests of their constituents" and "sentinels placed by them over the ministers of the federal government, to shield it from their encroachments, or at least to sound an alarm when it is threatened with invasion"). This 1790 declaration is an important link in the historical chain connecting the antiparliamentary activity of colonial legislatures before 1776 with the resolutions of 1798. Note especially the use of the revealing word "ministers" to describe federal officers.

"Revolution of 1800" fused rhetoric of federalism and freedom: the Alien and Sedition Acts were seen as violating both the First and the Tenth Amendments. Although many other state legislatures rejected Kentucky's open-ended claims that a state could nullify a federal law, state legislatures as a whole played a central role in the denouement of the new nation's first constitutional crisis. Through their power to select senators and presidential electors, state lawmakers helped sweep the high-Federalist friends of the Alien and Sedition Acts out of national office in the election of 1800, replacing them with Jeffersonians who allowed the repressive Acts to expire.

Madison was careful to identify the limits, as well as the affirmative scope, of states' rights. State governments could monitor the federal one, and mobilize political opposition to federal laws seen as oppressive, but no state entity could unilaterally nullify those laws or secede from the Union. Moreover, Madison's scheme gave the federal government a crucial role in protecting citizens from abusive state governments. Later spokesmen for the states' rights position, such as John C. Calhoun, Jefferson Davis, and Alexander Stephens, disregarded these vital limits to states' rights. Not only did their arguments on behalf of nullification and secession misread the Constitution's federal structure, but these arguments were deployed on behalf of slavery, the ultimate violation of human dignity. Once again, a war was fought on American soil over intertwined issues of states' rights and human rights, but with a critical difference. In sharp contrast to the Revolutionaries' rhetoric of the 1770s, the Rebels' rhetoric of federalism in the 1860s came to be seen as conflicting with, rather than supportive of, true freedom.

Americans are still living with the legacy of the Civil War, with modern rhetorical battle lines tracking those laid down a century and a half ago. Thus, in the tradition of the Radical Republicans of the 1860s, modern nationalists recognize the need for a strong national government to protect individuals against abusive state governments, but often miss the threat posed by a monstrous central regime unchecked by competing power centers. Conversely, in the tradition of Jefferson Davis, modern states' rightists wax eloquent about the dangers of a national government run rampant, but too often deploy the rhetoric of states' rights to defend states' wrongs. Sadly, "states' rights" and "federalism" have repeatedly served as code words for racial injustice and disregard for the rights of local minorities – code words for a world view far closer to Jefferson Davis' than James Madison's.

What has been lost in this modern debate is the crucial Madisonian insight that localism and liberty can sometimes work together, rather than at cross-purposes. This is one of the themes that will emerge from a fresh look at Madison's Bill of Rights, which I hope to offer in the first half of this essay.

In the second half of this essay, I shall bring Lincoln's generation – the aforementioned Reconstruction Republicans – into the frame of analysis. Through the Fourteenth Amendment, almost all the provisions of the Bill of Rights have come to be "incorporated" against the states. Although generally sound, the process of incorporation has had the unfortunate effect of blinding us to the ways in which the Bill has thereby been transformed. Originally a set of largely structural guarantees applying only against the federal government, the Bill has become a body of rights against all government conduct. Originally centered on protecting a majority of the people from a possibly unrepresentative government, the Bill has been pressed into the service of protecting vulnerable minorities from dominant social majorities. Given the core concerns of the Fourteenth Amendment, all this is fitting, but because of the peculiar logistics of incorporation, the Fourteenth Amendment itself often seems to drop out of the analysis. We appear to be applying the Bill of Rights directly; the Civil War Amendment is mentioned only in passing or not at all. Like people with spectacles who often forget they are wearing them, most lawyers read the Bill of Rights through the lens of the Fourteenth Amendment without realizing how powerfully that lens has refracted what they see.

It is time, then, to take off these spectacles, and try to see what the Bill of Rights in general – and the First Amendment in particular – looked like before Reconstruction. This is what I invite us to do in the first half of this essay. And then, in the second half, we shall put the spectacles back on and take a second look.

Let us begin by considering the second half of the First Amendment: "Congress shall make no law ... abridging the freedom of speech, or of the press; or the right of the people peaceably to assemble, and to petition the Government for a redress of grievances."

This declaration sounds in structure, and focuses (at least in part) on the representational linkage between Congress and its constituents. The body that is restrained is not a hostile majority of the people, but Congress; and we should recall that congressional majorities may at times have "aristocratical" and self-interested views in opposition to views held by a majority of the people. Thus, while the Amendment's text is broad enough to protect the rights of unpopular minorities (such as Jehovah's Witnesses and Communists), the Amendment's historical and structural core was to safeguard the rights of popular majorities (such as the Republicans of the late 1790s) against a possibly unrepresentative and self-interested Congress.

Consider in this regard Madison's distinction in The Federalist No. 51 between the two main problems of republican government – first, protecting citizens generally from government officials pursuing their own self-interested agendas at the expense of their constituents; and second, protecting individuals and minorities from tyrannical majority factions of fellow citizens. As originally worded, the First Amendment betrayed more concern about the first issue than the second. Recall the Amendment's first word. "Congress" was restrained but not state legislatures. Yet, as Madison's Federalist No. 10 reminds us, the danger of majority oppression of minorities (the second issue) was far greater at the state than at the national level. Of course, this was largely because state legislative representation was so much less attenuated than congressional representation, making state legislative majorities far more likely to reflect the unrefined sentiments of popular majorities. Thus, the fact that our First Amendment restrained only Congress suggests that its primary target was attenuated representation, not overweening majoritarianism. Congress was singled out precisely because it was less likely to reflect majority will.

Madison himself had a rather different goal. As part of his initial proposed Bill of Rights, he included an amendment proscribing states from violating "freedom of the press," and went on to declare:

> But I confess that I do conceive, that in a Government modified like this of the United States, the great danger lies rather in the abuse of the community than in the legislative body. The prescriptions in favor of liberty ought to be levelled against that quarter where the greatest danger lies, namely, that which possesses the highest prerogative of power. But this is not found in either the executive or the legislative departments of Government, but in the body of the people, operating by the majority against the minority.[4]

Madison's proposed amendment also obliged state governments to protect "equal rights of conscience" and "trial by jury in criminal cases," and was soon reworded to protect "speech" as well as "press" from state interference. When the package came up for discussion on the floor of the House, Madison described it as "the most valuable amendment in the whole list. If there was any reason to restrain the Government of the United States from infringing upon these essential rights, it was equally necessary that they should be secured against the State Governments."[5]

Madison's proposal passed the House of Representatives (as the original Fourteenth Amendment!) but died in the Senate. Of course, to the extent that principles of free speech and a free press were implicit in the republican structure

[4] *Annals of* Congress 1789, 452, 454–55; Edward Dumbauld, *The Bill of Rights and What it Means Today* (Greenwood: Praeger, 1979), p. 208. Madison had previously expressed the same view in a letter to Jefferson on the subject of a possible bill of rights: "In our Governments the real power lies in the majority of the Community, and the invasion of private rights is chiefly [sic] to be apprehended, not from acts of Government contrary to the sense of its constituents, but from acts in which the Government is the mere instrument of the major number of the constituents." "James Madison to Thomas Jefferson 17 October 1788," The Founders' Constitution, Volume 1, Chapter 14, Document 47, accessed August 18, 2015, http://press-pubs.uchicago.edu/founders/documents/v1ch14s47.html. Yet Madison's views were atypical, as his next sentence reveals: "This is a truth of great importance, but not yet sufficiently attended to …." Madison went on to say that a Bill of Rights would probably be most effective where unpopular and unrepresentative government action was at issue. "[T]here may be occasions on which the evil may spring from [government self-interest]; and on such, a bill of rights will be a good ground for an appeal to the sense of the community." *Id. at 299.*

[5] Dumbauld, *The Bill of Rights*, pp. 208, 211; *Annals of Congress* 1789, 78.

of the original Constitution, state legislatures were already bound to observe those principles – especially where citizens sought to speak out about issues of national concern. (Any state effort to stifle this debate would seem vulnerable on supremacy clause grounds.) However, full vindication of the Madisonian vision did not occur until the adoption of our Fourteenth Amendment after the Civil War. The equal protection clause of that Amendment, directed at state governments, obviously focuses more on overweening majoritarianism than attenuated representation. And, as we shall see later, strong arguments support a reading of the privileges-or-immunities clause as incorporating most of the provisions of the Bill of Rights, including the speech and press clauses, against the states.

Although many modern speech theorists echo Madison's 1789 fear of popular majorities, we must remember that the First Amendment tradition of "uninhibited, robust, and wide-open" criticism of government celebrated by *New York Times* v. *Sullivan* was born when Madison and Jefferson successfully appealed to a popular majority during 1798–1800. No court invalidated the Alien and Sedition Acts (unless one cheats by counting the *Sullivan* court itself, 150 odd years later, or the "court of history" it invoked). Rather, a popular majority adjudicated the First Amendment question in the election of 1800, by throwing out the haughty and aristocratic rascals who had tried to shield themselves from popular criticism. (The Sedition Act itself was a textbook example of attempted self-dealing among the people's agents; it criminalized libel of incumbents, but not challengers. Yet another dead giveaway: the Act conveniently provided for its own expiration after the next election.) If we see the First Amendment as primarily about minority rights, Jefferson's strategy of appealing to a popular majority seems odd indeed. But once we see the Amendment's populist roots, its vindication by the election of 1800 borders on the poetic.

It becomes even clearer that popular speech was the paradigm of our First Amendment when we recall its historic connection to jury trial; popular bodies outside regular government would protect popular speech criticizing government. The historic common law rule against prior restraint – courts could not enjoin a publisher from printing offensive material, but could entertain civil and criminal prosecutions for libel and sedition afterwards – had bite largely because of the structural differences between the two proceedings. The ban on prior restraints constrained equity courts, presided at by permanent government officials on the government payroll (chancellors), but libel and sedition lawsuits typically required the intervention of ordinary citizens (jurors) who could vote for the publisher without reprisal. In the colonies, the celebrated 1730s trial of the New York publisher John Peter Zenger had placed the issue of the jury's role at center stage in libel cases, and it continued to remain there even after the Revolution and Constitution: Publishers prosecuted under the Alien and Sedition Acts in the late 1790s tried to plead their First Amendment defense to jurors. The judges, after all, had been appointed by the very same (increasingly unpopular) Adams administration that the defendants had attacked in the press.

This episode contrasts sharply with today's practice, where friends of the First Amendment often seek to limit the power of juries on speech questions, such as obscenity vel non, by appealing to Article III judges. Since the First Amendment's center of gravity has (appropriately in light of the later Fourteenth Amendment) shifted to protection of unpopular, minority speech, its natural institutional guardian has become an insulated judiciary rather than the popular jury.

Similarly, today's First Amendment champions tend to see state and local "community standards" of discourse as the paradigmatic threat to free speech; but the Amendment's defenders in the 1790s turned to local juries and state legislatures for refuge. After congressional enactment of the Sedition Act, where could opponents vigorously voice their criticism of the Act without fear of prosecution under the Act itself? In state legislatures, of course. Even if, as the high Federalists claimed, freedom for partisan publishers was not absolute but limited to freedom from prior restraint, who would dare claim that absolute "freedom of speech" did not obtain within constitutionally recognized legislative bodies? Indeed, the very notion of free speech for citizens had grown out of an older tradition establishing legislative "speech and debate" immunity from prosecution.[6] The Articles of Confederation had explicitly used the phrase "freedom of speech" to immunize members of the federal Congress from state libel law, and the Virginia and Kentucky legislatures in 1798 were simply returning the compliment. Thus, even as the Virginia and Kentucky legislators themselves invoked both First and Tenth Amendment protections in arguing that the Alien and Sedition Acts were unconstitutional, their own speech was specially protected by a states' rights gloss on the free speech clause.

In the end, the individual rights vision of the speech and press clauses powerfully illuminates a vital part of our constitutional tradition, but only by obscuring other parts. The special structural role of freedom of speech in a representative democracy; the localist and majoritarian accent of the First Amendment circa 1800; the massive transformation brought about by the Fourteenth Amendment; the competing claims of judge, jury, and electorate to define the boundaries of "free speech"; the obvious problem of incumbent

[6] See, e.g., MD. Const. of 1776 (Declaration of Rights), pt. I, art. X; MA. Const. of 1780, pt. I, art. XXI; N.H. Const. of 1784, pt. I, art I, § XXX; see also an act for declaring the rights and liberties of the subject and settling the succession of the crown (Bill of Rights), 1689, 1 W. & M. ch. 2, § 9; Leonard Levy, *Emergence of a Free Press* (Oxford: Oxford University Press, 1985), pp. 102–03. Indeed, of the original 13 colonies, only Pennsylvania's 1776 constitution extended "freedom of speech" beyond the legislature, id. at 5. And as Gordon Wood has shown, the unusual unicameral legislative system in Pennsylvania can be understood as constituting the citizens themselves as the implicit lower house. See Gordon S. Wood, *The Creation of the American Republic, 1776–1787* (Chapel Hill: University of North Carolina Press, 1998), pp. 231–32, 249–51.

self-dealing at the heart of the Sedition Act; the special role of free speech in state legislatures – all this and much more are simply bleached out of the standard sketch drawn from the individual rights perspective.

When we turn our attention to the assembly and petition clauses, a similar pattern emerges. Both clauses obviously protect individuals and minority groups, but the clauses contain a majoritarian core that contemporary scholarship has tended to slight. The right of the people to assemble does not simply protect the ability of self-selected clusters of individuals to meet together; it is also an express reservation of the collective right of "We the People" to assemble in a future convention and exercise our sovereign right to alter or abolish our government.

Read carefully the remarks of President Edmund Pendleton of the Virginia ratifying convention of 1788:

> We, the people, possessing all power, form a government, such as we think will secure happiness: and suppose, in adopting this plan, we should be mistaken in the end; where is the cause of alarm on that quarter? In the same plan we point out an easy and quiet method of reforming what may be found amiss. No, but, say gentlemen, we have put the introduction of that method in the hands of our servants, who will interrupt it from motives of self-interest. What then? ... Who shall dare to resist the people? No, we will assemble in Convention; wholly recall our delegated powers, or reform them so as to prevent such abuse.[7]

This rich paragraph has it all: primary attention to the problem of government self-dealing, dogged unwillingness to equate Congress with a majority of the people, and keen appreciation of the collective right of the people to bring wayward government to heel by assembling in convention. Pendleton saw that the ever-present possibility of governmental self-dealing meant that future amendments might be necessary to bring government under control. Obviously, ordinary government officials – Congress, state legislatures, and so on – could not be given a monopoly over the amendment process, for that would enable them to thwart desperately needed change by self-interested inaction. Hence the need to keep open the special channel of the popular convention acting outside of all ordinary government, convenable, if necessary, by popular petition. (Indeed, it was the very threat of a second constitutional convention that induced many Federalists in the First Congress to support a Bill of Rights limiting their own powers, lest a new convention propose even more stringent amendments.)

Pendleton's language reveals the obvious bridge between the Preamble's invocation of "the People" and the reemergence of that phrase in our First Amendment. The Preamble's dramatic opening words, quoted by Pendleton, trumpeted the Constitution's underlying theory of popular sovereignty. Those words and that theory implied a right of "the People" (acting by majority vote

[7] See *Constitution Society*, www.constitution.org/rc/rat_va_04.htm.

in special conventions) to alter or abolish their government whenever they deemed proper: what "the People" had "Ordain[ed] and establish[ed]" (using popular conventions), they or their "posterity" could dis-establish at will (similarly using conventions). To good lawyers of the late 1780s, Pendleton was merely restating first principles.

In the First Congress, Madison's very first proposed amendment was a prefix to the Preamble that similarly declared: "[T]he people have an indubitable, unalienable, and indefeasible right to reform or change their Government ...." Not a single Representative quarreled with Madison on the substance of this claim, although some considered any prefix superfluous. When Congress eventually decided to add amendments to the end of the document rather than interweave them into the original text, the prefix was abandoned; but the underlying idea survived, repackaged as a guarantee of the right of "the people to assemble."[8]

Members of the First Congress shared Pendleton's understanding that constitutional conventions were paradigmatic exercises of this right. As Gordon Wood has observed, "conventions ... of the people ... were closely allied in English thought with the people's right to assemble ...." Thus, our First Amendment's language of "the right of the people to assemble" simply made explicit at the end of the Constitution what Pendleton and others already saw as implicit in its opening.[9] (Many other provisions of the Bill of Rights were also understood as declaratory, inserted simply out of an abundance of caution to clarify preexisting constitutional understandings. Indeed, the congressional resolution accompanying the Bill explicitly described it as containing "declaratory" as well as "restrictive" provisions. Our Tenth Amendment is an obvious example, and was so understood from the outset.)[10]

Pendleton's language about the people's right to assemble was echoed by the Declaration of Rights adopted by the Virginia convention, which included the following language: "That the people have a right peaceably to assemble together to consult for the common good, or to instruct their representatives." This was neither the first nor the last time that the people's asserted rights of assembly and instruction were yoked together. The same pairing had appeared in the Pennsylvania and North Carolina state Constitutions of 1776, the Vermont Constitutions of 1777 and 1786, the Massachusetts Constitution of 1780, and the New Hampshire Constitution of 1784; and

[8] *Annals of Congress* 1789, 451; id. at 741, 746 (remarks of James Jackson, John Page, and James Madison) (August 13–14, 1789).

[9] See, e.g., *ibid.* 446 (reference to "assembling of a convention") (remarks of John Page) (June 8, 1789); James G. Pope, "Republican Moments: The Role of Direct Popular Power in the American Constitutional Order," *U. PA. L. REV.* 139 (1990), 287 (connecting people's right to assemble to conventions and other forms of popular sovereignty and mass mobilization); Wood, *Creation of the American Republic*, p. 312.

[10] See *Annals of Congress* 1789 (remarks of James Madison admitting that his proto-Tenth Amendment "may be considered as superfluous").

would later appear in the Declaration of Rights of the New York, North Carolina, and Rhode Island ratifying conventions. When Madison proposed the assembly clause to the First Congress, Thomas Tucker of South Carolina quickly moved to add to it an express right of the people "to instruct their Representatives."[11]

The juxtaposition of assembly and instruction is illuminating. Both clauses have strong majoritarian components, and reflect the Anti-Federalist concern with attenuated representation in Congress. Yet there is a vital difference between the two rights – a difference that led Madison and his fellow Federalists to embrace the former while successfully opposing the latter. Instruction would have completely undermined the Madisonian system of deliberation among refined representatives – a system aiming for a Congress populated by leading statesmen far more knowledgeable and broadminded than the ordinary voter back home. All the advantages of representational refinement would be lost if each representative could be bound by his relatively uninformed and parochial constituents rather than his conscience, enlightened by full discussions with his fellow representatives bringing information and ideas from other parts of the country. As Garry Wills has pointed out, all of Madison's central arguments in The Federalist No. 10 are premised on a repudiation of the idea of instruction.[12]

By contrast, Madison and his fellow Federalists could and did embrace the idea of a popular right to assemble in convention. Unlike instruction, such a right would not continually undermine ordinary congressional deliberation on day-to-day affairs, but would simply reserve to the people the right to meet in future conventions to consider amending the Constitution in situations where government had become truly dysfunctional – just as the people had assembled in convention in the previous months to ratify the Constitution proposed by Madison and his fellow Federalists.

A similarly populist story may be told about the petition clause. One key textual point to note is that the Amendment explicitly guarantees "the right of the people" to petition – a formulation that decisively signals its connection to popular sovereignty theory and underscores Gordon Wood's observation

[11] Jonathan Elliot, *Elliot's Debates, on the Adoption of the Federal Constitution* (Philadelphia: J. B. Lippincott, 1937), pp. 658–59 (Virginia); PA. Const. of 1776 (Declaration of Rights), art. XVI; N.C. Const. of 1776 (Declaration of Rights), art. XVIII; VT. Const. of 1777, ch. 1, § XVIII; MA. Const. of 1780, pt. I, art. XIX; N.H. CONST. OF 1784, pt. I, art. I, § XXXII; VT. CONST. of 1786, ch.1, § XXII; Elliot, *Elliot's Debates*, p. 328 (New York); *id.* at 335 (Rhode Island); 4 id. at 244 (North Carolina); *Annals of Congress*, 1789, 761.

[12] See, e.g., *Annals of Congress* 1789, 767 (remarks of Michael Jenifer Stone) (instruction "would change the Government entirely" from one "founded upon representation" into a "democracy of singular properties"); Garry Wills, *Explaining America: The Federalist* (London: Penguin Books, 2001), pp. 216–30; see also James Madison, "The Federalist No. 63," Constitution Society, accessed August 18, 2015, http://constitution.org/fed/federa63.htm. Only after the instruction debate in the First Congress did state constitutions begin to sever the rights of instruction and assembly. See, e.g., KY. Const. of 1792, art. XII, § 22.

that the ideas of petition, assembly, and convention were tightly intertwined in eighteenth-century America.[13]

The precursors of the petition clause suggested by state ratifying conventions had obscured these connections. Each of the four conventions spoke of the "people's" right to "assemble" or to alter or abolish government (and as we have seen, these two rights were closely linked); yet each convention described the right of petition in purely individualistic language – a right of "every freeman," "every person," or "every man."[14] Under these formulations, petition appeared less a political than a civil right, akin to the right to sue in court and receive due process. The language and structure of our First Amendment suggest otherwise. As with assembly, the core right of "the people" to petition is collective and popular.

To be sure, like its companion assembly clause, the petition clause also protects individuals and minority groups. But to focus only on minority invocations of the right to petition is to miss at least half of the clause's meaning, even if we put to one side its momentous implications for constitutional amendment. Like the other provisions of the First Amendment, the clause is not solely concerned with the problem of overweening majoritarianism; it is at least equally concerned with the danger of attenuated representation. Legal scholar Stephen Higginson has shown that part of the purpose and effect of the petitions was to help inform representatives about local conditions. In eighteenth-century Virginia, for example, more than half of the statutes ultimately enacted by the state legislature originated in the form of popular petitions. And at the Founding, Congress's relatively small size gave rise to special concern about whether representatives would have adequate knowledge of their constituents' wants and needs.[15]

Indeed, the populist possibilities implicit in the petition clause should be evident from a simple side-by-side comparison of the First Amendment's language with English precedent. According to Blackstone's *Commentaries*, in England,

> no petition to the king, or either house of parliament, for any alterations in church or state, shall be signed by above twenty persons, unless the matter thereof be approved by three justices of the peace, or the major part of the grand jury, in the country; and in

[13] Wood, *Creation of the American Republic*, p. 312; See also Dumbauld, *The Bill of Rights*, 103–05 (linking assembly, petition, conventions, and rights "of the people"); Norman B. Smith, "Shall Make No Law Abridging ...": An Analysis of the Neglected, But Nearly Absolute, Right of Petition, *U. CIN. L. REV.* 54 (1986), 1153, 1179 (petition right "inextricably linked to the emergence of popular sovereignty").

[14] Elliott, *Elliot's Debates*, p. 328 (New York); 2 id. at 553 (proposals of Maryland convention committee minority); 3 id. at 658–59 (Virginia); 4 id. at 244 (North Carolina).

[15] See Stephen A. Higginson, "A Short History of the Right to Petition Government for the Redress of Grievances," *YALE L.J.* 96 (1986) 142, 158–66; Smith, "Shall Make No Law Abridging," 1178–79; Raymond C. Bailey, *Popular Influence Upon Public Policy: Petitioning in Eighteenth-Century Virginia* (Greenwood: Praeger, 1979), p. 64.

London by the lord mayor, alderman, and common council; nor shall any petition be presented by more than ten persons at a time.

In his American edition of Blackstone, St. George Tucker took obvious satisfaction in reminding his readers that, "In America, there is no such restraint."[16]

Like their speech and press clause counterparts, the rights of petition and assembly became applicable against state governments only after the adoption of the Fourteenth Amendment. As we shall see presently, incorporation of these guarantees against state governments makes a good deal of sense in light of the Amendment's text, its historical purpose of safeguarding vulnerable minorities against majority oppression, and the overall structure of federalism implied by that amendment – namely, that those citizen rights formerly protected against the national government should also be protected against state governments. Nor should we forget the central role the right of petition played in abolitionist thought and practice in the antebellum era.

What has to some critics made less sense, however, is the Supreme Court's attempt to fully "incorporate" the First Amendment's establishment clause against states. To that clause, and its free exercise counterpart, we now turn.

The establishment clause did more than prohibit Congress from establishing a national church. Its mandate that Congress shall make no law "respecting an establishment of religion" also prohibited the national legislature from interfering with, or trying to dis-establish, churches established by state and local governments. The key point is not simply that, as with the rest of the First Amendment, the establishment clause limited only Congress and not the states. As we have seen, that point is obvious on the face of the Amendment, and is confirmed by its legislative history. (It also, of course, has the imprimatur of Chief Justice Marshall's opinion in *Barron* v. *Baltimore*.) Nor is the main point exhausted once we recognize that state governments are in part the special beneficiaries of, and rights-holders under, the clause. As we have also seen, the same thing could be said, to some degree, about the free speech clause. The special prick of the point is this: the nature of the states' establishment clause right against federal dis-establishment makes it rather awkward to fully "incorporate" the clause against the states via the Fourteenth Amendment. Incorporation of the free speech clause against states does not negate state legislators' own First Amendment rights to freedom of speech in the legislative assembly. But mechanical incorporation of the establishment clause has precisely this kind of effect; to apply the clause against a state government is precisely to eliminate its right to choose whether to establish a religion – a right explicitly confirmed by the establishment clause itself!

We shall ponder this puzzle more carefully very soon – when we put on the Fourteenth Amendment's spectacles and see how powerfully these constitutional

[16] William Blackstone, *Blackstone's Commentaries: With Notes of Reference to the Constitution and Laws, of the Federal Government of the United States, and of the Commonwealth of Virginia* (Philadelphia: William Young Birch, and Abraham Small, 1803), pp. 299–300.

spectacles have refracted the Bill of Rights as originally understood; but for just a moment more, let's continue to try to see the world through the eyes of the Founding generation.

A federalism-inspired reading of the First Amendment has profound implications for the original meaning of the free-exercise clause. If the phrase "Congress shall make no law" really meant that Congress simply lacked enumerated power to intrude on religious freedom in the several states, the kind of intrusion prohibited must have been a congressional law that sought to abridge religious liberty *as such* – a congressional law *targeted* at the free exercise of religion. Such a law simply lay beyond Congress's legitimate province – it was not a necessary-and-proper exercise of Congress's secular enumerated powers – and it thus could be flatly barred: "no law ... prohibiting the free exercise" of region meant no law *designed* to prohibit religious freedom. A law that regulated worship qua worship would be unconstitutional from the very moment of its enacting – its "*mak[ing]*" – and so would an artful sham phrased in seemingly secular terms but motivated by an attempt to target a given religion. (The sham would offend the *McCulloch* pretext test.) Though enforceable in courts after the fact, the First Amendment's first addressee – its first word – was Congress, and it commanded conscientious congressmen to vote against offending bills, to "make no law" of a certain sort.

On this analysis, general laws designed to serve secular purposes enumerated in Article I would be a very different matter, even if, in operation, they had the effect of impairing some particular group's religious practices. Imagine, for example, a congressional ban on the importation of some drug that a particular religion deemed central to its worship practice. The Congress that made the law might not even know that such practice existed; indeed, the practice might well have arisen only after the law was passed. And surely some religious practices, even if bona fide, must yield to neutral congressional laws. (Consider for example, human sacrifice of nonbelievers seeking to vote in federal elections.) But once some neutral laws trump contrary religious practices, why not all neutral laws? The apparent absolutist grammar and logic of the clause do not seem to invite a balancing of the federal interest against the religious interest. Rather, the clause seems to invite careful attention to the purpose of a given federal law, and its nexus to legitimate, secular, enumerated powers in Article I.

On this reading, the controversial Supreme Court decision in the 1990 case of *Employment Division* v. *Smith* would appear to have even more textual, structural, and historical support than its author, Justice Antonin Scalia, claimed for it. In limiting the protection of the free-exercise clause to laws targeting religion, the Court said only that "[a]s a textual matter, we do not think the words [of the First Amendment] must be given [a broader] meaning" that would enable some religious practices to trump neutral, general, secular laws.

But *Smith* involved a state law, not a federal law. The true constitutional provision at issue was the Fourteenth Amendment, not the First. (Justice Scalia forgot that he was wearing glasses!) And perhaps – as we shall soon see – a sensitive reading of text, history, and structure of the Reconstruction Amendment calls for a broader protection of some forms of religious worship, even against neutral secular laws. There are reasons to think that the federalism-based reading of the First Amendment may not have been foremost in the minds of the Reconstruction Congress as it reglossed the federal Bill of Rights and made its freedoms, and other fundamental privileges and rights, applicable against states. Though the language of the Fourteenth Amendment in several ways tracks that of the First – "*No* state shall *make* or enforce any *law* which *shall abridge* the privileges or immunities of citizens" – it fact, subtle differences exist that might support critics of Smith. To begin with, the Fourteenth focuses not just on *making* laws but also on *enforcing* them. Perhaps this wording invites us to pay close attention to the clash between church and state not just at the time of enactment but also at the moment of application. And perhaps some religious practices that affect only the religious community itself (with no externalities imposed on religious nonbelievers) might be deemed "privileges" and "immunities" – islands of institutional privacy and communal autonomy against general laws. On this view, the precise text of the Fourteenth Amendment might enable sensitive interpreters to distinguish among different types of religious exercise in a principled and textually defensible way – once we remember, as Justice Scalia did not, quite, that the key text in almost all "First Amendment" cases is in fact – the Fourteenth Amendment.

It is thus time to take a second look at everything that we have considered thus far – this time, viewing the matter through the lens of Fourteenth Amendment's privileges-or-immunities clause, which, to repeat, reads as follows: "No State shall make or enforce any law which shall abridge the privileges or immunities of citizens of the United States." In a nutshell, these words were designed to make applicable against states – to incorporate, if you well – all fundamental civil "rights," "freedoms," "privileges," and "immunities." (The four quoted words were largely synonymous to the Reconstruction Republicans who drafted and ratified this amendment.) Where would judges and other interpreters find such fundamental rights? In part, in the US Constitution itself, and in its early amendments.

But not everything in the Constitution was incorporated against states. For example, presidents must be 35 years old but governors need not be. Only the basic rights and freedoms mentioned in the federal Constitution (and in other source-documents such as the Declaration of Independence and state constitutions) apply, thanks to the Fourteenth Amendment, against states. But sometimes – as in the First Amendment itself – rights (which do properly incorporate) and structural rules (which don't) are intertwined in the federal Constitution's text. Thus, faithful interpreters must carefully sift the Constitution to separate and refine out various rights and freedoms from the mixed textual ore in which these rights were initially embedded. Elsewhere, I have labeled this process "refined incorporation" and the First Amendment's provisions provide a nice series of case studies to illustrate the proper technique of sifting and refining.

"Congress shall make no law ... abridging the freedom of speech, or of the press; or the right of the people peaceably to assemble, and to petition the Government for a redress of grievances." Textually, the argument for applying these rights against states via the Fourteenth Amendment is wonderfully straightforward. The First Amendment explicitly speaks of "right[s]" and "freedom[s]" – entitlements also known as "privileges" and "immunities" – and the Amendment's words that these rights "shall" not be "abridg[ed]" by "law" perfectly harmonize with their echoes in the key sentence of Section One: "No state shall make ... any law which *shall abridge* ..." Nor can it be argued that these "rights" and "freedoms" are somehow not private rights of individual citizens. Though narrower in scope than their American counterparts, the freedoms of press, petition, and peaceable assembly were, according to Blackstone, core common-law rights "of persons" and of "every freeman."[17] As we have seen, these traditional common-law rights were broadened in the 1780s by American popular sovereignty theory, which also extended to ordinary citizens the freedom of speech previously enjoyed only by legislators.

Of course, federalism played an important role in the original First Amendment, but not in a way that impedes incorporation of its explicit rights and freedoms. Even if we assume that freedom of speech in state legislatures enjoyed special First Amendment status above and beyond the freedom of ordinary citizens, nothing about incorporation takes away state legislatures' freedom of speech; incorporation simply limits their freedom to use state law to silence ordinary citizens, and that freedom is not in any way protected by the First Amendment. For example, the Amendment nowhere forbids Congress to "make any law *protecting* freedom of speech" and so on against repressive state action. On the contrary, a strong argument can be made that Congress at the Founding was empowered and perhaps required to pass precisely these sorts of laws to vindicate the Article IV guarantee that each state would have a republican government. Could such a government ever punish citizens for speaking, writing, peaceably assembling, or petitioning against it?

Many antebellum critics of *Barron v Baltimore* – critics whom I have elsewhere playfully labeled "*Barron* contrarians" – thought not. Today, we might at first wonder how faithful interpreters of the First Amendment could earnestly argue, even before 1866, that its protections of free expression could bind states; but few moderns have any problem seeing a presidential censorship edict, or a judicial contempt order imprisoning a reporter critical of the court, as raising "First Amendment" concerns. To be sure, the Amendment speaks only of "Congress"; but any automatic *expressio unius* inference that citizens therefore lack analogous rights against the president or federal judges – or states – flies in the face of the Ninth Amendment. Thus, when supporters of the Fourteenth Amendment described its provisions as "declaratory" of the existing Constitution, properly construed, we must not assume that they necessarily

[17] 1 Blackstone, *Blackstone Commentaries*, p. 143 (petition and assembly); 4 id. at 152 (2016).

meant to include only those generally worded provisions of the Bill of Rights and to exclude those clauses explicitly linked to "Congress."

Thus, neither the First Amendment's arguably special protection of state legislative speech, nor its use of the word "Congress" presents any stumbling block to incorporation. But a third federalism component of the original Amendment does raise an interesting incorporation question. The particularly absolutist phrasing of the First Amendment – "Congress shall make no law" – may well have reflected a widespread understanding in 1789 that Congress simply lacked enumerated power to suppress speech, etc. To this extent, the First Amendment resembled the Tenth, specifying not a private right of citizens based on personal liberty, but a state right rooted in federalism. And under the model of refined incorporation, the federalism aspect of First Amendment absolutism does not sensibly incorporate against states. But then, we are left with a seeming paradox: the First Amendment might constrain Congress more strictly than the Fourteenth constrains states even though both Amendments seem to speak with one voice, that the freedom of speech, etc., "shall" not be "abridg[ed]" by "law."

The paradox is more apparent than real. As a practical matter, we must of course remember that the federalism-based argument for First Amendment absolutism has never been taken seriously by federal courts and is unlikely to be revived in the modern era. But if the theory ever were taken seriously, it could indeed permit differential treatment of state and federal governments. Even if couched as an interpretation of the First Amendment, federalism-based absolutism is ultimately rooted elsewhere – in a strict interpretation of Article I, Section 8 claiming that Congress lacks enumerated power to censor. But nothing in the text, history, or logic of the Fourteenth Amendment suggests that the federal system of enumerated powers should be overlaid on – incorporated against – states. Put another way, if we take federalism seriously, even before we reach the question whether federal power is trumped by the First Amendment in a given area, we must ask an analytically prior question: does the Constitution in fact grant the federal government power here? And if the answer is no, we must not assume that state governments also necessarily lack power – for perhaps Congress is denied a particular power precisely because the Constitution meant to leave it to the states.

At first, the federalism-based reading of the First Amendment might seem tailor-made for Hugo Black, who championed First Amendment absolutism, preached fidelity to the Founders' original intent, and also proved willing to invalidate acts of Congress on federalism grounds. Yet Black never relied on federalism to bolster his First Amendment absolutism, and with good reason. Such a move would have driven an analytic wedge between the First and Fourteenth Amendments, thereby destroying Black's own theory of mechanical incorporation – a theory that everything in Amendments One through Eight now applies against states in every respect. This wedge would not necessarily require abandonment of absolutism in free speech cases involving states: Black could well have defended First Amendment absolutism on grounds of *both* federalism *and* freedom, and the latter set of arguments clearly would apply equally against states. But if Black had ever admitted that any of the provisions of Amendments I–VIII had any federalism component whatsoever, he would have been forced to admit the analytical possibility that perhaps not all of his (redefined) Bill of Rights sensibly incorporated jot for jot. The entire analytic structure of his total-incorporation approach would have crumbled.

But even if Black's precise analytic path to incorporation of speech, press, petition, and assembly cut a few corners, he ended up in the right place: as a matter of constitutional text and structure, these clauses are indeed easy cases for full application against states via the Fourteenth Amendment. An ounce of history here provides powerful confirmation. From the 1830s on, the abolitionist crusaders had understood that freedom of speech for all men and women went hand in hand with freedom of bodily liberty for slaves. The Slave Power posed a threat to Freedom – of all kinds – and could support itself only through suppression of opposition speech, with gag rules on anti-slavery petitions, bans on "incendiary" publications, intrusions on the right of peaceable assembly, and so on. This global theory of Freedom was not limited to a few lawyers or theorists spearheading the crusade, but was quite literally the popular platform of the anti-slavery movement, perhaps best exemplified by an 1856 Republican Party campaign slogan: "Free Speech, Free Press, Free Men, Free Labor, Free Territory, and Fremont."[18]

During the Thirty-eighth and Thirty-ninth Congresses, Republicans invoked speech, press, petition, and assembly rights over and over – more frequently than any other right, with the possible exception of due process. These invocations occurred in a variety of overlapping contexts: as glosses on the "civil rights" to be protected by the Civil Rights Act and Freedman's Bureau Act (both of which were closely tied to the Fourteenth Amendment), as part of the definition of republican government (whose violation justified continued Southern exclusion from the national legislature), as "fundamental rights" of all citizens, and as paradigmatic "privileges or immunities" of national citizenship and/or interstate comity.[19]

[18] See generally Clement Eaton, *The Freedom-Of-Thought Struggle in the Old South* (New York: Harper Torchbooks, 1964); Russel B. Nye, *Fettered Freedom, Civil Liberties and the Slavery Controversy 1830–1860* (Lansing: Michigan State University Press, 1963); William S. Savage, *The Controversy Over the Distribution of Abolition Literature, 1830–1860* (New York: Negro Universities Press, 1968).

[19] See, e.g., *Cong. Globe*, 38th Cong., 1st Sess. 1202, 1313, 1439, 2615, 2990 (1864) (remarks of Rep. James Wilson, Sens. Lyman Trumbull and James Harlan, and Reps. Daniel Morris and Ebon Ingersoll); *Cong. Globe*, 38th Cong., 2d Sess. 138, 193, 237 (1864) (remarks of Reps. James Ashley, John Kasson, and Green Smith); *Cong. Globe*, 39th Cong., 1st Sess. 474–75, 1066, 1072, 1263, 1617 (1866) (remarks of Sen. Lyman Trumbull, Rep. Hiram Price, Sen. James Nye, and Reps. John Broomall and Samuel Moulton).

The centrality of these rights was not an idea limited to a few leading lawyers or theorists, but was widely understood by the polity. Various petitions from ordinary constituents to Congress in 1866 stressed the importance of the rights of "speech," "press," and "assembly" (while of course embodying the interrelated right of petition); the *New York Evening Post* noted that the freedoms of speech and of the press were guaranteed by the Civil Rights Act (even though the Act did not explicitly speak of those freedoms) and later read Section One of the proposed Amendment as covering the same ground; the *Philadelphia North American and United States Gazette* in September 1866 listed freedoms of speech, press, and assembly as paradigmatic "privileges and immunities" of citizenship within the meaning of the then-pending Amendment; various prominent Congressmen on the campaign trail in 1866 (including John Bingham, James Wilson, and Speaker of the House Schuyler Colfax) emphasized the Amendment's protection of freedom of speech; state politicians in leading northern states – including Wisconsin, Pennsylvania, Ohio, Massachusetts, and New York – linked the Amendment to freedom of discussion; and various popular 1866 conventions, both northern and southern, not only embodied the right to peaceably assemble, but used these occasions to reaffirm the importance of speech, press, petition, and assembly rights.[20]

Thus far, the refined incorporation model and Black's total incorporation approach appear to converge. But refined incorporation can help us to see what Black's approach obscured: how the very meaning of freedom of speech, press, petition, and assembly was subtly redefined in the process of being incorporated. In the eighteenth century the paradigmatic speaker was someone like John Peter Zenger or James Callender, a relatively popular publisher saying relatively popular things critical of less popular government officials. In the mid-nineteenth century the paradigm shifted to the Unionist, the abolitionist, and the freedman: to speakers like Samuel Hoar, Harriet Beecher Stowe, and Frederick Douglass. Hoar was a Massachusetts lawyer who in 1844 went to South Carolina with his daughter to defend the rights of free blacks, only to be literally ridden out of town on a rail by an enraged populace after the South Carolina legislature passed an act of attainder and banishment. A generation later, Hoar's cause célèbre still burned brightly in the memories of members of

[20] *Cong. Globe*, 39th Cong., 1st Sess. 337, 436, 494 (1866) (petitions presented by Sens. Charles Sumner, Lyman Trumbull, and Jacob Howard); Horace E. Flack, *The Adoption of the Fourteenth Amendment* (Hoboken: Wylie Press, 2008), pp. 42, 143, 149; Chester J. Antieau, *The Original Understanding of the Fourteenth Amendment* (Charleston: Mid-America Press, 1981), pp. 24–25, 30–33; Michael K. Curtis, *No State Shall Abridge: The Fourteenth Amendment and the Bill of Rights* (Durham: Duke University Press, 1990), pp. 138–40, 144–53 (Bingham, Wilson, Delano, Reps. William D. Kelly and William Boyd Allison, and Sen. Richard Yates); id. at 135 (quoting appeal from convention of Southern loyalists denouncing slave state violations of "constitutional guarantees of the right to peaceably assemble and petition for redress of grievances" and of "constitutional guarantees of freedom and free speech and a free press").

Congress who repeatedly cited the incident.[21] Stowe, of course, authored the "incendiary" bestseller *Uncle Tom's Cabin* in the 1850s – a novel that outraged the pro-slavery South and inspired the anti-slavery North, leading Lincoln to describe her as "the little woman who wrote the book that made this great war."[22] Frederick Douglass escaped from slavery in Maryland in 1838, published a daring autobiography in 1845, founded and edited a leading abolitionist newspaper over the next two decades, and became a preeminent orator on behalf of civil rights and suffrage for both women and freedmen.

The shift from Zenger and Callender to Hoar, Stowe, and Douglass was subtle but significant. All can be seen as "outsiders," but with an important difference. As representatives of the Fourth Estate, Zenger and Callender were "outside" the government that sought to censor them, but Hoar, Stowe, and Douglass were outsiders in a much deeper sense. Vis-à-vis the southern society trying to suppress their speech, Hoar, Stowe, and Douglass were geographic, cultural, and ethnic outsiders who were critical of dominant social institutions and opinions. Put another way, this shift directs us away from Madison's first concern in The Federalist No. 51 (the problem of protecting the people against unrepresentative government), toward his second concern (protecting minorities from factional majority tyranny). The new First/Fourteenth Amendment tradition is less majoritarian and more libertarian. To recast this point in a temporal frame, the abolitionist experience dramatized why even majoritarians should logically support strong First Amendment protections for offensive and provocative speech of fringe groups. For if allowed to freely preach their gospel, a zealous fringe group in one era (like proponents of abolition, equality, and black suffrage in 1830) could conceivably convert enough souls to their crusade to become a respectable or even dominant political force over the next generation (like the Republican Party of the 1860s).

My language here – "preach," "gospel," "zealous," "convert," "souls," and "crusade" – reflects the religious inspiration of many abolitionists. For example, Stowe's husband, father, and many brothers were famous New England clergymen. The well publicized martyrdom of Elijah Lovejoy also dramatized the centrality of religious speech. Lovejoy, a Presbyterian minister, used his church weekly to condemn slavery. His writings cost him his life in 1837 when he was murdered by an angry mob bent on silencing his press.

Reconstruction Republicans naturally understood the religious roots of abolitionism, and often stressed the need to protect religious speech. In 1859,

[21] See *Cong. Globe*, 38th Cong., 1st Sess. 2984 (1864) (remarks of Rep. William Kelley); *Cong. Globe*, 38th Cong., 2d Sess. 193, 237 (1865) (remarks of Reps. John Kasson and Green Smith); *Cong. Globe*, 39th Cong., 1st Sess. 41, 157, 475 (1865–1866) (remarks of Sen. John Sherman, Rep. John Bingham and Sen. Lyman Trumbull); id. at 142 app. (remarks of Sen. Henry Wilson); see also Antieau, *The Original Understanding*, p. 24 (quoting 1866 remarks of Rep. Columbus Delano).

[22] Charles E. Stowe and Lyman B. Stowe, *Harriet Beecher Stowe: The Story of her Life* (Boston: Houghton Mifflin, 1911).

John Bingham, the future lead author of the Fourteenth Amendment's opening language, had borrowed from an earlier John – Milton – in proclaiming the centrality of the right to "utter according to conscience." On the campaign trail in 1866 Bingham reminded his audience that men had been imprisoned in Georgia for teaching the Bible, and made clear that the Fourteenth Amendment would put an end to such state action, a theme to which he returned in a key speech on the Amendment before the House in 1871.[23] In early 1866, Lyman Trumbull introduced his Civil Rights Bill by stressing the need to protect the freedom "to teach" and "to preach," citing a Mississippi Black Code punishing any "free negroes and mulattoes" who dared to "exercis[e] the functions of a minister of the Gospel." Similarly, in 1865, Representative James M. Ashley linked religion to freedom of speech in the following way: "[The Slave Power] has silenced every free pulpit within its control ... and *made free speech and a free press impossible within its domain* ...."[24]

In 1789, the freedoms of speech and press had been yoked with religious freedoms largely for reasons of federalism: both religious regulation and press censorship were seen as beyond Congress's enumerated powers. This federalism-based reading of the original First Amendment draws support from the dramatic fact that no previous state constitution had linked these two sets of rights in a single provision. But once yoked together in the federal Bill, these clauses helped reinforce a libertarian theory of freedom of all expression – political, religious, and even artistic (*Uncle Tom's Cabin* was of course all three). By the 1860s, libertarianism had displaced federalism and majoritarianism as the dominant, unifying theme of the First Amendment's freedoms.

The centrality of religious speech in the 1860s proved especially significant for women. Though excluded from exercising the formal political rights of voting, holding public office, and serving on juries or militias, women could and did play leading roles in religious organizations. Moreover, these organizations engaged in moral crusades with obvious political overtones: temperance, abolition, and (eventually) suffrage. As a result, the voice of women was much harder to ignore in the 1860s than it had been in the 1790s.

In the debates over the Constitution and Bill of Rights, only one woman – Mercy Otis Warren – had participated prominently, and even then under a pseudonym. (Indeed, her most important pamphlet during the ratification debates was long ascribed to Elbridge Gerry, and was not credited to her until 1932.)[25] In 1866, however, the most widely read condemnation of slavery had

[23] *Cong. Globe*, 35th Cong., 2d Sess. 983–85 (1859); Antieau, *The Original Understanding*, p. 24; *Cong. Globe*, 42d Cong., 1st Sess. 84 app. (1871).

[24] *Cong. Globe*, 39th Cong., 1st Sess. 474–75 (1866); *Cong. Globe*, 38th Cong., 2d Sess. 138 (1865); see also *Cong. Globe*, 38th Cong., 1st Sess. 2615 (1864) (remarks of Congressman Daniel Morris discussing incarceration of "Christian men and women for teaching the alphabet;" emphasis added).

[25] See Charles Warren, *Elbridge Gerry, James Warren, Mercy Warren and the Ratification of the Federal Constitution in Massachusetts* (Boston: Massachusetts Historical Society, 1932).

been authored by a woman (Stowe); and in a campaign orchestrated by Susan B. Anthony and Elizabeth Cady Stanton, thousands and thousands of women flooded the Thirty-ninth Congress with petitions on the issue of women's suffrage, which had been largely a nonissue for the Founding Fathers. At least five petitions from women on the suffrage issue were presented on the floor of Congress in the first two months of 1866 alone. Women were therefore central exercisers of First Amendment freedoms in the Reconstruction era in a way they had not been at the Founding – yet another example of the rising importance of "outsider" speech. Interestingly, in discussing the Hoar affair before the Thirty-eighth Congress, Representative William D. Kelley pointedly spoke of not only Samuel Hoar, but also his "beautiful and accomplished daughter." So, too, Representative John Kasson noted that "innocent ladies, cultivated, intelligent, Christian women, have been driven from the cities and States of the South ... because they had dared to say something offensive to this intolerant spirit of slavery," and Representative Morris reminded his audience that Southern states had "incarcerated Christian men and women for teaching the alphabet."[26]

Just as the centrality of religious speech helped bring women into the core of the First Amendment, it also helped blacks. As with women, the exclusion of blacks from formal political rights like voting underscored the importance of their participation in other organizations, like churches, that could help focus the voice of the community. Southern governments, of course, were all too aware of the "incendiary" dangers posed by any assembly of blacks, even (or perhaps especially) an assembly of God. After all, Nat Turner, who had led a famous slave revolt in the 1830s, had been a black preacher – hence the Mississippi Black Code cited by Trumbull, prescribing thirty-nine lashes for any black exercising the functions of a minister. But Republicans like Trumbull strongly affirmed the "civil" rights of blacks to assemble and preach, even as these same Republicans in 1866 disclaimed any intent to confer "political" rights like the franchise upon blacks. Charles Sumner provided the Joint Committee on Reconstruction yet another dramatic example of black speech, laying before the Committee a petition "from the colored citizens of South Carolina," claiming to represent "four hundred and two thousand citizens of that State, being a very large majority of the population." Unsurprisingly, the petition prayed for "constitutional protection in keeping arms, in holding public assemblies, and in complete liberty of speech and of the press."[27]

The gloss of the Fourteenth Amendment experience on the First Amendment text has important doctrinal implications. As the paradigmatic speech in need of constitutional protection shifts from a localist criticizing the central

[26] See Nina Morais, "Sex Discrimination and the Fourteenth Amendment: Lost History," *YALE L.J.* 97 (1988), 1153, 1155–56. *Cong. Globe*, 38th Cong., 1st Sess. 2984 (1864); *Cong. Globe*, 38th Cong., 2d Sess. 193 (1865); *Cong. Globe*, 38th Cong., 1st Sess. 2615 (1864).

[27] *Cong. Globe*, 39th Cong., 1st Sess. 337 (1866).

government to a Unionist defending its Reconstruction policies, carpetbagging federal judges appointed in Washington, D.C. become more trustworthy guardians of First Amendment freedoms than localist juries. When the core of the Amendment was protection of the people collectively from unrepresentative government, perhaps an unelected federal judge on the federal payroll was a more suspect sentry; but when the central mission of free speech shifted to protection of currently unpopular ideas from a current majority, an Article III officer with life tenure, sheltered from current political winds and sensitive to the long-term value of free speech, enjoyed certain advantages over a jury structured to reflect today's dominant community sentiment. If women and blacks were central speakers in the Reconstruction paradigm, would a jury of twelve white men be in every sense a jury of their "peers"? And if not, there was less reason to expect that such a jury would represent their interests and rights any better than would a federal judge.

Thus, it is largely the Fourteenth Amendment experience, I submit, that best justifies the emphasis in modern First Amendment doctrine on federal judges, rather than juries, as guardians of free speech. Yet the reigning doctrinal approach of jot for jot incorporation has obscured the significance of the Fourteenth Amendment, which all but drops out of the free speech picture. Advocates and scholars focus all their analytic and narrative attention on the Founding, not the Reconstruction. Thus, in championing the rights of Communists and Jehovah's Witnesses in the twentieth century, the ACLU has analogized to Zenger more than to the abolitionists – who are the truer forebears of modern political and religious speakers perceived as "nuts" and "cranks" by the dominant culture.

Similarly, in the landmark First Amendment case of our era, *New York Times Co. v. Sullivan*, Justice Brennan quoted Madison and thoughtfully reflected on the lessons of the Alien and Sedition Acts controversy, but said virtually nothing about the Reconstruction Amendment except that it incorporated the First Amendment against states (presumably jot for jot). Yet the facts before the Court in *Sullivan* almost cried out for comparison with the Reconstruction era. Southern followers of the Reverend Martin Luther King, many of them black and many of them religious, had used a northern newspaper to criticize southern officials; and a southern jury composed of good ole boys had socked the speakers with massively punitive damages. Many of the doctrinal rules crafted by *Sullivan* and its progeny reflect obvious suspicion of juries – resulting, for example, in various issues being classified as legal questions or mixed questions of law and fact inappropriate for unconstrained jury determination – yet that suspicion is much better justified by the Reconstruction experience than by the Founding.

We can chart similar Reconstruction-inspired shifts in "the right of the people peaceably to assemble, and to petition." These words, as originally written, linked up tightly to popular sovereignty theory. In its strictest sense, "the people" encompassed voters – the same adult male citizens who, roughly speaking, constituted "the militia" equated with "the people" in the very next sentence of the Bill of Rights. And the paradigmatic exercise of (We) "the [P]eople's" right to assemble was a constitutional convention called by political rights-holders (adult male citizens) to alter or abolish government. Other meanings of "the people" and "assembly" were also encompassed at the Founding, but popular-sovereignty theory colored the Amendment's core.

By 1866, all this had subtly changed. The phrase "the people" was still read relatively strictly – for example, the Senate refused to allow foreigners to petition – but clearly encompassed those who were not political rights-holders. American women deluged the 1866 Congress with petitions precisely because they were *not* voters. So too, Sumner's petition from the South Carolina "convention" of "colored citizens" came from a group excluded from the vote, the militia, and the jury – excluded from the polity, strictly defined. Likewise, while the debate on the Fourteenth Amendment was drawing to a close in the Thirty-ninth Congress, another prominent convention of nonvoters – the Eleventh Women's Rights Convention – was meeting in New York City.

In introducing a women's suffrage petition in 1866, Senator Thomas Henderson sharply distinguished between the rights of suffrage and petition: "The right of petition is a sacred right, and whatever may be thought of giving the ballot to women, the right to ask it of the Government [by petition] cannot be denied them." Though dubious of granting women the political right of the vote, Henderson declared that "no civil right," presumably including the right to petition, "can be denied her."[28]

In a similar vein, the Republican *New York Evening Post* rejected the notion that the Civil Rights Act embraced political rights like jury service and office holding, but cheerfully conceded that the rights of speech, press, petition, and assembly, though unenumerated, were clearly covered by the Act. So too, in Professor tenBroek's rich account of abolitionist theory in the antebellum era, the core right of assembly at issue seems to be the right of blacks "to assemble peaceably on the Sabbath for the worship of [the] Creator."[29]

In a nutshell, the hybrid rights of petition and assembly were increasingly being characterized as civil, not political rights – a shift reflected in and perhaps caused by the exercise of these rights by women and blacks. Petitions and assemblies by the disenfranchised were no longer seen as peripheral to, or derivative of, a popular sovereignty core celebrating the right of the (political) people to (re)assemble, through specially elected representatives, in constitutional conventions. Whereas the lived experience of 1787–89, with precisely such conventions of "the people" actually assembling, glossed the text with popular-sovereignty theory, a different lived experience in the 1860s offered a different, civil-rights gloss on the very same words.

[28] *Cong. Globe*, 39th Cong., 1st Sess. 952 (1866).

[29] Flack, *The Adoption of the Fourteenth Amendment*, p. 42; Jacobus tenBroek, *Equal under law* (Springfield: Collier Books, 1965), pp. 124–25.

Having seen how, in the cases of speech, press, petition, and assembly, the same words meant slightly different things when first inscribed into the Constitution in the 1790s and when later reglossed in the 1860s, it remains to see how the same thing is true of the establishment and free-exercise clause.

Begin with the establishment clause text prohibiting Congress from making any law "respecting an establishment of religion." We have seen that these words, as originally written, stood as a pure federalism provision. Congress could make "no law respecting [state] establishment [policy]" – that is, no law either establishing a national church or dis-establishing a state church. On this reading, the clause was utterly agnostic on the substantive issue of establishment; it simply mandated that the issue be decided state by state and that Congress keep its hands off, that Congress make no law "respecting" – that is, no law on the topic of – the vexed question. In short, the original establishment clause was a home-rule local option provision mandating imperial neutrality, a late eighteenth-century American version of the 1648 European Treaty of Westphalia echoing the 1555 Peace of Augsburg: *Cuius regio, eius religio*.

Home rule and imperial neutrality made a good deal of political sense in 1789 America (much as these concepts had made sense in central Europe a century and a half earlier). At the Founding, half the states in the new fledgling Union gave specified sects privileged status and half didn't. Pro-establishment New Hampshiremen and anti-establishment Virginians might sharply disagree on the substantive issue of church–state relations but could agree on the jurisdictional idea that Congress should keep out: this was the lowest common denominator.

But America's local church–state practices changed considerably over the ensuing decades. Formal state establishments were abandoned in state after state. In 1833, Massachusetts made it unanimous, becoming the last state to abolish state financial support for a legally privileged sect.

In the 1780s half the states featured sectarian establishments; by the 1860s none did. Virtually all states in the mid-nineteenth century favored religion generally, and some privileged Christianity or Protestantism above other religions in various ways, but none singled out one Christian sect for special favor. The common denominator among states had shifted dramatically, and popular understandings of the establishment clause reflected this shift. What began as an agnostic but strict federalism rule – *no law* intermeddling with religion in the states – was gradually mutating into a soft substantive rule: religion in general could be promoted, but not one sect at the expense of others.[30]

30 Joseph Story's influential 1833 treatise nicely straddled the issue, featuring both the older federalism-based, agnostic-absolutist reading and the more modern soft-substantive reading of the establishment clause. See Joseph Story, *Commentaries on the Constitution of the United States*, edited by Thomas Cooley (Boston: Little, Brown and Company, 1873) at § 1871, p. 731 ("The whole power over the subject of religion is left exclusively to the state governments"); id. § 1871, p. 728 ("The real object of the amendment was, not to countenance, much less to advance, Mahometanism, or Judaism, or infidelity, by prostrating Christianity; but to exclude all rivalry among Christian sects").

Whereas one of the key concerns of the Founding Fathers in the 1780s was congressional power in the *states*; by the 1850s Americans were fighting out many of the most intense constitutional issues of the day in and over the *territories*. Whereas the original Bill of Rights had in many cases borrowed language from older state constitutions, newer states were now returning the compliment by borrowing from (and in the process redefining) the words of the federal Bill of Rights. By 1866 half the states had begun as federal territories; the typical state was no longer Madison's Virginia, but Bingham's Ohio.

And in various territories-turned-states, the original federalism reading of the establishment clause faded away, and gave rise to a more substantive anti-establishment principle. As territorial legislatures matured into state legislatures, it seemed natural to bind them to the same non-establishment rule to which Congress was bound, using language borrowed from the First Amendment. For example, when Iowa gained statehood in 1846, its first state constitution proclaimed in its Bill of Rights that "[t]he general assembly shall make no law respecting an establishment of religion or prohibiting the free exercise thereof," words repeated verbatim in its Constitution of 1857.[31] Virtually identical phrases appeared in the territorial Constitution of Deseret in 1849, and its successor Utah Territory draft constitution of 1860.[32] Similarly, in the 1859 Constitution of the Jefferson Territory (today known as Colorado), we find the following clause: "The General Assembly shall make no laws respecting an establishment of religion, nor shall any religious test be required of any citizen."[33] And in his influential constitutional treatise of 1868, the respected Michigan jurist Thomas Cooley likewise wrote that, under prevailing state constitutions, state legislatures were barred from creating "[a]ny law respecting an establishment of religion."[34]

But even if by 1866 the establishment clause was no longer a state right, pure and simple, can we really say that it was a true "privilege" – a private right of certain individuals, as opposed to a general rule of governance, akin to the rule that presidents be age 35 or above? To the extent that a state created a *coercive* establishment, decreeing that individuals profess a state creed or attend a state service or pay money directly to a state church, such coercion would threaten the bodily liberty and property of individuals and would thus obviously intrude upon the privileges and immunities of citizens. But what of a noncoercive establishment – say, a simple state declaration on a state seal proclaiming Utah "the Mormon State"?

[31] IA. Const. of 1846, art. II, §3; IA. Const. of 1857, art. I, §3.

[32] See William F. Swindler, *Sources and Documents of United States Constitutions* (Dobbs Ferry: Oceana, 1973) p. 380 (reprinting Constitution of the State of Deseret, art. VII, §3); *id.* at 388 (reprinting Utah Draft Constitution of 1860, art. II, §3).

[33] 2 *id.* at 18 (reprinting Constitution of Jefferson Territory, art. I, §3).

[34] Thomas M. Cooley, *A Treatise on the Constitutional Limitations which Rest upon the Legislative Power of the States of the American Union* (Boston: Little, Brown, 1868), p. 469.

If we look to Blackstone, we will not find this kind of non-establishment right classified as a common-law "privilege" or "immunity." And the historical evidence from the 1860s and early 1870s is somewhat sparse and rather mixed. However, strong support for the argument that there is a non-establishment right even against the noncoercive establishment of religion by a state came from Thomas Cooley's widely influential 1868 treatise. Under prevailing state constitutions, wrote Cooley, states generally could not enact "[a]ny law respecting an establishment of religion ... There is not religious *liberty* where any one sect is favored by the State ... It is not toleration which is established in our system, but religious *equality*."[35] Even a noncoercive establishment, Cooley suggested, violated principles of religious liberty and religious equality – violated norms of equal rights and privileges.

And once we see this, it turns out that the question – should we incorporate the establishment clause? – may not matter all that much, because even if we did not, principles of religious liberty and religious equality could be vindicated by the free-exercise clause (whose text, history, and logic make it a paradigmatic case for incorporation) and the equal-protection clause (which frowns upon state laws that unjustifiably single out some folks for special privileges and relegate other folks to second-class status). Surely Alabama could not adopt a state motto proclaiming itself "the White Supremacy State." Such a motto would offend basic principles of equal citizenship and equal protection. And so a law that proclaimed Utah a Mormon state should be suspect whether we call this a violation of non-establishment principles, free-exercise principles, equal-protection principles, equal-citizenship principles, or religious liberty principles. Once we remember that we are not (*pace* Hugo Black) mechanically incorporating clauses but reconstructing and refining rights, we reach the unsurprising but satisfying conclusion that our basic touchstones should be the animating Fourteenth Amendment ideals of liberty and equality.

Let us now, finally, turn to the First Amendment's free-exercise principle and trace how it, too, was reconstructed by the Fourteenth Amendment.

Outraged by decades of religious persecution in the antebellum South, prominent Republicans in the Thirty-eighth and Thirty-ninth Congresses repeatedly stressed the need to protect "freedom of religious opinion," "a free exercise of religion," "freedom of conscience," "freedom in the exercise of religion," and "the free exercise of religion."[36] In some form or other, they insisted that henceforth this basic First Amendment freedom apply against states.

[35] Cooley, *A Treatise on the Constitutional Limitations*, p. 469. Cooley went on to defend nonpreferential, nonsectarian governmental endorsements of religion, such as government-sponsored fast days and thanksgivings, while warning that care must "be taken to avoid discrimination in favor of any one denomination or sect." *Id.* at 471.

[36] See, e.g., *Cong. Globe*, 38th Cong., 1st Sess. 1202 (1864) (remarks of Rep. James Wilson); *Cong. Globe*, 39th Cong., 1st Sess. 156–57, 1072, 1629 (1866) (remarks of Rep. John Bingham, Sen. James Nye, and Rep. Roswell Hart). See generally *Cong. Globe*, 36th Cong., 1st Sess. 198

But in what form, exactly? The original free-exercise clause of the First Amendment merely barred laws targeted at religious exercise as such; its letter and spirit allowed Congress to make genuinely secular laws, even though those laws might obstruct particular religious practices.

But perhaps the Fourteenth Amendment sweeps more broadly in its language of *privileges*. Where only believers in a specific religion are involved in a religious practice – with no direct invasions of the lives, limbs, or property of nonbelievers – such a religious practice could be deemed suitably "priv[ate]" and hence "privilege[d]" from intruding legislation.[37] Under this definition, a secular law like, say, murder, would take precedence over the religious claims of a cult that demanded human sacrifice of nonbelievers; but the Catholic Church would be constitutionally "privileged" to employ only male priests regardless of general laws outlawing sex discrimination in employment.[38]

Professor Kurt Lash has argued that this textually possible reconstruction of free exercise is also historically plausible.[39] Reconstruction Republicans, Lash argues, at times sought to shield religion even from secular laws. Southern laws making it a crime to teach blacks to read were secular enough, but these laws outraged Republicans because of their devastating effect on (Protestant) religion; they outlawed teaching blacks to read the Holy Bible, the word of God.[40]

If, as Lash claims, "freedom of religion" in the 1860s meant autonomy from governmental intrusion in ways that it did not in the 1790s, this shift fits snugly into our overall story of rights reconstruction. Under the Founding Fathers' vision of free exercise in 1791, Congress might, but need not, choose to exempt a given religious practice from a general secular law. At that time,

app. (1860) (remarks of Rep. W. E. Simms); *Cong. Globe*, 42d Cong., 1st Sess. 84–85 app., 475 (1871) (remarks of Reps. John Bingham and Henry Dawes); see also M. CURTIS, *supra* note 29 (quoting similar speeches outside of Congress by Judge Lorenzo Sherwood and Judge Preston Davis); *United States* v. *Hall*, 26 F. Cas. 79, 81 (C. C. S. D. Ala. 1871) (No. 15,282) (Woods, J.) (stressing speech, press, assembly, and free-exercise rights as Fourteenth Amendment privileges and immunities while omitting mention of establishment clause); William D. Guthrie, *Lectures on the Fourteenth Article of Amendment to the Constitution of the United States* (Boston: Little, Brown and Company, 1898) (defining as Fourteenth Amendment privileges and immunities each of the five rights and freedoms of the First Amendment, but omitting non-establishment).

37 For a somewhat similar suggestion, see Michael W. McConnell, "Free Exercise Revisionism and the Smith Decision," 57 *U. CHI. L. REV.* 1109, (1990), 1145–46.

38 What if a religious group indulged voluntary sacrifice of its own adult members? If we strictly applied the autonomy principle, these acts of religious "suicides" and "suicide assistance" could be criminalized only in the event that the volunteers were mentally incompetent. Otherwise, how could government bar an adult of sound mind from literally dedicating his life to God in an act of supreme sacrifice? This hypothetical may tempt us to bend the autonomy principle here, but before we do, we should remember that many churches were built by martyrs who gave up their earthly lives to win something they deemed even more precious.

39 See Kurt T. Lash, "The Second Adoption of the Free Exercise Clause: Religious Exemptions Under the Fourteenth Amendment," *NW. U. L. REV.* 88 (1994), 1106.

40 See *supra* text accompanying note; *Cong. Globe*, 39th Cong., 1st Sess. 783 (remarks of Rep. Hamilton Wood).

large, politically powerful religions consisting of a majority of voters could win exemptions more easily than could fringe minority sects. But the Fourteenth Amendment accentuated minority liberty, and this accent perhaps invites special judicial accommodation of minority sects.

Regardless of how this specific issue is resolved, a larger point – the central point of this essay – remains: In pondering the proper meaning of "the First Amendment" today, interpreters must always remember the Fourteenth as well. Just as Christians read the Old Testament through the prism of the New, so faithful constitutionalists must attend not just to the creation of the Bill of Rights, but also to its reconstruction.

4

Recasting the argument for religious freedom

Hadley Arkes

We meet in dark times for the defense of religious freedom against the government of the day. Even people experienced in politics were jolted to discover that the Obama Administration had deliberately chosen, as a political stroke, to pick up a fight with the Catholic Church by compelling Catholic institutions and Catholic businessmen to cover abortifacients and contraceptives in the medical insurance they offer to their employees. And what can be said here, of course, in regard to Catholics will be said just as well for Mormons and Evangelicals. The religious, now embattled in the courts, are persistently invoking the First Amendment: that "Congress shall make no law respecting an establishment of religion, or prohibiting the free exercise thereof." And yet it seems to be coming as a surprise to the religious and their lawyers, so late in the seasons of our experience, as to how thin and equivocal the First Amendment would be as a support for their religious freedom.

The quickest way of delivering some sobering news here would come by recalling for a moment a case that has slipped into the fog of distant memory: the case of Fr. Permoli in New Orleans in the 1840s. At the direction of his bishop, Fr. Permoli performed a funeral mass with an open casket in the Church of St. Augustin in the French Quarter in November 1842. With this act he violated an ordinance of the city that forbade such funerals with open caskets at all Catholic churches in the city, apart from one designated mortuary chapel. The law was passed supposedly as a measure for the public health. New Orleans had been afflicted with recurring epidemics of yellow fever, and it was thought at the time that the disease could be fed by the noxious effects of decaying plants and animals. New Orleans was one of the rare places in this country, at the time, with a high density of Catholics. And the City council that passed the ordinance was composed predominantly of Catholics. Therein lies a fuller story – a story of conflicts within the Catholic community, but that story is best left to another time.

Fr. Permoli was prosecuted and fined $50 for violating the law. His supporters helped to carry his appeal all the way to the Supreme Court of the United States, with Fr. Permoli invoking his rights under the First Amendment to the "free exercise" of religion. But the appeal was dispatched by the Supreme Court in a quick stroke: The Court simply explained that it had no jurisdiction to hear the case because, as everyone knew, those first eight amendments to the Constitution – the amendments that became known as the "Bill of Rights" – were restraints solely on the *federal* government.[1] They were never meant to apply to the States. For the Anti-Federalists, who had been resisting a new, strong national government, the main danger to freedom would emanate from that distant central government. And that was the government they sought to restrain with a Bill of Rights.

It seems to come as a surprise even to lawyers and judges to learn that there was a serious argument at the beginning about a "Bill of Rights," and the gravest reservations had not come from the men who were reserved about rights. The concern rather was that a Bill of Rights would misinform the American people about the very ground of their rights: People would come to believe that they bore those rights because they were "posited," set down, enacted in the text of the Constitution. And so we commonly hear people speak of those rights they have "through the First Amendment" – as though in the absence of that Amendment, they would not have the right to speak and assemble, or to engage in the "free exercise of religion." As Alexander Hamilton put it, "The sacred rights of mankind are not to be rummaged for among old parchments or musty records. They are written, as with a sunbeam, in the whole volume of human nature." They were a species of "natural rights," not rights conferred by those in power.

It is an arguable point, best left to another time, which the Bill of Rights has actually worked to obscure or disparage certain rights and the persons who bear them (e.g., the right of an unborn child to the protections of the law).[2] As Justice Scalia has pointed out, the Founders did not seek to protect rights by proclaiming rights on paper, and indeed no Constitution had been more chock full of those "rights" set down in paper than the old Soviet Constitution. The Founders created a "structure" that would secure rights – mainly through the device of arming the people themselves with the vote. People concerned about their rights would have a lever for warding off or removing the politicians who would threaten those rights.

As it turned out, it was not until 1925 that the provisions on free speech in the First Amendment would be applied by the Supreme Court to the States.

[1] See *Permoli* v. *Municipality No. 1 of the City of New Orleans* 44 U.S. 3 How. 589 (1845).

[2] See Hadley Arkes, "On That 'Superintending Principle' That Was There before the Laws," in *The Future of Religion in American Politics*, ed. Charles W. Dunn (Lexington, KY: University of Kentucky Press, 2009), pp. 47–60 and Arkes,*Beyond the Constitution* (Princeton: Princeton University Press, 1990), ch. 4.

As the line went, certain parts of the Bill of Rights were thought to be "incorporated" and applied to the States through the Due Process Clause of the Fourteenth Amendment. It wasn't until 1940, in *Cantwell* v. *Connecticut*[3] that the Court would apply to the States the provision on the "free exercise" of religion. Up to that time, we may ask, what protected religious freedom in this country – other than the people themselves, who made manifest in different ways that they took that freedom seriously? And yet only seven years later, in the Everson case,[4] Justice Hugo Black took the First Amendment as his lever for inverting the Establishment Clause. Instead of a clause barring the federal government from interfering with religion in the States, the clause would be converted by Black and his colleagues into a clause that would work toward driving religion – and the religious – out of the public square altogether.

Indeed, it is one of the unnoticed ironies in the history of our law that it was the political process, as Scalia caught it, which worked to dis-establish religion in the separate States before Justice Black transmuted the Establishment Clause in 1947. And in recent years that political process has worked to rescue religious freedom as the judges and the political class have sought to purge religion altogether from our public life. Mark DeWolfe Howe, in his fine book, *The Garden and the Wilderness*,[5] noted the forces that had been working to remove religious establishments in States as different as Massachusetts, New York, and South Carolina. We often forget that the "establishment" of religion could often mean simply that communities found it important to support churches and religious instruction for the same reason that they would come later to support public schools. The good done by churches was not seen to hinge on whether they could make the profits necessary to support the teaching of their ministers. If it were thought that the teaching was quite important in shaping the moral literacy of the community, it made sense to support the churches as public institutions. But the problem came when, over time, a community became dominantly Unitarian, and voters would bridle at the notion of being taxed to support Trinitarian churches. Whether it was north or south, Massachusetts or South Carolina, the very character of this regime, a regime of elections, worked to remove the support of the churches from taxpayers, paying into the public treasury. That support would be transferred then to the private realm, with the funds supplied by the members of the church.

And on the other side, we find that the principle of equality has been working to protect religious freedom in certain cases even when the authorities have been fired by a new passion to remove every vestige of religion from the support of public funds. Young James Zobrest in Tucson, Arizona, afflicted with deafness, was given generous provision of an interpreter when he was in the public schools. Those benefits for deaf students flowed to him both from the policies

[3] *Cantwell* v. *Connecticut* 310 U.S. 296 (1940).

[4] *Everson* v. *Board of Education* 330 U.S. 1 (1947).

[5] Chicago: University of Chicago Press, 1967.

of the national government, and from his own State of Arizona. And yet when James's parents decided to move him, for high school, to the Salpointe Catholic High School, the County Attorney refused to permit the support to continue.[6] He assumed that the modern understanding of the Establishment Clause would bar any such support to students in Catholic schools. The Supreme Court struck down that judgment in one of the rare victories for the religious. The decision was rendered a bit equivocal as Chief Justice Rehnquist mulled over such questions as whether the aid was direct or indirect, or just how "substantial" it really was. But I would suggest that the understanding emerging here would run in this way: There may be no obligation on the part of the voters, local or national, to provide aid to local schools, public and private, much less to provide generous services for the deaf. But if such aid flows to deaf students through the laws, it would be a distinct disability based on religion if that aid were denied to a student solely on the ground that his parents had placed him in a Catholic school. This proposition, if it takes hold, can have a profound effect on the cases in our law. But I would point out that this proposition or principle is nowhere set down explicitly in the Constitution, neither in the First Amendment nor in Art. VI, barring any religious test for office.

There have been trends, then, working to protect the religious, and yet they may have little to do with any protections set down for religion explicitly in the Constitution, much less a reverence for religious "belief." In fact, since the time that the Court lifted the provisions on religion to the level of clauses enforced against the States, the trend produced by the liberal mind has been one of reducing religion to a body of "beliefs" with no claim to truth, and no claim to be taken seriously by anyone who does not share those beliefs. It may be no surprise, then, that we find no ready refuge now in invoking the First Amendment in defending religious freedom. A more sober view would tell us that it is indeed time to start recasting the argument for religious freedom, to undo the work of the judges and the way they have misshaped, in turn, the understanding of the public. If the crisis brought by Obamacare actually moves us to the work of rethinking the argument, it will not have been a disaster wholly unalloyed, though we might wish that Providence had found a defter Hand in doing its work.

Ordinary folks may invoke their rights under the First Amendment without quite realizing that they are appealing merely to the positive law of the Constitution. But clearly, their understanding runs deeper. In their natural understanding, they do seem to think that they are appealing to something in principle right, something closer than to a natural right, which would be there even without the Constitution. In that notable letter, so characteristically terse, and yet with it all, magnificent, George Washington remarked to the Hebrew Congregation in Newport that "it is now no more that toleration is spoken of as if it were the indulgence of one class of people that another enjoyed the

[6] *Zobrest* v. *Catalina Foothills School Dist.* 509 U.S. 1 (1993).

exercise of their inherent natural rights." Several years earlier James Madison had invoked a comparable notion of the freedom of religion as nothing less than a natural right. In his "Memorial and Remonstrance Against Religious Assessments" (1785), Madison insisted that "this right [of religious freedom] is in its nature an unalienable right."

Of course, that "natural right" to be left undisturbed in the religious life did not necessarily entail the fuller set of "civil" rights that attached to citizens. And it certainly did not entail "political rights," for Jews could not yet vote or hold public office in Rhode Island. It also went without saying that the natural right to practice one's religion would be governed and restrained by the laws that were rightly binding on everyone else, because they sprang from the same ground of natural law and moral reasoning that entailed the freedom of religion. And so the laws that barred homicide would bar the burning of wives on the funeral pyres of husbands even if the act were done in accord with a religious code. Not everything that people professed themselves "obliged" to do by their understanding of God's commands, or the commands of their religion, would be honored merely because people professed to believe earnestly in the source of the obligation and their duty to respect it.

And yet the complications run deeper than that: If we take seriously the claims to freedom of religion as a "natural right," we discover, with a sobering jolt, that the conventional and familiar arguments for religious freedom in the courts suffer a critical embarrassment. For those arguments are not offered in the currency of "natural rights," with reasons that are accessible even to people who do not share the convictions of the religious. The defenders of religious freedom offer foremost an avowal of their earnest *beliefs*, sincerely held. But in that way, the advocates for religion find themselves backing precisely into that libel of religion that John Courtney Murray warned about years ago: they are willing to identify religion with a set of "beliefs," which is to say "imperfect knowledge," with no claim to a truth or validity for anyone who does not share those beliefs. On the other hand, if we take seriously the properties of religious freedom as a natural right, we are led to a recognition that the defenders of religious freedom these days may find quite as jarring, or at least uncongenial or impolitic: for we would be led to the recognition that not everything that calls itself "religion" has a claim to be taken seriously with the same respect or invested with the same cluster of "rights" to their practice.

The pieces begin to sort themselves as soon as we remind ourselves of the logic that attaches to natural law and natural rights. Aquinas observed that the divine law we know through revelation, but the natural law we know through that reason that is accessible to human beings as human beings – the reason, we might say, that is distinctly "natural" to human beings. Washington's letter cannot be misunderstood on this cardinal point: To say that Jews had a natural right to be left undisturbed in the practice of their religion was to say that Jews possessed a right here that had a claim to be respected even by people who did not take seriously for a moment the revelation recorded in the Hebrew bible.

Somehow, those who were not Jewish had to be able to grasp *through reason alone* why they were obliged to respect the freedom of Jews to practice their religion, even if those gentiles understood and respected nothing in the religion that they were enjoined now to respect.

But when we tender respect to people *we respect the way in which they understand themselves*, or the principles that animate their acts. As Kant put it, we summon a certain reverence for that "law" of which they happen to be examples. On what ground, then would people "respect" the "natural right" of Christians and Jews to live their religious lives when those other people do not even remotely understand or credit the truth understood by Christians and Jews, the truth that commands them to lead Christian and Jewish lives?

In explaining the reasoning of natural law, I've found no example simpler or clearer – or understood more readily – than that fragment Lincoln wrote for himself, when he imagined himself engaged in a conversation with the owner of black slaves. And the question was, Why are you justified in making a slave of a black man?:

> You say A. is white, and B. is black. It is color, then: the lighter having the right to enslave the darker? Take care. By this rule, you are to be slave to the first man you meet, with a fairer skin than your own.
>
> You do not mean color exactly? – You mean the whites are intellectually the superiors of the blacks, and therefore have the right to enslave them? Take care again. By this rule, you are to be slave to the first man you meet, with an intellect superior to your own.
>
> But, say you, it is a question of interest; and, if you can make it your interest, you have the right to enslave another. Very well. And if he can make it his interest, he has the right to enslave you.[7]

The upshot was that there was nothing one could cite to disqualify the black man as a human being that would not apply to many whites as well. And at no point in the chain of reasoning was there an appeal to faith or belief or revelation. The argument is carried forward simply as a matter of "principled reasoning," the reasoning access to ordinary human beings, quite apart from faith.

In the same way, those of us on the pro-life side usually draw on the same form of Lincoln's argument for the sake of rebutting that chief, unsinkable cliché: that we are appealing to religious faith or belief. We insist on approaching the problem through a combination of embryology and principled reasoning. And so, in the style of Lincoln, we ask ourselves questions: Why is that offspring of Homo sapiens in the womb anything less than a human being? It doesn't speak? Neither do deaf mutes? It has yet no arms or legs? Well, other people lose arms or legs in the course of their lives without losing their standing as human beings in receiving the protections of the law. The upshot here is that there is nothing one could cite to disqualify the

[7] *The Collected Works of Abraham Lincoln*, ed. Roy P. Basler (New Brunswick: Rutgers University Press, 1953), Vol. II, p. 222.

child in the womb as a human being that would not apply to many people walking about well outside the womb.

Once again, there is no appeal to faith or beliefs. In other words, one doesn't have to be Catholic or religious in order to understand this argument – and that has been precisely the argument of the Church, that this is a matter that turns on the moral reasoning of the natural law.

And so it was telling in this respect when Bishop William Lori spoke for the Conference of Catholic Bishops in resisting those controversial mandates under Obamacare on contraception and abortion. Bishop Lori made it clear that Catholics were not seeking an *exemption* from the mandate on contraception. They were pronouncing the mandates to constitute an "unjust law, no law at all," and therefore *rightly binding on no one*. This was not, he said, a Catholic or Protestant position, but an American position.

It is worth noticing that Bishop Lori cast the argument for religious freedom around the claims of "conscience," but not "conscience" as it has been talked about commonly in a manner purged of its moral content. The Archbishop insisted that he was not using "conscience" as it has been used – and virtually unraveled over the years – in the claims of "conscientious objection," where it has been taken to mean any conviction that a person holds with earnest passion.[8] The Bishop was appealing, rather, to "conscience" in the sense once explained with exquisite care by John Paul II in *Veritatis Splendor*: conscience as an understanding ordered to a body of objective moral truths. John Paul II remarked on that facile tendency to accord to the "individual conscience the status of a supreme tribunal of moral judgment which hands down categorical and infallible decisions about good and evil." But in this way the inescapable claims of truth disappear, yielding their place to criteria of sincerity, authenticity, and 'being at peace with oneself', so much so that some have come to adopt a radically subjectivistic conception of moral judgment. [Par. 32]

What is lost then is the recognition that conscience is not directed inward to the self and one's feelings, but outward to the natural law: The "natural law discloses the objective and universal demands of the moral good," and the function of conscience is "the application of the law to a particular case." But with the corrupted or "relativized" version of "conscience" and religion, religious moral teaching can be reduced simply to "beliefs," in the modern, vulgar sense and hence the line grown familiar among Catholic political figures from Edward Kennedy and Mario Cuomo to John Kerry and Joseph Biden: that they have an aversion to abortion but they would not impose their Catholic "beliefs" through the law. (In fact, of course, as the joke ran, they would not even impose these beliefs on themselves.) That kind of refrain marks a disfiguring of the very logic of a moral judgment, but it is also a deep scandal, for it involves the most egregious misreading of Catholic teaching, for that teaching,

[8] See Hadley Arkes, *First Things* (Princeton: Princeton University Press, 1986), pp. 192–96.

as I have had many occasions to point out, has been a teaching in natural law, accessible to people across the religious divisions.

But when we are clear that the argument for religious freedom is cast now as an argument in natural law, moving beyond "beliefs," and appealing now to objective moral norms, accessible to our reason, the problem of Obamacare and its mandates become transformed. And by "transformed" I mean a shift that suddenly alters, for lawyers and judges, the landscape before them and leaves them uncertain about the terms that would guide them. Consider this problem of two owners of businesses: Both of them object on moral grounds to the mandates of Obamacare on abortion and contraception. One is a Catholic, whose understanding has been informed by the Catholic reasoning on these matters. The other man claims no religious attachment; he has formed a moral objection to abortion, say, solely on the grounds of that principled reasoning that the Church teaches as a teaching in natural law.[9] Would we actually say that the Catholic businessman had a stronger claim to challenge the law on grounds of religious freedom, when his reasoning was in no way different from that of the businessman who reached his moral conclusion with the same weave of the empirical evidence of embryology, amplified by moral reasoning? Are the claims distinguishable on any grounds that matter? And does one position claim a certain dignity, as a claim of "religious conviction" or religious freedom, which is not available to the man standing against the law with the same moral reasoning used by the Church?

We might ask then, with the labels stripped away, is one man being deprived of his religious freedom, and the other deprived of nothing of comparable moral or constitutional standing?

This confusion over beliefs and reasoning was on display in a notable victory for the religious in the summer of 2013 when a federal appellate court in Colorado went to the aid of the Green Family, the owners of the Hobby Lobby "craft" stores and Mardel, a chain of Christian bookstores. This was the case that would later make its way to the Supreme Court, with the position of the Green family sustained, in the narrowest vote, but with an outcome highly celebrated.[10] The Greens offer a program of health insurance to their employees, and under Obamacare the Greens would have been obliged to cover, in their plans, contraceptives and abortifacients. The Greens asserted that they could not do that without violating their religious convictions. The appellate court preserved for the Greens the possibility of sustaining their suit and holding at bay the barrage of fines that the government was prepared to

[9] We have had this kind of problem in the past – most notably in the argument years ago over the Civil Rights Restoration Act, where the proponents offered to exempt Catholic or religious hospitals from the obligation to perform abortions. But it turned out that there were many hospitals that refused abortion on moral grounds to perform abortions, even though they claimed no religious character. See Arkes, *Beyond the Constitution*, pp. 220–30.

[10] See *Burwell* v. *Hobby Lobby Stores, Inc.* 573 U.S. ___ (2014).

unload on them. But if this was a victory, it was a melancholy win, for it was argued within the cast of the Religious Freedom Restoration Act, and it would foretell in that way, the ground of the later victory in the Supreme Court, along with the things that would make that later victory rather melancholy as well. According to Judge Tymkovich and his colleagues in the appellate panel, the Greens asserted, among their "sincere beliefs," a "belief that human life begins when sperm fertilizes an egg."[11] A "belief"? That would surely come as news to the authors of all of the texts in embryology, who report that point as one of their anchoring truths. The Greens also professed to "believe" that they would be "facilitating harms toward human beings" if they helped to provide drugs that prevent implantation on the uterine wall. Since the blocking of implantation does kill the nascent life, we may ask, what is the part that belongs here to "belief" rather than truth?

Our friends litigating religious freedom feel pressed to argue within the grooves of "sincere beliefs," because they are the terms that the courts have confirmed and the judges recognize. But in this way they plug into a trend of cases that has seen "conscience" reduced, or relativized, to virtually anything that a person sincerely believes, and religion itself relativized until it is detached from any notion of God and the laws springing from that God. Well into the nineteenth century the judges could invoke Madison's understanding of religion as "the duty which we owe to our Creator and the manner of discharging it." But as the judges dealt with claims of conscientious objection, the "conscience" they were protecting did not require the commands of a Lawgiver, nor did it require an elaborate body of theology – for late revelations may be as valid as early revelations. "Religion" did not require a body of moral teachings with a claim to truth, and in fact a religious sense could be supplied simply by passions that were thought to offer the functional equivalent of religious convictions.[12] The truth that dare not speak its name is that even many friends of religious freedom have been content to argue for that freedom on terms that accept this reduction of religion to "beliefs" untested by reason, for our friends don't wish to put themselves in the position of speaking the uncomfortable truth: that not everything that calls itself religion in this country may be regarded as a legitimate religion. And so we try to vindicate a "ministerial exception" to the laws on employment – we insist that churches must be free to determine who counts as a minister according to their own criteria and teaching. But does that freedom from the intrusion of the government apply as well to the ministers appointed under the Church of the Flying Spaghetti Monster, or even worse, does it apply to Satanists claiming the standing of a religion?

We cannot detach ourselves from judging Satanism, or radical evil, and in the same measure we cannot detach ourselves from the task of discriminating

[11] See *Hobby Lobby Stores* v. *Sebelius* (10th Federal Circuit, June 27, 2013).

[12] See *Welsh* v. *United States* 398 U.S. 333 (1970).

between religions that are more or less plausible, more or less legitimate, based on the substance of what they teach.

Return for a moment to that example of the two owners of businesses, who reach the same conclusion on abortion with the same reasoning, but one of them is Catholic. The Catholic may say that he thinks that his position has been enjoined upon him by God as the Author of the moral law. But we have other people who think that their God or gods enjoin them to burn widows on funeral pyres, or they carry out the rituals prescribed by Satan. Are we to recognize all such claims of "conscience," as though conscience were indeed relativized and we gave the same respect to anything people claimed to believe? Or do we follow the logic of John Paul II and say that we would have to make a judgment on whether a just God would enjoin such things as the burning of widows? But that judgment – about the policies and about the God from whom they are thought to spring – that judgment could be made only as we finally judge the *reasons* we are given for the rightness or wrongness of the act, not on the basis merely of "beliefs." Once again, the judgment on what God would plausibly will, will have to hinge on the reasons.

The canons of reason will ever be woven into the law on religion because, as Michael Novak has pointed out so powerfully, they have been bound up, from the beginning of the American law, with the Creator who endowed us with rights.[13] That was the Creator mentioned in the Declaration of Independence, the Author of the "Laws of Nature," including the moral laws. That was the God of the logos, of reason, who was understood to have brought forth, as the peak of His creation, those creatures with the capacity to give and understand reasons over matters of right and wrong. There is no understanding of religion more bound up with the deep principles of the American regime *and the very ground of our laws*. That is not to say that we would be retreating to some notion of "the god of the place," the God associated with this *tribe of Americans*. The God of the Declaration was not a local god. Serious Protestants, Catholics, and Jews understood the God of the Creation as a God with a universal jurisdiction, the Author of moral commands universal in their reach. Not only was that God and his Laws comprehensible, but there was also accessible to us, through the reason, the case for the existence of God, whether it was put forth as a First Cause, the uncaused cause of all things contingent on a chain of happenings, or whether it was put forth in the style of an argument based on probabilities.[14] We can put that decorously to the side, though, as an argument not likely to be sounded in the Courts; but we can return the matter to the very ground of the polis and the law.

Aristotle taught us that the mark of the polis, the political order, was the presence of law, and law sprang distinctly from the nature of that creature who can give and understand reasons over matters of right and wrong. Aristotle

[13] See Michael Novak, *On Two Wings* (San Francisco: Encounter Books, 2002).

[14] *Vide* Richard Swinburne, *The Existence of God* (Oxford: Clarendon Press, 2004).

expressed in that way the classic understanding of the moral ground of the law, and what I would argue here is that the freedom of religion may find its firmer ground by insisting again on that connection between reasoning and the law, between the reasons that support our religious convictions and the religious freedom we would protect through the law. The beginning of the argument would be to remind people of that connection, so clear and yet so unknown these days, the connection between the very logic of a moral judgment and the logic of law: In the strictest sense, a "moral" judgment moves beyond statements of merely personal taste or private beliefs; it speaks to the things that are right or wrong, just or unjust more generally or universally – for others as well as ourselves. In the corresponding way, the law moves by overriding claims of private choice, personal freedom, subjective belief. It imposes a rule of justice that claims to hold for everyone who comes within the reach of the law. The laws that bar the killing of the innocent override claims of personal convenience and private interest, and even "sincere beliefs" that the victim is not really human. In the classic understanding, we do a portentous thing when we impose laws on other people, and that move will always call for a *justification*, an explanation of what makes it *just* or rightful for others as well as ourselves. It used to be understood that those creatures we call "moral agents" have the capacity to reason about the grounds of their well-being – and the rightful limits to their own freedom. They have a presumptive claim to all dimensions of their freedom, and the burden lies with the law in supplying a moral justification for overriding that freedom.

When we view the law through that kind of lens, the burdens of justification for the law would be altered – and deepened. And so, before the law would impose the mandates on Obamacare on the owners of the Hobby Lobby stores, the law should bear the burden of showing that there is something deeply unreasonable about the understanding held by the Greens: that lives destroyed in abortions cannot be anything other than human lives; that those lives are inescapably innocent in the sense that they cannot be the source of any intentional wrongdoing; that the standing of these offspring as human beings cannot be in any way contingent on their height or weight, or whether they are speaking yet in sentences. And unless there is a new right to kill for one's own private interest, the justifications that must be offered for the taking of these human lives must be on the same plane as the justifications we would demand in any other case for the taking of any other human life. Unless the government can have something plausible to say on these points, it should back away from any presumptuous willingness to displace the moral code of this family with policies that cannot supply more than a rough version of utility or a claim to serve something only vaguely called a "public good."

The moral argument here may be deepened by pointing out the claims that the Greens had forgone: They did not make the kinds of arguments we have seen in the past on the part of people who object "conscientiously" to the fact that the money they are compelled to pay in taxes is being used for policies they find deeply repugnant: the support of the United Nations, the provision of welfare to unmarried mothers or – even more keenly – the support for abortion. The Greens understood that they were already committed, through the nexus of the tax system, to the support of abortions funded and promoted by the government. But the question then was just why the Greens should be compelled to support abortion more directly and personally through the medical services they fund for their employees. In another day, the very notion of the public authority compelling a private person A to make payments, or transfer his property, to private person B, would have been marked as the plainest example of "class legislation" and a form of legalized theft. If done by the federal government, it would have come clearly under the Fifth Amendment as a "taking of property" without due process of law. Chief Justice Chase caught the sense of this matter many years earlier in the famous Legal Tender cases when he remarked that,

> [the provision on the taking of property] does not, in terms, prohibit legislation which appropriates the private property of one class of citizens to the use of another class; but if such property cannot be taken for the benefit of all, without compensation, it is difficult to understand how it can be so taken for the benefit of a part without violating the spirit of the prohibition.[15]

The principle here was that we may not take private property for public use without just compensation: Do we get around that principle entirely by taking property not for public use, but for benefits delivered to particular persons or classes of persons? And after all, if a service is mandated by the federal government, the federal government should be required to fund that service, not transfer a public service to private persons to bear at private expense. That convenient maneuver simply manages to avoid the discipline of constitutionalism, for it frees the government from the need to raise the money to cover its own commitments, and justify to the voters the added taxes that it is laying upon them. In the case of abortion, the surgery is readily affordable by most people who desire to have it, and if an additional child is really seen as an economic burden, then it would make even more sense to borrow money for the abortion as to borrow money to pay for a car or a smart phone.

When we bring together these points, the case for imposing on private persons the obligation to fund abortions for other persons would not survive the tests of justification that were once thought to spring into place for any measure that could be imposed on the public with the force of law. The readiest, general rationale is that the measure would be necessary for the public safety or health. But abortion is not a procedure that relieves any illness or cures any disease, for pregnancy is not a state of illness. And if the offspring in the womb cannot be anything other than human, then it could hardly enhance the

[15] *Hepburn* v. *Griswold* (8 Wallace 603, at 624, 1870).

"public safety" by withdrawing the protections of the law from this class of human beings.

For the partisans of abortion in this country, the logic has long ago moved from a regrettable private choice to a positive public good, which deserves to be promoted and expanded with public funds. And yet it is plain that there is no need for public provision or subsidy for this service, for the moral barriers have been swept away, and the surgery is easily afforded. But that want of any necessity for a public provision takes the argument to another, telling level – perhaps the final, telling level. In a recent case in New Mexico, Elaine and Jonathan Huguenin were fined, penalized, for declining to take photos at the "wedding" of two women. No one could seriously claim that the lesbian couple would be deprived of photographs of their memorable moment. There was no want of photographers to pick up the business. The only reason to punish the Huguenins sprang from the moral passion to insist that Elaine and Jonathan Huguenin be marked as wrongdoers. The people who have made their signature tune the denial of moral truths, or the denial of any grounds for casting judgments on others, have shown that the "logic of morals" is something they have quite absorbed in their natural understanding – and they apply it now with a vengeance: As Aquinas caught that logic, the good is to be sought and evil avoided. What is rightful should be encouraged and promoted; what is wrongful should be condemned and punished. The passion at work here – the passion that explains why it was worth pursuing and punishing this young couple in New Mexico – was the passion to compel people to confess the rightness of same-marriage, and to waive all moral reservations about the homosexual life. Lincoln captured that sense of the matter exactly when he observed that, "if slavery is right, all words, acts, laws, and constitutions against it, are themselves wrong, and should be silenced, and swept away."[16] And he remarked about the forces pressing the rightness of slavery that they will not be satisfied if others simply acquiesce in silence: We must be "avowedly with them," he said. For "this, and this only [would assure them]: cease to call slavery wrong, and join them in calling it right."[17] The activists for gay rights and same-sex marriage have identified their adversaries as the religious, and they will not feel unthreatened until the teaching that animates the religious is renounced at the core. The religious will need to recant. But the religious, with a certain sympathy and humility, steer away from demanding that their adversaries abase themselves in this way. The passion to demand that abasement marks an unlovely expression of fanaticism in our law.

I find it notable, in that respect, that the libertarian professor of law, Eugene Volokh, likened this case to the case on compelled speech under the First Amendment. I find that interesting because Professor Volokh surely appreciated

[16] Abraham Lincoln, "Speech at the Cooper Union in New York, February 1860," in *Collected Works*, vol. 3, p. 549.

[17] *Ibid.* at 547–48.

that the Huguenins were not strictly being required to speak words, say, as the children of Jehovah's Witnesses were once compelled to speak and perform the pledge to the flag. But what Volokh apparently noticed here was that the moral insistence on punishing could be explained mainly by the desire to humble these people before a new orthodoxy, demanding now its place as a principle commanding reverence. And for the judges, the case should offer a telling sign of precisely the kind of intemperate passion that the Founders were seeking to avert on either side. That intemperance could be found on the side of irreligious no less than the side of the religious, as they became untethered from an anchoring prudence. It was a religious and constitutional temperance that the Founders were aiming at as they sought to put the levers of official power at a more salutary distance from our religious life.

The argument, as I've made it so far, has not depended, in any of its parts, on appeals to faith or "religious belief." It would move entirely through moral reasoning and the principles of constitutionalism. And yet these principles *are* touched by our religious understanding, though touched in ways so deep that most people may hardly be aware any longer of their source. For the deep truth of the matter is that the religious tradition does not come into our law and our lives as a set of eccentric "beliefs," merely begging for indulgence and exemptions to the laws laid down for others. But rather, our religious tradition has formed the deep moral reservoir on which the law has drawn. Our language of law speaks of persons, of their rights and wrongs and their "injuries," the unjustified harms they absorb. These terms are part of the logic of law, and they were woven in the laws before the advent of Christianity. But these terms are given a deeper resonance by our religious tradition. For something else comes into play to tell us what is so deeply portentous about the taking of a human life, or why it is hardly trivial to restrict the freedom, or take the property, of those beings we call "moral agents," those beings who alone can impart a moral purpose to property and to inanimate matter. At the center of everything is that remarkable creature, as John Paul II described him: the "human person." And nothing has enlarged our sense of the moral meaning of the human person than the teaching, long preserved, that that "person" was made in the image of something higher. What other teaching could have shaped Lincoln's understanding when he remarked that "nothing stamped with the Divine image and likeness was sent into the world to be trodden on, and degraded, and imbruted by its fellows?" [18] The law has lived, and continues to live, on the moral capital of our religious teaching, even while the awareness of that connection has fled the memory of most lawyers, or been happily put out of mind by them.

Some of my colleagues have taken as their signature tune that line from Nietzsche, amplified by Dostoevsky, that "God is dead" and that everything is

[18] Abraham Lincoln, *Speech in Lewistown, Illinois* (August 17, 1858), *Collected Works*, vol. 2, p. 546.

permitted, presumably because there is no ground on which to cast a moral judgment. And yet these same colleagues will look at that homeless man in the street, who has broken his own life, and say that he has about him nevertheless a certain "dignity" or even "sanctity." Sanctity? Of the sacred? That is redolent of You-know-who. That perspective made sense to those of us whose understanding was shaped by the notion that these human beings, however impaired or diminished or even morally broken, were made in the image of something higher.

In my book *Natural Rights & the Right to Choose*,[19] I recalled this incident from years back, when I'd been commissioned to do a piece on the newly opened Holocaust Museum in Washington. As I moved through the halls with a friend, I suddenly came upon a scene that has been encountered by many visitors to the museum: a vast vat filled with shoes. They were the shoes of the victims, as the Nazis sought to extract anything they could use again or sell. And what came flashing back instantly, at that moment, were those searing lines of Justice McLean, in his dissenting opinion in the Dred Scott case: You may think that the black man is merely chattel, but "He bears the impress of his Maker, [he] is amenable to the laws of God and man; and he is destined to an endless existence."[20] He has, in other words, a soul, which is imperishable; it will not decompose when his material existence comes to an end. The sufficient measure of things here is that the Nazis looked at their victims and thought that the shoes were the real *durables*.

My colleagues in Amherst and the academy are people of large natures, and they are prepared to engage their sympathies for all species of hurts suffered by the mass of mankind. But even they would have to concede that they cannot give the same account of the wrong of slavery or the wrong of genocide that Justice McLean was able to give. They cannot give the same account that serious Christians and Jews can give.

My argument today is that we have backed ourselves into a rather impoverished and self-defeating mode of argument – and understanding – as we have been content to settle in with appeals for religious freedom based upon "sincere beliefs" – as though any beliefs sincerely held had a claim to our respect. As anyone will tell you, the zealots who flew those planes into the World Trade Center on September 11 no doubt earnestly believed the doctrines that had taken hold of their lives; but our respect is not summoned or commanded by the report they held to their beliefs with a tenacious sincerity.

And yet, when the Green family finally prevailed in the Supreme Court, in June 2014, the decisive accent was still placed on the "sincerity" of "belief," quite detached from claims of truth. Justice Alito, writing for the majority, went even further. The Green family had avowed its "belief" that human life begins at "conception," and Justice Alito held that "it is not for us to say that their religious beliefs are mistaken or insubstantial." Justice Alito echoed here a

[19] Cambridge: Cambridge University Press, 2002, pp. 174–75.

[20] *Scott* v. *Sandford* 60 U.S. 393, at 550 (1857).

train of expressions cast up by judges, as though they could overcome, through repetition, what was immanently implausible. With this reasoning in place, it is hard to see the ground on which to challenge the "sincere beliefs" of those who were convinced that widows should be burned on the funeral pyres of their husbands. Or more recently: On what ground would we quibble with those people who "sincerely believe" that infants in the womb do not count yet as "human" – especially when that belief seems to be credited so widely now in the climate of opinion that sustains abortion. But Justice Alito was willing to draw yet again, in this vein, on the case of *Thomas* v. *Review Board* (1981). In that case, a worker in a factory refused on religious ground to participate in making turrets for tanks. His draft board couldn't quite see that there was a notable difference between the work in a factory making sheet metal, and the work that shaped the same sheet metal into turrets for a tank. But the Supreme Court was willing to make a retreat into this epistemic relativism when it came to the religious: "it is not for us to say that the line [Thomas] drew was an unreasonable one."

That the Court was willing to indulge this kind of credulity, that it would continue to mention "sincerity" as the threshold question, was another mark of the fact that the Court would not challenge the standing of anything that called itself "religion" by judging the substance of what was taught in its name. And that was simply a confirmation of the dominant fact that the case was being litigated under the Religious Freedom Restoration Act (1993). Under that Act, the religious may be given a certain exemption even from laws of "general applicability," laws thought to be valid for everyone who came under their terms (such as the laws on traffic, or on homicide). The claim is that, under certain conditions, the religious may be given a release from these laws even when those laws reveal no animus directed at the religious. The triggering condition is the holding of "sincere" beliefs. And in that event a heavier burden is shifted to the side of the law. The law must offer a "compelling interest" that animates the statute, and then the law would be obliged to use "the least restrictive means of furthering [that] compelling interest" when it came to "burdening" religious freedom.

In the run-up to the Hobby Lobby case, in the federal appellate courts, Judges Diane Sykes and Janice Rogers Brown showed us how it was done. In the companion cases of *Korte* v. *Department of Health & Human Services*, and *Grote* v. *Sebelius*,[21] Judge Sykes dealt, once again, with the Catholic owners of private businesses. And once again it was a matter of compelling Catholic owners to become accomplices in policies that were deeply at odds with the moral teaching they had absorbed as Catholics. As Judges Sykes observed, the government identified "two public interests – 'public health' and 'gender equality' ": As the argument ran, the wider availability of contraceptives would be

[21] Seventh Federal Circuit, November 8, 2013.

useful for public health and for "promoting the autonomy of women" by liberating women, no less than men, from the "risks" of pregnancy and childbirth.[22]

But as Judge Sykes pointed out, contraceptives could be diffused to the population at large in many other ways: The government could provide "contraception insurance"; it could "give tax incentives to contraception suppliers to provide these medications and services at no cost to consumers; it can give tax incentives to consumers of contraception and sterilization services."[23]

The government could also buy the contraceptives and give them away, but with funds it has to raise from the public by justifying taxes. In other words, these ends of public policy can be accomplished quite readily without compelling any particular person to buy contraceptives for anyone else – and compelling him at the same time to violate the moral principles taught in his Church.

But at the same time, as Judge Sykes pointed out, the government sets a trap for itself when it offers as a justification some airy notion of a "public interest." Such a statement, so blurry in its content and boundaries, "guarantees," as she said, that the mandate will flunk the test:

> Strict scrutiny requires a substantial congruity – a close "fit" – between the governmental interest and the means chosen to further that interest. Stating the governmental interests at such a high level of generality makes it impossible to show that the mandate is the least restrictive means of furthering them. There are many ways to promote public health and gender equality, almost all of them less burdensome on religious liberty.[24]

Or, we might say, less burdensome on economic liberty, or any other liberty that may be equally worthy of the protection of the judges.

Judge Brown in the D.C. Circuit dealt with the case of *Gilardi* v. *U.S. Department of Health and Human Services*,[25] a case involving two brothers, owners of Freshway Foods and Freshway Logistics. The Gilardis offer a self-insured plan of medical care for the 400 people they employed. And they would be forced under Obamacare to become accomplices in policies they been taught to regard as serious wrongs. Judge Brown argued that the government should be compelled then to meet a standard more demanding than something "vaguely called" the public interest or safety. Even if there is a "right" on the part of people to contraception, Judge Brown made the elementary – and, in an earlier time, decisive – point that the Gilardis were not blocking the access of anyone to contraception. And so, as Judge Brown observed, "the government has failed to demonstrate how such a right – whether described as noninterference, privacy, or autonomy – can extend to the compelled subsidization of a woman's procreative practices. Again, our searching examination is impossible unless the government describes its purposes with precision."[26]

[22] *Id.* at 61 in the. Nos. 12-3841 & 13-1077

[23] *Id.* at 63.

[24] *Id.* at 61.

[25] U.S. Court of Appeals, DC Circuit, November 1, 2013.

[26] *Id.* at 26 in the slip opinion.

Both Judges Sykes and Brown professed to be writing within the cast of cases being argued under the Religious Freedom Restoration Act (RFRA). And yet, Judge Brown's argument offered a telling path outside this framework. The case was being argued under RFRA, but the Judge noted at the outset what was "not at issue": the case was not about "the sincerity of the Gilardis' religious beliefs, nor does it concern the theology behind Catholic precepts on contraception." Judge Brown argued that a right to contraception simply did not entail a right to compel the Gilardis to buy contraceptives for other people. In other words, she recognized the action here as a classic case of "taking" the property or assets of person A and transferring them to person B. That principle was with us long before the advent of RFRA, and it would be part of a constitutional order even if RFRA were repealed. What could be said here is that RFRA has brought back, for the religious, the kinds of protections that used to be available to everyone else in this country. Or rather, they were available when the judges took far more seriously the notion that the freedom of people in control of their own assets and property was a freedom that warranted their guardianship no less than any other dimension of our freedom.

The lesson taught in Judge Brown's opinion would come out, in its deeper importance, if we connected it to the problem I raised earlier about the "two owners": One was Catholic and avowed his "religious belief" that life began at conception. The other owner professed no religious attachments, but he reasoned about abortion precisely along the same lines of moral reasoning used by the Church. Some of us may indeed celebrate the outcome of the Hobby Lobby case as it bore on the Green family, but the cast of logic there left us with this state of affairs: that RFRA would work to protect the Green family, or that first owner, but leave quite unprotected that businessman who reached the same moral judgment, with the same moral reasoning used by the Church, and yet professed no religion. But Judge Brown's argument, moving gently, without trumpeting its deeper lesson, would work just as powerfully to protect all other businessmen, even those who are not Catholic.

If I'm right in spotting the real tension or the problem of coherence in the arguments here, we would indeed need, as I've suggested, some serious work in recasting the arguments that the defenders of religious freedom have been making in the courts. The job may be made easier by the fact that this task of recasting simply requires us to restore the things that were once known widely among lawyers, and which can never be coherently denied: namely, that necessary connection between "the logic of morals" and the "logic of law," and the demanding burdens then that the law should have to face before it imposed these mandates on abortion and contraception, on either the religious, or the people who are irreligious. The task is made slightly more difficult by the fact that, for several generations now, lawyers and graduates of universities, have been led away from that classic understanding, as they have been led away from the notion of natural law and objective moral truths.

In a speech four years ago on natural law, Pope Benedict countered the famous positivist Hans Kelsen, who argued that moral norms can come only from will, and we cannot find in bare nature the presence of that will. To which Benedict said, "Is it really pointless to wonder whether the objective reason that manifests itself in nature does not presuppose a creative reason, a *Creator Spiritus*?"[27] Where did we get the Laws of Reason except from the same Author of the Laws of Nature, including the moral laws? Why is it so hard to grasp that the Creation does contain the laws of reason along with those creatures uniquely gifted with reason; the creatures who marked the peak of Creation? Why, then – we must ask – would even conservative judges think that we bring in something distant from the law, not properly within the law or the kit of judges, if we began to speak again of the reasoning that underpins our religious understanding and explains, more fully, what we take ourselves to be defending when we are defending religious freedom?

It is especially telling, I fear, that even the conservative judges and lawyers, spooked with a fear of natural law, defend religious conviction mainly as something "traditional," something that claims its plausibility and legitimacy among us mainly because it has been taken seriously by our people for such a long time. But in that path of argument we may find again the flight of conservatives from reason and natural law. They will defend religion as something traditional, but they will not think of weaving into their opinions the reasons that have made that teaching compelling to the people who have been summoned by it. Those teachings, we might say, are about first causes, about a universe containing laws of nature, including a moral world more fitted for creatures of reason, and the intrinsic worth of human life. They tell us that we cast moral judgments only in the domain of freedom, where people have control of their own acts, and we don't hold people blameworthy for acts they were powerless to affect. They tell us that we can tell the difference between assaults that are justified and unjustified, and therefore, that we can speak seriously of innocence and guilt. And from there we can spin out axioms of law that have the force of necessity, axioms that would have to be in place in anything we could rightly call the "rule of law."

A fine teacher of natural law, J. Budziszewski, has remarked that these teachings involve the things we *cannot not know*; the things we can never help knowing. But then it may be the hardest thing of all to teach again what we as a people, and lawyers, have been taught *not* to understand. And yet it is not hard to teach the underlying logic anew, because that logic has never been purged. No matter how far we may have traveled to places distant and exotic, no matter how distorted the conventions of our so-called culture become, the natural law will always be with us. It will always be there, tucked away in our

[27] Benedict XVI, Address to the Bundestag in Berlin, September 22, 2011: "The Listening Heart: Reflections on the Foundations of Law."

souls, and in the style of Plato's *Meno*, it will be readily awakened and called forth when we raise again the right questions.

If the task of teaching anew seems daunting we should remind ourselves that some of us have seen, in our own lifetimes, Justice Hugo Black recasting the law on the Establishment of religion and the very meaning of religion, beginning in 1947 with the Everson case. It was a deeply false teaching – false in its historical construction of the meaning of the First Amendment on the Establishment, and false in the understanding that would remove religion from our public discourse and political life. And yet, so deeply did that recasting take hold that Justices like David Souter would refer to it as a firmly settled part of our jurisprudence, as though it had been part of the original text of the Constitution. Justice Scalia set off years ago to teach us how to talk about "originalism," and Clarence Thomas on how to recover the Commerce Clause as it was. If we think these things are worth doing, the judges are in a unique position for teaching, and if we are to teach anew, we might as well start now.

In our own case, there is no need to contrive anything new; it truly is a matter of teaching anew the things that judges once used to know, and could easily know again, because these truths have always been there. It may indeed be the case that judges will cast their arguments in terms of "beliefs," because that is what they have become used to hearing and writing. But to give an account of the reasoning and the truths that form the ground of our religious conviction is to give a more accurate and more faithful account of the life we are seeking to describe, and a more coherent account of the jurisprudence we would seek to shape. And a jurisprudence that can explain its moral ground is a jurisprudence that does not back away from explaining the justice it seeks to do.

5

Let us pray: Greece *v.* Galloway

Gerard V. Bradley

In the run-up to the Supreme Court's decision in *Town of Greece* v. *Galloway*, many observers expected the Court to uphold Greece, New York's practice of opening its council meetings with a prayer. Many observers figured, too, that Justice Kennedy would write the Court's opinion. His was likely to be the deciding vote. He had also proved in prior cases to be the justice who was the most ambivalent about public displays of religion. Any opinion of the Court would therefore have to abide his caution. Justices Alito, Scalia, and Thomas would struggle mightily – it surely seemed – to write an opinion within Kennedy's comfort zone.[1] So might Chief Justice Roberts.

It was thus no great surprise when, on May 5, 2014, the Court upheld Greece's customary prayer. Nor was it curious that Anthony Kennedy wrote for the five-man majority.[2] The surprise – and it is a big one – is that Justice Kennedy did not stick to the limited permission for legislative prayers provided by the Court's only precedent on point, the 1983 decision in *Marsh* v. *Chambers*.[3] Kennedy did not equivocate or dither. He did not rely upon vague generalities or conclusory assertions to support the Court's decision. Justice Kennedy instead delivered a bold, cogent, and mostly perspicuous opinion. His opinion in *Greece* v. *Galloway* secures a wide constitutional berth for legislative prayer, including those that are robustly "sectarian" (as most were in Greece).[4] Kennedy's opinion

[1] In the event, Scalia subscribed to most of a Thomas concurrence which would have upheld Greece's practice on grounds more sweeping than those articulated by Justice Kennedy. I take up the Thomas concurrence in Part V of this chapter. Justice Alito wrote another concurrence, in which Scalia joined. Alito's opinion was not sweeping. It was, however, a persuasive critique of Justice Kagan's breathtakingly broad dissenting opinion for all four Justices in the minority. I analyze the dissent and Alito's criticisms of it in Part III.

[2] Because the official report is not yet available, all citations here to *Greece* v. *Galloway* are from the slip opinion issued by the Supreme Court.

[3] 463 U.S. 783 (1983).

[4] See Part VII, *infra*.

distances the Court from its prevailing Establishment Clause principle of "neutrality" between religion and what the Court usually calls "non-religion." It also brings non-establishment doctrine into closer alignment with the historical meaning of the First Amendment.[5]

Greece v. *Galloway* is a significant departure in church-state constitutional law. It portends additional significant changes down the road. It is the best Establishment Clause opinion of the Court in decades.

I

The case arose in Greece, New York, located just outside Rochester. For many years the town council opened its monthly meetings with prayers delivered by community religious leaders. An overwhelming majority of these prayer-givers were Christians, praying as Christians are wont to do. The lower appellate court found that "[a] substantial majority of the prayers in the record contained uniquely Christian language. Roughly two-thirds contained references to 'Jesus Christ,' 'Jesus,' 'Your Son,' or the 'Holy Spirit.' "[6]

This proportion was no surprise; the town invited local leaders to deliver the prayer, and the vast majority of Greece's residents were Christians, as were all of the local religious congregations.[7] The nearly inescapable preponderance of Christian prayer-givers was nonetheless the basis for the Second Circuit's ruling against Greece. In an opinion by former Yale Law Dean Guido Calabresi, that court declared that the "steady drumbeat of ... specifically sectarian Christian prayers" improperly "affiliate[ed]" the town with Christianity, in violation of the First Amendment prohibition upon laws "respecting an establishment of religion."[8]

In fact, the Greece Town Board utilized a random process to recruit its opening prayer-givers. That process and the information provided to those selected to give invocations was informal and somewhat *ad hoc*. However, the record makes clear that invitees were free to speak as they pleased, and that the board wanted them to maintain a spirit of respect for the views of everyone present at the monthly gatherings.

The Second Circuit's "affiliation" finding was for these reasons a bit improbable. It is more curious in light of the fact that Calabresi ascribed "no religious animus to the town or its leaders,"[9] and found "no evidence" that the town would not have accepted "any and all volunteers who asked to give the prayer."[10] In fact, sometime around 2008 a Buddhist temple

[5] See Part VI, *infra*.

[6] *Galloway* v. *Greece*, 681 F.3d 20, 24 (2d. Cir 2012).

[7] *Ibid*.

[8] *Ibid*. at 32.

[9] *Ibid*.

[10] *Ibid*. at 31.

opened up within town borders. Soon the board invited a representative to offer a prayer, then two Jews, and later a Wiccan priestess. She invoked the Olympian gods, not because anybody in Greece believed in them, but because of the town's name.

The Second Circuit also concluded that the prayers given did not "preach conversion, threaten damnation to nonbelievers, [or] downgrade other faiths."[11] Even though there had been no proselytizing in roughly 130 invocations over an eleven-year period, the court worried about the possibility of proselytization. Calabresi warned that public bodies have "few means to forestall the prayer-giver who cannot resist the urge" to do so.[12] He seems to have supposed that the Constitution's was utterly risk averse on the subject. *Any* possibility of "proselytizing" was too great to permit. In his scale of the goods at stake, it surely seems that asking God to guide lawmakers ranked very low indeed.

The plaintiffs in *Greece* v. *Galloway* were Susan Galloway and Linda Stephens. They had lived in or near the town for more than thirty years. Both testified that they were unaware of any non-Christian places of worship in the town. During the course of their litigation, the *Galloway* plaintiffs "expressly abandoned the argument that the town intentionally discriminated against non-Christians in its selection of prayer-givers."[13] Galloway and Stephens objected not only that the prayers "violated their religious or philosophical views (their views were not described in the appellate opinions, and nothing in them depended upon what the plaintiffs actually believed)," but they also asserted that the prayers were "offensive," "intolerant," and an affront to a "diverse community" – which, by all accounts, Greece, New York was not.

II

All of the justices in *Greece* v. *Galloway* agreed that they had resolved a constitutional dispute concerning sincere invocations of divine blessings and assistance, of heart-felt expressions of gratitude for previous blessings bestowed, and of candid recognition of God's continuing care for the world and everyone in it. Although they split almost evenly about whether Greece behaved in a constitutionally permissible way, they all agreed that they disagreed about (genuine) *prayer*.

One might reasonably ask, "What is the alternative?" The Court has on other occasions said that expressions like "under God" in the Pledge of Allegiance and the Court's own opening declaration – "God Save this Honorable Court" – are examples of language which time has stripped of literal meaning. Familiarity has bleached them of religious content. These expressions linger without valid objection because (to use phrases from the Court's *Greece* opinion) they "lend

[11] *Ibid.* at 31–32.
[12] *Ibid.* at 34.
[13] 681 F.3d at 26.

gravity to the occasion," and "reflect values long part of the Nation's heritage." The Supreme Court has sometimes called these expressions examples of "ceremonial deism." The dissenters in *Greece* referred to pieties which are part of "our expressive idiom" and "our heritage and tradition" – with emphasis on *our*, precisely to indicate a badge of social solidarity rather than, well, real prayers.

Chief Justice Roberts drew the attention of Greece's lawyer to this way of thinking about religious expression during the oral argument.[14] The Chief used the term "historical artifact." He then drew a distinction, using the example of our national motto, between a civic inheritance and a civic initiative. "[W]e [would] look at it differently if there were a proposal today for the first time, to say let's adopt the motto "In God We Trust." Even if a particular practice were affirmed today because it has long been in place, "it doesn't mean that it would be okay to adopt a seal today that would have a cross on it, does it?"

Why not? What is the difference between *keeping* a seal with a cross and *adopting* one? The difference presupposed by the Chief Justice seems to be that any *initiative* would inescapably be caught up in a troublesome, if not simply prohibited, genuine religious sentiment, while leaving the *status quo* undisturbed evidently would not be so entangled. If America's President announced tonight that he would henceforth commence each of his state speeches with the phrase "God bless America," the suspicion might arise that he sincerely wished that God would bless America. But if the President tomorrow ignored the canned version of Kate Smith's *God Bless America* which has played from time out of mind each morning on the White House PA system, it would – we are invited to believe – signal indifference, not eager embrace.

Or maybe not. One problem with the Chief Justice's suggestion is that its presumptions are not apparently sound. Persons and communities possessed of no particular religious motive might well wish to reconnect – today, anew – with their pasts, even where and notwithstanding that the past is a hallowed one. This retro impulse could simply be a "new traditionalism." On the other hand, persons and communities might retain a religious marker, not as a connection with the past but due to a pungent present belief in what the marker signifies. In American society at least, there is no evident basis for presuming one rather than the other.

The second problem with the Chief Justice's suggestion is the ambiguity of "artifact." One sense of the term looks horizontally at the present; the other looks vertically at the past. Neither is materially religious, though both are formally so.

In the first sense, we could imagine that all those assembled exhibit solidarity by expressing a common religious refrain, just as besotted alums might do when they sing and sway to the alma mater of a once-Presbyterian (or Methodist or Episcopalian or Catholic) university during reunion weekend.

[14] All excerpts from the *Galloway* oral argument are taken from the Court's official transcript of it.

The meaning of the words chanted is irrelevant. What matters is that these are *our* words. The value of saying or singing them is that the words strike the same mystical chord in each person present. The recitation fosters and even actualizes the group's identity.

In the second sense, we could imagine that those present affirm their solidarity with those who have gone before, just the way besotted alums might do when they sing together on the chapel steps. They would affirm their link with all those former Crimson or Elis or Fighting Irish who have stood on the same ground and recited the same words. In both cases, the hallowed phrases constitute a ritual. Saying or singing them reaffirms the identity of those present, including how they identify with all their predecessors. We do as they did.

Any court upholding pageantry honeycombed with hosannas along either the vertical or the horizontal axis could say that it expresses social solidarity, not sincere supplication. Any court could reach the same conclusion if the hosannas fell along both axes.

The catalog of ways by which the genuinely prayerful content of a prayer might be neutered is much larger than a reunion songbook. Calabresi criticized Greece's council for not "explain[ing] that it intended the prayers to solemnize Board meetings rather than to affiliate the town with any particular creed."[15] Here Calabresi made a gratuitous assumption, one very likely motivated by his conviction that the Constitution prohibited public *prayers* except where they were recited for a non-religious purpose. He asserted that the town "desire[d] to mark the solemnity of the proceedings with a prayer."[16] Not so. It could hardly be clearer that the town leaders really wanted divine guidance, and that they sought the prayers of local citizens to help them get it. They did not mean to "mark solemnity" by and through a "prayer." It was quite the other way around. Any "solemnizing" – in the non-religious sense of setting a sober tone for the proceedings – was a welcome byproduct of really praying. For them, praying was the point of praying.

Besides, there are many ways besides prayer to solemnize public events. Given how fraught with grave peril Calabresi (and, as we shall see, the *Greece v. Galloway* dissenters) believes public prayers to be, it is a wonder that he (or they) do not simply forbid them as needlessly risky. If the aim is to "solemnize" one could instigate a reading of Whitman's *Leaves of Grass* or a Maya Angelou composition. Those assembled could be treated to a rousing recital of the Gettysburg Address. They could listen to *The Battle Hymn of the Republic*. They could be led to a moment of silent reflection by the oldest person present. If the point is to get those present to recollect themselves, any of these potentially edifying exercises will do the job. If the point is, however, to seek God's blessing and guidance, none will.

[15] 681 F. 3d at 32.
[16] *Ibid.*

Judge Calabresi also lamented that in Greece "most prayer-givers appeared to speak on behalf of the town, rather than on behalf of themselves."[17] Of course they did. All of the prayer-givers were invited *by* the town to pray *for* the town, its board, and the pending deliberations, and *in* their presence. The opening prayer slot at Greece town board meetings was not supposed to be an open microphone for volunteers to express their views about whatever might strike their fancy. Justice Kennedy rightly saw that the "principal audience for these invocations is not, indeed, the public but the lawmakers themselves."[18] Calabresi is inclined to transpose the town's prayers into a series of speeches delivered by private persons in a limited public forum, where the town's public officials just happen to be present. But this is not to uphold legislative prayer. It is to replace it with karaoke.

What all these ways of thinking about legislative prayer have in common is the redescription of "prayer" as something religious in form but not in substance. "God Save this Honorable Court" is thus a signal that business is about to get underway, so fold up your newspapers and put your cell phones on silent. "In God We Trust" is an emblem of national identity, and there is an end to it. Its presence on our currency possesses no more genuine religious character than do the many seals, escutcheons, and maces that university marshals carry every graduation day. These university insignia may teem with Latin hosannas to the Almighty. Few of those present bother to read them. Fewer still understand. Almost no one cares.

Prayer may work as an ice-breaker, or as a sonorous gong, or as a meaningless but cherished totemic slogan or brand for a certain contingent solidarity. Prayers could function as instigators of recollection, as could the reading of letters from Iwo Jima or singing *Auld Lang Syne*. But none of these possible uses, effects, and redescriptions capture what the people in Greece did.

At a few points in *Greece* Justice Kennedy seemed to be slipping into this way of thinking of "prayer" as a non-religious act that happens to consist of religious-sounding phrases. Kennedy described Greece's prayers as "symbolic expression[s]" that possessed some instrumental value.[19] He wrote that "the reasonable observer" of goings-on in Greece is "presumed [to be] acquainted with this tradition and understands that its purposes are to lend gravity to public proceedings and to acknowledge the place religion holds in the lives of many private citizens"[20] – as if the "prayer" functioned to "solemnize" the occasion and to merely "acknowledge" ambient private religious sentiment.

The great bulk of the Court's descriptions of Greece's opening acts leaves no doubt, however, that the justices viewed them as real *prayers*. The many specimens of Greece prayers cataloged by Kennedy were especially pious. They

[17] *Ibid.*

[18] *Town of Greece* v. *Galloway*, No. 12–696, slip op. (Kennedy) at 19 (U.S. May 5, 2014).

[19] *Ibid.* at 6.

[20] *Ibid.* at 19.

could not honestly be assimilated to a non-religious category – solemnizing expressions, vestiges of a more God-fearing past, or stamps of social solidarity. The majority described Greece's prayers as "invo[cations of] divine guidance in town affairs." The Court said that they were surely "religious in nature" and largely in a "Christian idiom." And the Court relied extensively upon *Marsh* v. *Chambers*, which affirmed the constitutionality precisely of "invok[ing] Divine guidance on a public body entrusted with making the laws." Of the very largely Christian content of the prayers splayed across that record the Marsh Court wrote that they were "a tolerable acknowledgement of beliefs widely held among the people of this country."[21]

III

The four *Greece* dissenters called for a regimen more "inclusive" than that practiced by the town and upheld by the Court's majority. Their opinion, written by Justice Kagan, is unfortunately incoherent. It would lead exactly where Justice Alito said that it would: no genuine prayer as part of a legislative (and, presumably, other public) proceeding could be constitutional. The *Greece* dissenters are guilty of the sin that Calabresi protested *he* did not commit: "adopting a test that permits prayers in theory but makes it impossible for a town in practice to avoid Establishment Clause problems."[22] (For the record: Calabresi committed it, too.)

Justice Kagan interrupted the town's lawyer about thirty seconds into his oral argument. She challenged him to reply to the concern that turned out to be the heart of her dissenting opinion. She recited a hypothetical scenario in which the chief justice invited a minister to pray before the Court. The minister might ask everyone present to bow his or head. Then he would say, "We acknowledge the saving sacrifice of Jesus on the cross."

Justice Kagan demanded to know whether this scenario could pass constitutional muster. The lawyer did not summon the obviously correct answer: it is impossible on the facts given to say. Has the chief justice instructed this minister to bring all those present to a personal encounter with the Risen Lord? Has the chief chosen all invitees from the directory of Christian evangelical ministers in the DC area? (Both?) Or is this minister the thirtieth "prayer-giver" of the term, where none of his randomly selected predecessors has offered a Christian invocation? Is he a Wiccan priest, who has decided to pander to the fantastical beliefs of the majority? (Both?)

The force of Kagan's hypothetical entirely depends on *assuming* that "sectarian" prayer is inherently unconstitutional. Professor Doug Laycock argued *Greece* for the plaintiffs, and he pressed the same point. "[Y]ou cannot have

[21] These spare but muscular phrases made an utterly inconsequential cameo in Calabresi's opinion. He quoted this decisive passage and paddled past it as if the words were written in an inscrutable dialect.

[22] 681 F. 3d at 34.

sectarian prayer." There were three notations of "laughter" in the oral argument transcript, though, as Laycock struggled to answer the challenge thrown down by Justices Alito, Scalia, and the Chief Justice: give us an example of a "non-sectarian" prayer, which the justices further described as – as did Professor Laycock – one acceptable to all believers.

Laycock never answered the question. His futility included an especially mirth-provoking question about whether "devil-worshippers" had to be invited to pray for legislators. Laycock drew laughs with a reply, "They might be okay. But they're probably out." No one stated the obvious truth that, if there is a devil, it would be no business of any legislative body to seek *its* guidance.

In his brief concurring opinion Justice Alito sought to establish that looking for a "non-sectarian" prayer (especially one "acceptable to all") is less promising than looking for the Holy Grail. The dissent, he said, "really consists of two very different but intertwined opinions. One is quite narrow."[23] (A few pages later he describes it as "niggling."[24]) "The other is sweeping." Alito rightly criticized Kagan's two "narrow" pathways to constitutionally acceptable legislative prayer. Looking at the many conditions with which the dissenters hedged in their prayer permission, Alito said: the "effect of requiring such [Kaganian] exactitude would be to pressure towns to foreswear altogether the practice of having a prayer before meetings of the town council."[25]

The deeper "logic" of the dissent, Alito also argued, suggested that prayer was "*never* permissible prior to meetings of local government legislative bodies."[26] Alito's view of the dissent's "sweep" is correct. But he did not quite get to the bottom of *why* the dissent had a rendezvous with empty religious formalities. He did not see clearly how the dissenters' reasoning was utterly incompatible with any possibility of genuine legislative prayer.

Here is the heart of the *Greece* dissent:

> A person's response to the doctrine, language, and imagery contained in these invocations reveals a core aspect of identity – who that person is and how she faces the world. And the responses of different individuals, in Greece, and across this country, of course vary. Contrary to the majority's apparent view, such sectarian prayers are not "part of our expressive idiom" or "part of our heritage and tradition," assuming the word "our" refers to all Americans. They express beliefs that are fundamental to some, foreign to others – and because that is so they carry the ever-present potential to both exclude and divide.[27]

Here is ground-zero for all the many jurists, professors, and pundits who say that they approve legislative *prayer* but in truth approve only legislative "prayer." Here is ground-zero of Establishment Clause doctrine up to

[23] *Town of Greece* v. *Galloway*, No. 12–696, slip op. (Alito) at 1.
[24] *Ibid.* at 4.
[25] *Ibid.* at 7.
[26] *Ibid.*
[27] Kagan slip opinion at 23.

Greece: government must not associate itself with religion if doing so causes any "reasonable" observer to feel like an outsider, like a second-class citizen – except that Kagan's (admittedly) brief explanation makes no reference whatsoever to any observer's "reasonableness." For Kagan, it is evidently subjectivity, all the way down: any person's "response" to public prayer "reveals a core aspect of identity," which "identity" is to be preserved from what that observer feels is "offensive," or unwelcome.

Here then is the utter incompatibility of the dissent with any legislative *prayer* practice. No real prayer could ever complete this constitutional gauntlet. Nothing in the Kagan excerpt turns upon "sectarian" content. Drop that word from the quoted sentences and the meaning of them changes not at all. "Foreign doctrine, language, and imagery" are the subjects of the critical sentence, and "foreign" there means, simply, "not mine" – or perhaps, just for the moment, unwelcome by someone present. Whether that which is "not mine" (or temporarily unwelcome) is "sectarian" makes no difference whatsoever.

IV

The truth is that the irreducibly "sectarian" quality of legislative prayer does not arise from any discrimination by public authorities, but is rather an ineradicable element of the undertaking. The legislative prayer practice upheld in *Marsh* v. *Chambers*, for example, affirmed a nested set of beliefs which are not and have never been shared by all Americans, or even by all Americans who profess religious faith.

Neither the prayers sanctioned by the *Marsh* Court nor those uttered in Greece amounted to some spiritual Esperanto, or religious least common denominator. All of these prayers (save, perhaps, the Wiccan's and Buddhist's) affirmed or presupposed a set of common but scarcely universally held propositions. Namely, that (i) there is a Supreme Being who (ii) has a continuing interest in human affairs, (iii) possesses the power to affect their course of human affairs, (iv) is benevolent (for the legislators assembled are obviously seeking some good effect by and through their prayer), and (v) actually listens and responds to people when they pray.

Many people do not hold beliefs such as these. Non-believers of course reject all such claims. Even some religious people deny or doubt some of them.

More than a few founding fathers, for example, have been described as Deists. Deists affirm the existence of a creator god. But they characteristically deny divine providence; that is, they profess belief in a "clockmaker" god who at the beginning of time set in motion a course of events which includes human affairs, but who remains forever after aloof from them. Deists of this description would not affirm the efficacy of prayers for God's guidance in deciding what people should do about earthly matters.

Buddhists are "Deists" in this one sense. Although Buddhism is a blend of some particular ancient traditions and practices, Buddhists characteristically do not believe in a creator god who remains interested in "guiding" or "assisting" human political affairs.[28] Buddhists would thus characteristically eschew the types of prayers upheld in *Marsh*.

Jehovah's Witnesses are well known to students of constitutional religious liberty, having served as plaintiffs in so many important Supreme Court cases. Jehovah's Witnesses are not Deists. They typically affirm, however, that God's undivided sovereignty over the whole universe renders human government so presumptuous as to be almost blasphemous. This is the theological basis for the Witnesses' famous refusal to salute the American flag. Given these beliefs, Jehovah's Witnesses are not likely candidates to seek divine assistance for a legislative assembly.

"Wicca" – a religion represented by the priestess who offered the ersatz Olympian invocation at a town of Greece board meeting – is an eclectic blend of beliefs and traditions, with origins and continued influence supplied by witchcraft. Wicca is perhaps most accurately described as a "nature" religion with certain magical elements, and its dominant form of belief is pantheistic. In any event, the possibility of a prayerful appeal to a personal supreme being for guidance in practical matters is practically unintelligible within this framework of thought.

Oral argument in *Greece* supplied an illustration of the truth that *any* class of invocations populated by genuine prayers for divine assistance to public authorities is bound to be (if you will) "sectarian." Justice Breyer asked the all-too-obliging lawyer for the town whether he – the obliging one – had "any objection to … publiciz[ing] rather thoroughly in the area that those who were not Christian, and perhaps not even religious are also welcome to appear and to have either a prayer or the equivalent if they're not religious?" "Certainly not," was the lawyer's reply. Minutes later Justice Scalia asked the same attorney: "What is the equivalent of prayer for somebody who is not religious?" His reply began – "It would be some invocation of guidance and wisdom from …" and the justice interrupted: "From what?" Answer: "I don't know." The transcript then reads: "Laughter."[29]

[28] See Rupert Gethin, *Foundations of Buddhism* (Oxford: Oxford University Press, 1998), 65–66.

[29] Justice Scalia described the inescapable particularity of governmental prayer, in his dissent in one of the 2005 Ten Commandments cases. See *McCreary*, 545 U.S. at 893 (Scalia, J., dissenting).

> If religion in the public forum had to be entirely nondenominational, there could be no religion in the public forum at all. One cannot say the word "God," or "the Almighty," one cannot offer public supplication or thanksgiving, without contradicting the beliefs of some people that there are many gods, or that God or the gods pay no attention to human affairs … Historical practices … demonstrate that there is a distance between the acknowledgment of a single Creator and the establishment of a religion.

As Judge Paul Niemeyer said, dissenting in another recent legislative prayer case: "Prayer includes the articulation of words addressed to the Divine Being in accordance with the beliefs of the prayer-giver's religion." Thus, "[w]hatever name is spoken, it is spoken by the religious leader in accord with the leader's religion to call on the Divine Being." See *Joyner* v. *Forsyth County*, 653 F. 3d 341, 355 (4th Cir. 2011).

As a matter of contingent fact, a legislative prayer offered at a certain date and time could, I suppose, resonate with the "identity" of every one present. But even this Kumbaya moment would be unconstitutional for the *Greece* dissenters. For they seem to suppose that the relevant population of sensitive "identities" extends beyond those physically present to all those who reside in the relevant jurisdiction and, maybe, to "all Americans." The "our," which modifies the dissenters' use of "expressive idiom" and "heritage and tradition" does not necessarily pertain to some local community, much less to those who happen to be present at a specific public gathering. The "potential" to "both exclude and divide" is – on these suppositions – indeed "ever-present."

V

The dissenters effectively abandoned coercion as a necessary feature of an Establishment Clause violation. Justices Thomas and Scalia joined the *Greece* majority opinion, save for that part of it which discussed the "coercion" which the Establishment Clause prohibits. Their disagreement depended upon their judgment that "the municipal prayers at issue in this case bear no resemblance to the coercive state establishments that existed at the founding."[30] *Those* involved "coercion of religious orthodoxy and of financial support *by force of law and threat of penalty*."[31] The other three justices in the majority held that the Clause prohibits, too, more subtle (though perhaps no less real) psychological pressure to conform, as well as the threat of social ostracism. They had the weight of precedent behind them; these sorts of "coercion" have played an important role in cases of religious observances (organized prayer, devotional Bible readings, religious instruction) in primary and secondary public school classrooms. So, Justices Scalia and Thomas argued frankly for a doctrinal retrenchment upon the strength of the original understanding of the Establishment Clause – as they understood that history.

Now, either of the majority justices' understandings of "coercion" would lead to Establishment Clause outcomes greatly preferable to those ordained by the dissent. Justice Thomas' opinion would reduce even further the number and kinds of possible Establishment Clause violations, which – in very general terms – is welcome news to anyone (such as myself) who holds that the Court's modern doctrines here are fundamentally misguided. Nonetheless, my judgment is that neither majority wing is right about "coercion."

One reason for my judgment is that "coercion" was not a defining feature of Establishment Clause violations at the founding. For the Framers and for many after them, "coercion" was neither a necessary nor a sufficient feature of

[30] Thomas slip opinion at 5.

[31] *Ibid.*; emphasis original.

an establishment.[32] The defining feature of an "establishment" for the Framers (and for generations of Americans thereafter) was government preference for the peculiar rites or doctrines of a particular church or sect. What distinguished an "establishment of religion" was government favoritism. The core meaning of non-establishment was that public authority must not discriminate among the churches. None should receive unequal treatment or peculiar hostility.

The question then naturally arises (as it did in *Greece* v. *Galloway*): What sort of preference counts? Is it a skewed distribution of some valuable opportunity, tangible benefit, or privilege as a matter of fact? Does the requisite "neutrality" pertain, then, to outcomes or effects? Or is the constitutionally relevant disparity a matter of government intention or purposes? Is it about breaching a norm requiring a neutrality of *reasons* for state action? If it is to be this last sort of neutrality, what does (or could) that look like?

The original meaning of non-establishment was (again) "no sect-preference."[33] That meant more specifically that the government must remain neutral on finer points of theological doctrine, modes of worship, internal discipline, church polity, for these matters distinguished the many churches and religious groups from each other.[34] The distinguishing feature of an "establishment" was government action predicated on the truth (or falsity) of answers to such "sectarian" questions. Non-establishment as originally understood required government "neutrality" on what distinguished the various churches and sects from each other. "Neutrality" between religion (altogether and as such) and "non-religion" has been the core of court doctrines for decades. But it has absolutely no historical support as a reading of the Establishment Clause.

"Coercion of religious orthodoxy" (at least in its main sense of a legal obligation to affirm one's belief in, say, the Apostles' Creed) would surely have counted as an "establishment" at the founding, because it was the clearest case imaginable of government backing one church's tenets over all other churches' tenets. In fact, coercion of this sort was rare if not practically non-existent at the founding, as it has been ever since. Even the most intolerant-seeming legal practices of the time – such as requiring a license to preach or civil penalties for failing to keep the Sabbath – required no one to affirm as true anything they believed to be otherwise. The oaths or tests for office-holders, which were then

[32] The text addresses the question of the meaning of the Establishment Clause, as do the opinions in *Greece*. It is important to note that the requirements of an Article III case or controversy – such that a dispute about the meaning of the Establishment Clause comes properly before a federal court – might have an additional place for "coercion," however understood.

[33] For a book-length defense of this claim, see Gerard V. Bradley, *Church-State Relationships in America* (New York: Greenwood, 1987).

[34] The central meaning of the Establishment Clause is thus very similar to what the Court in 1990 attributed to the Free Exercise in *Oregon* v. *Smith:* a "neutrality" of reasons when it comes to religion. See, Gerard V. Bradley, "Beguiled: Free Exercise Exemptions and the Siren Song of Liberalism," 20 *Hofstra Law Review* 245 (1991).

commonplace in states' laws, and those conditionally required even today of court witnesses, similarly do not involve "coerced" confessions of faith.

Coerced tax support of religion, along with other legal obligations toward religion, were commonplace during the founding. Just so far described, they were not "establishmentarian" practices. The Founders' view was overwhelmingly that religion was part of the common good and that everyone had obligations to promote it regardless of one's personal convictions. Everyone benefited from living in a religiously observant society, not least because of the near-universal belief among the Founders that widespread piety was essential to the success of their experiment in free government. And so, notwithstanding anyone's personal convictions about God, everyone had to be respectful of the Sabbath, refrain from insulting religious faith, and contribute his fair share to the common funds which underwrote (on a sect-neutral basis) the necessities of worship (if circumstances called for such public subsidies).

When the First Amendment was enacted, taxation for religion was characteristic of an "establishment," *only where a taxpayer was obliged to support a manner of worship or sect to which he did not subscribe*. Making a Baptist pay for, say, Episcopal worship services or for the maintenance of Anglican ministers was a sure sign of an "establishment." But even this victimized Baptist would not be "coerced" into becoming an Anglican. The coerced support of religion in his case made for an establishment *because* it depended upon an obvious state preference for Anglicans over Baptists.

We might compare the Founders' views about the relationship of conscience, religion, and the common good to our views about Christian Scientists. These believers eschew scientific medicine. They are nevertheless obliged to support modern medicine (albeit short of being made to personally participate in procedures incompatible with Christian Science) by paying taxes, supporting public medical schools, and the like. Or we might compare the Founders' views to ours about Quaker pacifists, who must contribute to the common defense in ways short of being conscripted to actually fight. In fact, we have roughly the same views about Quakers that the Founders did. Our views about religion differ, in that we do not recognize a common good in religion. We regard it as a "private" matter.

The first section of Justice Thomas' concurrence expressed his views only.[35] In it he asked the question: Is the Establishment Clause – "Congress shall make no law respecting an establishment of religion" – rightly understood as a norm prohibiting an establishment of religion? Justice Thomas' answer is that, as an original matter, no.[36]

[35] Justice Scalia did not join this portion of Thomas' concurrence.

[36] Justice Thomas conceded (as he should) that forestalling the erection of a national church by Congress was part of what the Establishment Clause was meant to do.

Thomas maintained that the Establishment Clause is "best understood as a federalism provision."[37] This means (in his words, from his *Galloway* concurrence) that Congress "could not interfere with state establishments"; the Clause "effectively denied Congress any power to regulate state establishments"; the First Amendment was "agnostic on the subject of state establishments"; "[a]pplying the Clause against the states [by "incorporating" it as an interpretation of the Fourteenth Amendment Due Process Clause] eliminates their right to establish a religion free from federal interference."[38]

The central meaning in all these expressions is that the Establishment Clause deprives Congress of any power to dismantle state establishments (such as those that existed, according to Thomas, in at least six states in 1789). The main effect of this position is – according to Justice Thomas – to "resist" the incorporation of the Clause against the states; that is, to "resist" the view that the Establishment Clause should apply to state as well as federal government action.[39] Recognizing the practically quixotic nature of this "resistance," Justice Thomas concluded this part of his concurrence by saying that, given the "difficulties posed by incorporation," the burden of persuasion should rest upon anyone who would vary the meaning of it today from that which the Founders apprehended.[40]

There is no doubt that the Establishment Clause (along with the rest of the Bill of Rights) had no application to the state governments until after the Civil War. There is considerable dispute about how much of the Bill of Rights was thereafter "incorporated" by the Fourteenth Amendment. I should like to leave that large question aside for now. As to the narrower question – was the Establishment Clause "incorporated" – there is a lively disagreement, too. My judgment is that those who ratified the Fourteenth Amendment very likely did *not* think that they were applying the Establishment Clause to the states.

Yet I think that Justice Thomas is mistaken about the original meaning of the Establishment Clause.

Thomas is right that (in no technical legal or recondite sense) the Founders wanted to leave religion to the states. This they did principally by granting no power to the national government over religion. The Establishment Clause was nonetheless added to the Constitution, partly to confirm or to somehow give added force to that pre-existing state immunity. The Establishment Clause reiterated and bolstered this federal disability by forbidding Congress to establish a national church (which Justice Thomas recognizes to have been one purpose of the Clause).[41] Any national establishment would, by dint of the supremacy of federal over state law, wipe out state establishments of a different church,

[37] Thomas slip opinion at 1.

[38] *Ibid.* at 2–4.

[39] *Ibid.* at 1.

[40] *Ibid.* at 5.

[41] *Ibid.* at 1.

and introduce an established church into states that previously had none. That is, the Founders understood the Establishment Clause as mainly a non-establishment norm. The Clause so understood had the foreseeable (and welcome) effect of preserving church-state regimes – whatever they were – from federal interference.

Justice Thomas would tie the meaning of the Establishment Clause more tightly than this to the historically contingent state establishments. This is one problem with his view. To say that "Congress could not interfere with state establishments" is to say that the Clause had no relevance to seven states in 1789, and to none after 1833. (Justice Thomas reports that the last state establishment (Massachusetts') expired in 1833.) On Thomas' reading of the Clause, the argument about whether the Fourteenth Amendment "incorporated" the Clause would be a queer dispute indeed. By then there were no establishments. What would that argument be about? Indeed, on his view the Establishment Clause means nothing now unless we return to the question which he recognizes is still on the table: If the First Amendment prohibits an "established church," what does that mean?

Another set of historical considerations show that the Establishment Clause had an operative normative meaning at the founding, and that meaning is best expressed as "no-sect preference." Almost from the beginning of our nation's existence, national public officials in Congress, in the Executive, and (faintly) in the judiciary understood that the federal government labored under a restrictive non-establishment norm about religion – *entirely apart from any felt disability to regulate religion in the states*. These occasions included presidents thinking about national proclamations in favor of prayer and deciding about incorporating churches where federal law governed the matter. They included Congress thinking about supporting missionaries to the Indian tribes, debating whether to prohibit mail delivery on Sundays, deciding whether to recruit and pay Congressional chaplains, and providing tangible supports for religion in the newly organized Northwest Territories. In all of these instances and many more before the Civil War and immediately after it, national government officials exhibited unmistakably their felt obligation to abide the norm laid down by the Founders in the First Amendment – namely, that no favor be shown to any church, denomination, or sect due to the theological claims of that religious body.[42] The founders most certainly did *not* hold that such matters were not susceptible of being either true or false. They judged that the truth or falsity of church doctrines, modes of worship, and internal church governance could safely, and would wisely, be put beyond the competence of the national government to judge.

[42] For a fuller account of these early American, establishment-illumining practices, *see* Bradley, *supra* note 33, at 97–104, 121–134.

VI

The Second Circuit warned prayer-givers in Greece to "resist [the] temptation" to "convey their view of religious truth, and thereby run the risk of making others feel like outsiders."[43] Here the lower court sought to bring *prayer* in line with today's Establishment Clause master norm by claiming the public authority should do nothing to "endorse" religion, for doing *that* would breach the wall of neutrality between religion and non-religion, and doing *that* would signal to the non-religious that they are "outsiders" and "second-class citizens." It is easy to see that the Kagan dissent draws from the same reservoir of ideas and concerns.

We have already seen in Part IV that *this* undertaking is quixotic – there is no such thing as a "non-sectarian" prayer in the specific sense of being "acceptable to all." It is true of course that respect and tolerance are especially important in matters as personally defining as religious faith. But it is a failure of tolerance and respect if religious persons are expected to display respect and tolerance for others' beliefs by redefining religion so that it consists of personal feelings and private opinions – in short, so that religion is not concerned with the truth about reality.

Justice Kennedy mined a different store of ideas. "Offense … does not amount to coercion. Adults often encounter speech they find disagreeable; and an Establishment Clause violation is not made out any time a person experiences a sense of affront from the expression of contrary religious views in a legislative forum."[44]

Justice Kennedy took full measure in *Greece* of the Calabresi/Kagan rendition of truth and tolerance. His reply is worth extensive quotation because it strikes at the heart of the Court's whole approach to the Establishment Clause since around 1970, which is that public religion inescapably and gravely divides Americans.

> From the earliest days of the Nation, these invocations have been addressed to assemblies comprising many different creeds. These ceremonial prayers strive for the idea that people of many faiths may be united in a community of tolerance and devotion. Even those who disagree as to religious doctrine may find common ground in the desire to show respect for the divine in all aspects of their lives and being.[45]

The *Greece* Court did not, unfortunately, expressly abandon the "endorsement" test. But the majority did alter and improve Establishment Clause doctrine. In 1983, the *Marsh* Court said that "in light of the unambiguous and unbroken history of more than 200 years, there can be no doubt that the practice of opening legislative sessions with a prayer has become part of the fabric

[43] Kennedy slip opinion at 21.

[44] *Ibid.*

[45] *Ibid.* at 16.

of our society."[46] *Marsh* was widely thought to have simply put aside the usual constitutional tests in favor of what amounted to a one-off grandfathered exception to the normal rules for legislative prayer. The Court said in *Greece*, "*Marsh* must not be understood as permitting a practice that would amount to an Establishment Clause violation if not for its historical foundation."[47] "Any test the Court adopts must acknowledge a practice that was accepted by the Framers and has withstood the critical scrutiny of time and political change."[48]

Greece v. *Galloway* seems to have inaugurated – or renewed, with a fresh commitment – a partnership between constitutional doctrine and historical practice. It is too early to say where this alliance will take the law. It is not too early to say that it would preserve from Establishment Clause attack some important practices which, although presently lawful, would be vulnerable to any Supreme Court majority with views like those of the *Greece* dissenters. Among these potential targets are tax exemptions for churches and other religious institutions, a benefit which escaped Supreme Court invalidation in 1970 by dint of a poorly articulated historical exception.[49] Another potential target is the long-held tradition of *legislated* conscientious exemption from general laws (think of Hobby Lobby), a practice imperiled by any reading of the Establishment which relentlessly pursues an alleged neutrality between religion and "non-religion." Lastly, there is a host of public–religious collaborations in projects which serve the common good in terms of health, education, and welfare, a practice which dates back to the founding when most of what we now think of as "public" services were supplied (where they were supplied at all) by churches, often at public expense.

Some other practices now constitutionally endangered could be saved by *Greece*'s invitation to shape doctrine according to the data of history. The Court identified one such practice – prayer on special public school occasions, such as graduations, honors assemblies, sports banquets, and perhaps athletic contests. The majority worked hard to distinguish and to preserve its own precedents on the subject, which are mildly hospitable to *generic* prayers in such venues. *Greece* supplies ample bases for revisiting those precedents. Public manifestations of religion *other* than legislative prayer – including but not limited to Ten Commandments displays in public places – could be buttressed as well by *Greece*.

VII

Greece v. *Galloway* preserved some genuine prayers, most of them "sectarian," from practically all constitutional attacks. The Court declared, "So long

[46] 463 U.S. at 792.
[47] Kennedy slip opinion at 7.
[48] *Ibid.* at 8.
[49] See *Walz* v. *Tax Commission*, 397 U.S. 664 (1970).

as the town maintains a *policy* of nondiscrimination, the Constitution does not require it to search beyond its borders for non-Christian prayer givers in an effort to achieve religious balancing." [Emphasis added.] "The content of the prayers is no concern," said *Greece* affirming *Marsh*, so long as there is no indication that "the prayer opportunity has been exploited to proselytize or advance any one, or to disparage any other, faith or belief." An isolated "disparagement" would not suffice: "Absent a pattern of prayers that *over time* denigrate, proselytize, or betray an impermissible government purpose, a challenge based solely *on the content of a prayer* will not likely establish a constitutional violation." [Emphasis added.][50]

But legislative prayer does not inhabit a First Amendment free-range. On the contrary, there are several robust norms of constitutional limitation that must be observed by any praying public body. Those norms must make sense, however, in the legislative prayer context. A public body desiring to open its sessions with an invocation need look no further than *Greece* itself for these limiting principles. (I say "principles" and "norms" purposely, so as to leave aside tertiary considerations, such as the font-size of various paragraphs and ink colors and such matters, which some first-year associate might be commissioned to measure and compare, so as to calibrate to the last decimal point the even-handedness of the relevant public authority's dealings with the various ambient religions.)

First, the public authority must not act with an improper "motive" in selecting prayer-givers.[51] To require the public body to go beyond this requirement of proper motive – by requiring, as the Second Circuit did, that the town invite clergy from outside its borders – places burdens on the practice that the Constitution does not demand. Furthermore, such requirements are inconsistent with the definition of legislative prayer as a tolerable acknowledgment of beliefs widely held; the central aim of having legislative prayer in the first place ties the prayers to the sentiments of those actually present. For example, the prayer might recollect the assembly. It does so by putting those present in mind of the existence of a greater-than-human-source-of-meaning-and-value, of our creaturely status, of our dependence upon the divine and our desire to live in some kind of harmony with it. This is scarcely accomplished by recitations of poetry. Nor is it sought by an appeal to the devil. Consider too the prospect that the good citizens and lawmakers of Greece might be called to order by the solemn recitation of an Aztec fertility prayer, uttered in the native tongue. In what conceivable way would that advance the cause of obtaining divine guidance and favor for the assembly? Neither heavenly assistance nor the legislators'

50 Greece *v.* Galloway on JUSTIA U.S.https://supreme.justia.com/cases/federal/us/572/12-696/.

51 For example, although selecting a single minister to deliver the prayer at every meeting of a town board would not, standing alone, violate the Establishment Clause under *Marsh*, it would be impermissible if a majority of the board members were members of a particular church, and they selected their pastor with the intent to promote the church itself.

consciousness of their dependence upon the divine is effectively pursued by a judicial requirement that the prayer array must reflect the gorgeous mosaic of religious belief abroad in the state, or the country (or the globe). The whole point of having legislative prayer depends, in a certain important way, upon it being indigenous.

The second requirement under *Greece* v. *Galloway* – that the public body not exploit the prayer opportunity to proselytize or disparage a particular faith – flows from the expressed purpose of legislative prayer to seek divine guidance for the work of the relevant legislators or public officials. The acts of proselytizing and disparaging fall outside this purpose. Although the Court did not expressly require it, the public authority would be wise to advise invited speakers of the nature and purpose of the occasion – to invoke divine assistance upon the deliberations, and to give thanks for the blessings which heretofore have been bestowed – and that these aims naturally exclude "proselytizing" and "disparaging." The prayer-giver should be encouraged to pray according to his or her conscience as informed by the teaching of the prayer-giver's religion.

The prohibition against proselytizing does not mean that the prayer-giver may not convey his or her view of religious truth. It means that the prayer-giver may not try to argue listeners into converting to his or her faith.[52] If an individual prayer-giver should violate this guideline, or if he or she uses the opportunity to disparage other faiths, the public authority should decline to extend any further invitation to pray to that particular individual.

What counts as "proselytizing" or "disparaging"? We know one thing which does not count: the felt truth of what the speaker says. One circuit court of appeals recently expressed the same sentiment, albeit less directly, about legislative prayer: "[T]he deep beliefs of the speaker afford only more reason to respect the profound convictions of the listener. Free religious exercise posits broad religious tolerance."

The alarming suggestion is that the only way to display respect and tolerance for others' beliefs is for the prayer-giver to keep his real beliefs to himself, or to offer them as one opinion among many others. But every religious tradition – Christianity, Islam, Judaism, Hinduism, Buddhism, or any number of others – consists of a set of claims defining the particular religion's view of reality; that is, of *truth*. Inviting religious believers into the public square, asking them to "pray," and then telling them to avoid suggesting that they are speaking the truth from their hearts as they understand that truth to be, only promotes an artificial dialogue, a phony pluralism, and a platitudinous civil religion.

Greece v. *Galloway* could not have more resoundingly rejected this whole notion of self-censorship. The majority declared that "[o]nce it invites prayer into the public sphere, government must permit a prayer-giver to address his or

[52] Merriam-Webster defines "proselytize" as "to induce someone to convert to one's faith." See www.merriam-webster.com/dictionary/proselytize.

her own God or gods as conscience dictates, unfettered by what an administrator or judge considers to be nonsectarian."[53] The Court was not entertaining any empty civic ritual, or some politico-theological civil religion. Prayer-givers may speak from the heart ("conscience"). They may all speak in similar "sectarian" terms. They may all speak what they believe to be *true* for you and for me and for everybody.

CONCLUSION

Public prayer like that upheld in *Greece* v. *Galloway* implicitly but squarely affirms belief in divine providence, where belief is a valuable amenity to any political community. Belief in providence moderates any tendency to political utopianism. It supplies the foundation for limited government secured by a common understanding that the state's moral demands are subordinate to God's. It also fosters a deep sense of humans' creatureliness, which reinforces their political humility.

The penultimate paragraph of Justice Kennedy's *Greece* opinion is, finally, worth full quotation:

> "Ceremonial prayer" is but a recognition that, since this Nation was founded and until the present day, many Americans deem that their own existence must be understood by precepts far beyond the authority of government to alter or define and that willing participation in civic affairs can be consistent with a brief acknowledgement of their belief in a higher power, always with due respect for those who adhere to other beliefs.[54]

[53] Greece v. Galloway on JUSTIA U.S. https://supreme.justia.com/cases/federal/us/572/12-696/.

[54] Kennedy slip opinion at 23.

6

What are we really arguing about when we argue about the freedom of the church?

Michael P. Moreland

"Freedom of the church." For some, the phrase is one of the central concepts in Western political theory, redolent of names such as Becket, More, Gorostieta, and Bonhoeffer. *Libertas ecclesiae*, on this view, provides the necessary institutional alternative to aggrandizing civil authority, which always threatens to extend itself into the realm of the church and other subsidiary institutions. These institutions of civil society in general but churches in particular serve to check the state so that, in a phrase of Abraham Kuyper's, "it may never become an octopus, which stifles the whole of life."[1] Indeed, the heroes of the tale of the freedom of the church are often martyrs who died violent deaths at the hands of civil authorities.

For others, though, freedom of the church is a non-constitutional, outdated concept, dependent on a medieval understanding of ecclesial authority, now widely (and rightly) rejected in the wake of the Protestant Reformation and the Enlightenment. In the words of Richard Schragger and Micah Schwartzman in their article, "Against Religious Institutionalism," "nothing is left of the ancient idea that the church is uniquely sovereign in its relation to the secular state."[2] Freedom of the church, on this account, is as likely today to perpetuate misogynistic, homophobic, hierarchical, and authoritarian institutions as it is to be a means for protecting liberty. The sooner we get past the romantic and false view of the "freedom of the church" and move on to, say, individual freedom of conscience, the better.

These sharp differences over the freedom of the church – or, put more generally, institutional religious freedom – were on prominent display in the US Supreme Court's controversial decision in *Burwell* v. *Hobby Lobby*,[3] but the

[1] Abraham Kuyper, *Lectures on Calvinism* (Grand Rapids: WM. B. Eerdmans Publishing Company, 1931).

[2] Richard Schragger and Micah Schwartzman, "Against Religious Institutionalism," VA. L. REV. 99 (2013), 937.

[3] *Burwell* v. *Hobby Lobby Stores Inc.*, 134 S. Ct. 2751 (2014).

debate runs much deeper conceptually and historically. Legal discourse often coasts on the surface of much deeper disagreements. What divides those who assert the freedom of the church and those who reject it or are skeptical about it? More than in most constitutional debates, the differences between the two sides in the debate over the freedom of the church seem especially profound. For those advocating the freedom of the church, religious freedom, in any robust sense, *requires* something like the institutional expression of such freedom in the freedom of the church. As Rick Garnett writes, "this idea [of the freedom of the church] – or something like it – remains a crucial component of any plausible and attractive account of religious freedom under and through constitutionally limited government."[4] Skeptics of the freedom of the church, on the other hand, often do not seem merely to think that the balance of the argument is against the freedom of the church in American constitutional law – as we might disagree over whether, say, the Second Amendment protects an individual right to bear arms. Rather, opponents of the freedom of the church appear baffled by the very idea. Freedom of the church, they argue, simply makes no sense.

This is true, the argument goes, in at least two ways. One is that there is no place for the rights of the "church," as such, in American constitutional doctrine apart from the rights of natural, individual persons. As Schwartzman and Schragger put it, "It is ... a mistake to treat churches as if they had rights that are not derived from the rights of natural persons."[5] And so arguing over the freedom of the church in American constitutional law is like arguing over the Article II authority of the monarch. Furthermore, skeptics of the freedom of the church argue that the very idea is alien to a modern liberal democracy, which, on account of the freedom and equality of *individual* citizens, has no place for according special protection to groups and most especially religious groups.

There is, I think (and to borrow from Alasdair MacIntyre), a conceptual incommensurability between advocates and opponents of freedom of the church:

> Every one of the arguments is logically valid or can be easily expanded so as to be made so; the conclusions do indeed follow from the premises. But the rival premises are such that we possess no rational way of weighing the claims of one as against another. For each premise employs some quite different normative or evaluative concept from the others, so that the claims made upon us are of quite different kinds.[6]

As one would expect in such a debate, each side in the debate asserts that the other side is failing to be rational, and each side asserts that the other side has engaged in question-begging adoption of contestable premises. But we might

[4] Richard W. Garnett, "The Freedom of the Church," *J. Catholic Social Thought* 4 (2006), 59.

[5] Schragger and Schwartzman, "Against Religious Institutionalism," 967.

[6] Alasdair MacIntyre, *After Virtue: A Study in Moral Theory*, 2nd edition (Notre Dame: University of Notre Dame Press, 1984).

make some progress in the disagreement if we could unpack those underlying premises and hold them up for discussion and deliberation. I want to explore this disagreement and suggest some reasons *why* it is so deep and pervasive.

There are at least three aspects of the debate that give rise to this profound disagreement, which I will label "theological," "metaphysical," and "moral." Theologically, advocates and skeptics of the freedom of the church are divided over whether theological claims – not *apparently* theological claims that are actually claims about something else (say, rights of conscience or association) but *genuinely* theological claims – are legally cognizable and sensible. This is closely related to the ongoing debate over whether religion can be regarded in any way as "special" for constitutional and political philosophical purposes, as discussed in work by such figures as Chris Eisgruber and Larry Sager,[7] Brian Leiter,[8] and Micah Schwartzman.[9] Liberalism, particularly under certain Rawlsian formulations, cannot admit or adjudicate theological claims, so little wonder, the argument goes, that liberal starting points cannot admit that there are genuinely theological reasons for the formation of groups of believers in worship in the church. Any such theological reasons need to be, so the argument continues, translated into terms that are publicly reasonable.[10] The church, then, comes to be seen as, at most, a voluntary association (formed by the free consent of its members) and little or no different for legal purposes than any other such voluntary association.

That leads me to the second issue, what I am terming (loosely) the "metaphysical." For skeptics of the freedom of the church, churches are simply aggregations of individual believers. The religious freedom issue with regard to churches is nothing less but surely nothing more than a claim about the right to religious freedom of the individuals who happen to belong to the church. This reflects in some ways a deep reservation about the status of groups more generally and about whether we can make sense of groups as right- and duty-bearing entities. Though there has been growing interest in institutionalism in First Amendment doctrine – most notably in such work as Paul Horwitz's book *First Amendment Institutions*[11] – much remains to be said about why institutions rather than only individuals are worthy of constitutional protection. But

[7] Christopher L. Eisgruber and Lawrence G. Sager, *Religious Freedom and the constitution* (Cambridge: Harvard University Press, 2010).

[8] Brian Leiter, *Why Tolerate Religion?* (Princeton: Princeton University Press, 2012).

[9] Micah Schwartzman, "What If Religion Is Not Special?," *U. of Chicago L. Rev.* 79 (2012), 1351.

[10] See Richard Schragger and Micah Schwartzman, "Lost in Translation: A Dilemma for Freedom of the Church," *J. of Contemporary Legal Issues* 21 (2013), 15, 17 ("The dilemma, then, amounts to a choice between two bad options: (1) to be internally coherent, freedom of the church must be justified on traditional theological grounds, which makes the doctrine sectarian and unfit for use in constitutional argument; or (2) its justification can be translated into secular terms, which renders the idea incoherent.").

[11] Paul Horwitz, *First Amendment Institutions* (Cambridge: Harvard University Press, 2012).

that question opens up to a more difficult question about whether it is meaningful to talk about groups as such, groups with moral agency, intentions, and identities that are not reducible to the moral agency, intentions, and identities of individuals.[12]

Finally, the elephant in the room in many discussions of the freedom of the church is sex. Not all disputes over freedom of the church turn on sexual issues (certainly that has not been true historically),[13] but the current debate is unmistakably marked by divisions over sexuality in one form or another. I think this expresses something about the relation between certain institutional forms of religious belief and practice – most especially in Christianity – and their relation to sexual morality. The ways in which these fights about sex distort the debate over the freedom of the church will, then, be my third topic. I will suggest that sexual morality – while undoubtedly an important context in which the contemporary discussion of the freedom of the church is conducted – distorts that discussion. What we might consider instead is how to relate most appropriately a set of import concerns about sex in various contexts and subject to government regulation – including sexual abuse, family formation, reproduction, and so on – with the claims of religious believers and institutions to be free from interference by the state.

I acknowledge at the outset that I am writing from a standpoint that owes most to Christian ways of framing these matters, and I set aside for now whether this analysis can apply more broadly and to other institutional accounts of religious freedom. But perhaps one of the shortcomings in the current debate is that it does not take seriously and often enough the particularity of religion – never encountered as "religion" or "church" in a generic sense anywhere. What we do encounter is a Presbyterian church, a Catholic parish, a Muslim mosque, a Reformed Jewish synagogue, a Mormon ward, and so forth. Religion, where it exists, exists in and through particularity. When we encounter such particular expressions of what we, since 1700 or so, call "religion," it is on account of a group believing, credibly or not, that God is speaking in the world.[14] And

[12] Indeed, one of the issues in the Supreme Court's decision in *Hobby Lobby* dividing Justice Alito's opinion for the majority and Justice Ginsburg's dissent was over the ability of corporations (in that case, for-profit, closely held corporations) to "exercise religion," though both opinions seem to conclude that corporations serve to protect individual rights. See, e.g., *Burwell* v. *Hobby Lobby*, 134 S. Ct. at 2768 ("A corporation is simply a form of organization used by human beings to achieve desired ends .... When rights, whether constitutional or statutory, are extended to corporations, the purpose is to protect the rights of these people.") (majority opinion of Alito, J.) and 134 S. Ct. at 2795 ("Religious organizations exist to foster the interests of persons subscribing to the same religious faith.") (Ginsburg, J., dissenting).

[13] See Uta-Renate Blumenthal, *The Investiture Controversy: Church and Monarchy from the Ninth to the Twelfth Century* (Philadelphia: University of Pennsylvania Press, 1988).

[14] On the modern and historically contingent concept of "religion," see William T. Cavanaugh, *The Myth of Religious Violence: Secular Ideology and the Roots of Modern Conflict* (Oxford: Oxford University Press, 2009), pp. 57–122 and Nicholas Lash, *The Beginning and the End Of "Religion"* (Cambridge: Cambridge University Press, 1996), pp. 3–25.

so while not every account of the freedom of the church would emphasize the centrality of theological claims, the rights of groups, or divisions over sexual morality, these seem to me the most salient ways in which the debate is being framed today by both proponents and skeptics alike.[15]

GOD

Before the freedom of the church is a legal claim batted about by law professors, it is a theological claim of religious believers – a claim that God summons together people into a group for (primarily though not exclusively) worship. More particularly, it is a theological claim about language – what the word "God" (or its cognates) means and what is entailed when uttering such a word within a community. Part of the rejection of the freedom of the church depends upon a contestable view that (a) claims about "God" (and God's action in the world) are not admissible in deliberation about constitutional essentials because of the limitations of public reason, and (b) correlative ecclesiological claims that reject what I will call "voluntary membership ecclesiology" are similarly deemed inadmissible because of the individualistic doctrine of consent that is widely taken for granted.

Writing in 1940 amid the crisis of the freedom of the church in Nazi Germany, Karl Barth opens the second volume of his *Church Dogmatics* – arguably the greatest work in Christian theology of the twentieth century and since the Reformation – with these bracing words:

> In the Church of Jesus Christ men speak about God and men have to hear about God. About God the Father, the Son and the Holy Spirit; about God's grace and truth; about God's thoughts and works; about God's promises, ordinances and commandments; about God's kingdom, and about the state and life of man in the sphere of His lordship. But always and in all circumstances about God Himself, who is the presupposition, meaning and power of everything that is to be said and heard in the Church, the Subject who absolutely, originally and finally moves, produces, establishes and realises in this matter. In dogmatics it is the doctrine of God which deals with this Subject as such. In the doctrine of God we have to learn what we are saying when we say "God." In the doctrine of God we have to learn to say "God" in the correct sense. If we do not speak rightly of this Subject, how can we speak rightly of His predicates?[16]

Understanding the "church," then, requires that we understand rightly what we are saying when we say "God." An account of the church internal to the

[15] A complete account here would treat more fully the divisions in the Christian church. The best works in that vein today are Ephraim Radner's books, *A Brutal Unity: The Spiritual Politics of the Christian Church* (Waco: Baylor University Press, 2012) and *The End of the Church: A Pneumatology of Christian Division in the West* (Grand Rapids: William B. Eerdmans Publishing Co., 1998).

[16] Karl Barth, *Church Dogmatics*, II.1, trans. T. H. L. Parker and J. L. M. Haire (London: Bloomsbury T&T Clark, 1957).

church – an account articulated by those who affirm the claims of the Christian church – begins with "God." Accounts external to the church begin from some other standpoint – the sociology of groups, the psychology of religious belief, the history of religious practice. But this distinction between the internal and the external understanding of the church is no reason to dismiss, without more, the internal and theologically grounded account.

In a related vein, Stanley Hauerwas argues that the church is God's language in the world and overcomes the human divisions wrought by the Tower of Babel: "At Pentecost God created a new language, but it was a language that is more than words. It is instead a community whose memory of its Savior creates the miracle of being a people whose very differences contribute to their unity ... We call this new creation, church."[17] I do not mean to suggest that such claims on behalf of the church will be held to be true by all (or even many), but they are the theological claims on behalf of the church that some believers do, in fact, hold.

What are we to make of this? Skeptics of freedom of the church argue that claims regarding the "church" are reducible to (interchangeable with) claims of rights of conscience for individuals. But what would it mean to take seriously, if just for a moment, the claim affirmed by many that God acts in the world, sometimes in and through a community? One neglected aspect of the current debate is what to make of the very fact of "God-talk," whatever one's own views about the coherence, viability, or truth of such language.

For skeptics of the freedom of the church, this is all at best a black box but more likely delusional. As Brian Leiter has recently argued in his book *Why Tolerate Religion?*, but also familiar from Rawls's account of public reason, such theological claims are objectively unreasonable. To rely on them in, say, thinking about the freedom of the church (or indeed anything else) would be at odds with what liberal democracy requires. Let me be clear that my view does not require that those advocating the freedom of the church and doing so for genuinely theological reasons internal to the church are thereby committed to opposing liberal democracy.[18]

[17] Stanley Hauerwas, "The Church as God's New Language," in *Christian Existence Today: Essays on Church, World and Living in Between* (Grand Rapids: Brazos Press, 1988), pp. 53–4. Hauerwas goes on to note, "The creation of such a people is indeed dangerous, as we know from Babel. For the very strength that comes from our unity has too often led the church to believe that it can build the tower of unity through our own efforts. Not content to wait, in time we try to make God's unity a reality for all people through coercion rather than witness."

[18] For a defense of religious freedom and a rejection of religious coercion that is consistent both with certain aspects of liberalism and post-Vatican II Catholic doctrine on religious freedom, see John Finnis, "Reflection and Responses," in *Reason, Morality, and Law: The Philosophy of John Finnis*, ed. John Keown and Robert P. George (Oxford: Oxford University Press, 2013) p. 459 and Joseph Komonchak, "Vatican II and the Encounter Between Catholicism and Liberalism," in *Catholicism and Liberalism: Contributions to American Public Policy*, ed. R. Bruce Douglass and David Hollenbach (Cambridge: Cambridge University Press, 1994), p. 76.

Indeed, as Nicholas Wolterstorff argues, there is a (non-Rawlsian, to be sure) way to argue for permitting such reasons to be included among the reasons with which one deliberates about constitutional essentials.[19] For Wolterstorff, belief in God cannot be dismissed as outside the bounds of public reasonableness without adopting, in a question-begging move, some contestable account of what counts as "reasonable" and "justified belief" in the first place. Wolterstorff argues that foundationalist accounts ruling out religious belief through reliance on a view about what constitutes beliefs to which we are "entitled" or are epistemically "justified" in holding are dubious:

> [E]legant and admirable though it be, Locke's version of the liberal position will not do – fundamentally because its underlying epistemology, though admirably articulated, is nonetheless untenable. Since almost no one today would contest that claim, my critique will be brief.
>
> In the first place, the rationale Locke offers for restraint on the use of religious reasons is defective. Locke holds that only if one holds one's religious beliefs for reasons of that highly specific sort that he specifies is one entitled to those beliefs. The development in recent years, at the intersection of philosophy of religion and epistemology, of what has come to be known as "Reformed epistemology," is a powerful attack on that claim. Decisive, even – though I say this as one who has participated in the development. Not only is it not the case that one must hold one's religious beliefs for reasons of the Lockean sort to be entitled to them, it is not, in general, necessary that one hold them for any reasons at all. Something about the belief, the person, and the situation brings it about that the person is entitled to the belief. But that need not be another belief whose propositional content functions as reason for the religious belief. Entitlement simply does not effect the winnowing that Locke thought it would.[20]

If Wolterstorff is right that religious belief need not be accorded epistemological second-class status, then how should the claims of religious believers for a theological warrant for their ecclesial commitments be treated? One view noted already would hold that such views cannot be admissible when deliberating about law, most especially constitutional essentials such as liberty and rights – perhaps because, as Rawls suggests, to rely on such private forms of knowledge (revelation, ecclesial authority) would be to treat other citizens

[19] Nicholas Wolterstorff, "The Role of Religion in Decision and Discussion of Political Issues," in Robert Audi and Nicholas Wolsterstorff, *Religion in the Public Square: The Place of Religious Convictions in Political Debate* (Lanham: Rowman & Littlefield Publishers, Inc., 1996), pp. 67, 81.

> Let me make: clear that it is not the Idea of liberal democracy that I oppose; to the contrary, I firmly embrace it. What I oppose is *the liberal position:* the thesis that the role of citizen in a liberal democracy includes a restraint on the use of reasons, derived from one's religion, for one's decisions and discussions on political issues, and a requirement that citizens instead use an independent source. In due course I will explain and defend my alternative to the liberal position, which I will be calling the *consocial* position. I contend that the consocial position is fully harmonious with the Idea of liberal democracy.

[20] Wolterstorff, "The Role of Religion in Decision and Discussion of Political Issues," p. 87.

(who do not subscribe to such views) as unequal. The norm of equal respect, so the argument goes, requires excluding religious reasons from public debate, including religious commitments to a church and its liberty.

An alternative view would hold that equal respect in fact requires that such religious claims by religious believers on behalf of the liberty of religious institutions be treated, well, equally and respectfully. I am here suggesting that we cannot simply waive away such claims of theological particularity in the name of liberal canons of equal respect. As Wolterstorff puts it in his criticism of this aspect of the public reason view that excludes religious reasons:

> Are persons not often worth honoring in their religious particularities, in their national particularities, in their class particularities, in their gender particularities? Does such honoring not require that I invite them to tell me how politics looks from their perspective – and does it not require that I genuinely listen to what they say? We need a politics that not only honors us in our similarity as free and equal, but in our particularities. For our particularities – some of them [and here I would include membership in churches] – are constitutive of who we are, constitutive of our narrative identities.[21]

A corollary of theological claims about the church is that the church is not just another civic organization. Again, from a view internal to the life of the church, the decision to be part of the church is not a "decision" at all, but more like the "decision" to be born to your parents. Historically, one's belonging to the church was a response (a response itself conditioned by and made possible by grace) to a divine summons and a call to salvation. But lurking in the background of suspicion of the freedom of the church is what we might term "voluntary membership ecclesiology." On this account of the church, some people happen to choose to be members of a church, just like people happen to be members of any other group. That this is a view widely shared in liberalism and widely shared even among religious believers and adherents to churches today does not entail that such a view is true or the exclusive account of what a church might be.

There is a longer story to be told about how voluntary membership ecclesiology came to be the dominant understanding of the church from the standpoint of liberalism, even if it would not be the understanding internal to the church, certainly not the theological understanding in orthodox Christian doctrine. Locke's *A Letter Concerning Toleration* is the central text here and probably marks the historical turning point, though there are roots earlier in the Protestant Reformation.[22] As John Perry notes, "Locke is making a controversial *ecclesiological* claim when, in the *Letter*'s opening line, he [writes], 'Since you are pleased to inquire what are my thoughts about the mutual toleration of Christians in their different professions of religion, I must needs answer

[21] Wolterstorff, "The Role of Religion in Decision and Discussion of Political Issues," p. 111.

[22] See Brad S. Gregory, *The Unintended Reformation: How a Religious Revolution Secularized Society* (Cambridge: Belknap Press, 2012), pp. 129–79.

you freely that I esteem that toleration to be the chief characteristic mark of the true Church.' "[23] Locke's rhetoric of toleration and religious freedom in the *Letter* (for all except Catholics and atheists) is so broadly accepted today and the level of theological ignorance so high, we are inclined to accept such passages from the *Letter* without question. And so when we come to debate the freedom of the church, we do so from contestable, if widely held, Lockean premises.

As Perry goes on to note, though, "Locke's excurses into ecclesiology do not end there. It seems as though it should be sufficient for Locke's purposes to declare that, from the ruler's perspective, the church is not one voluntary society among many. However, he wants to go further to show that this is true from a perspective internal to the church."[24] My provisional suggestion here is that part of the current debate over the freedom of the church is fueled by the success of this Lockean account in convincing those inside the church to adopt the voluntary membership ecclesiology that Locke urged on the ruler(s) external to the church.

In concluding this section on the significance of theological claims on behalf of the freedom of the church, I should also note the contested terrain over whether freedom of the church is genuinely part of "freedom" (or "liberty"). As noted earlier, proponents of the freedom of the church argue that such forms of institutional freedom are indeed a necessary component of liberty. But as also noted, skeptics of the freedom of the church are inclined to see it as oppressive and giving special preference to one parochial form of group identity.

Here again, I will only suggest that we are working on terrain beset by assumptions that are subject to debate and disagreement. As Emile Perreau-Sassine notes:

> The theorists of secularization have portrayed the modern world as substituting political "autonomy" for religious "heteronomy," making democratic politicization part of a struggle against churches. But perhaps it is precisely acknowledgment of dependence on the divine that, by moderating the tyranny of the majority, makes political liberty possible. Religious life can go together with a wisdom to which democratic life does not give rise on its own, a wisdom that consists in recognizing limits to human autonomy.[25]

The suggestion here is that suspicion of the freedom of the church or of making room for theological claims is also skeptical of the liberty-enhancing property of the church and naïve about the state, while proponents of the freedom of the church are susceptible to the inverse set of prejudices – perhaps naïve about the church and the acceptance of theological claims, while suspicious of the liberal state.

[23] John Perry, *The Pretenses of Loyalty: Locke, Liberal Theory, and American Political Theology* (Oxford, Oxford University Press, 2011), p. 113.

[24] *Id.*

[25] Emile Perreau-Sassine, *Catholicism and Democracy: An Essay in the History of Political Thought*, trans. Richard Rex (Princeton: Princeton University Press, 2011), p. 152.

GROUPS

A second site of enduring disagreement on this topic is whether the law of religious freedom recognizes (or is primarily concerned about) individual, natural persons and their rights or whether it also applies to groups – groups not as mere aggregations of individuals, but groups as real entities, worthy of constitutional consideration. Now, a lot of work is done by the word "real" in that last phrase, so what do I mean?

If I say to you, "Let's meet at the hotel registration desk this evening and walk over to the restaurant together," what is the *shared* content of our intention to meet and to walk together? I start with this simple example adapted from Margaret Gilbert to suggest that there can be a sharing of intentions.[26] Sometimes, such a sharing of intentions is extended in time and space among large numbers of persons and sometimes such persons come together in a group on account of a shared religious belief. Recent work on groups and social practices by Raimo Tuomela in his books *The Philosophy of Sociality* and *The Philosophy of Social Practices* and by Philip Pettit and Christian List in *Group Agency* helpfully illuminates some aspects of this debate over group personality.

Tuomela's primary objective is to provide a framework for analyzing how groups influence action to complement the individualistic view that he argues is prevalent in social sciences generally. In both *The Philosophy of Sociality* and *The Philosophy of Social Practices*, Tuomela's approach can be viewed as a middle ground between a wholly reductive, individualistic account and an account that attributes full moral agency to groups. In contrast to these approaches, Tuomela recognizes that groups are composed of individuals, but, because they act in the same we-mode "for the group," one can attribute quasi-agency to the group. Accordingly, the most important aspect of Tuomela's approach is distinguishing between "I-mode groups" and "we-mode groups."

When a member of a group adopts that group's ethos, "defined as the set of the constitutive goals, values, beliefs, standards, norms, practices, and/or traditions that give motivating reasons for action,"[27] as his own end but for *private* reasons (i.e., reasons particular to that individual, such as joining a club to impress a romantic interest), then that person is acting in the I-mode. In contrast, a member of a group is acting in the we-mode when she has adopted the group's ethos, her main impetus for action is a group reason, and the desire to complete or achieve that action is "for the group." This distinction between we-mode and I-mode thus consists in the members' attitudes in relation to the

[26] Margaret Gilbert, "Walking Together: A Paradigmatic Social Phenomenon," *MIDWEST STUD. IN PHIL.* 15 (1990), 1, 7; see also J. David Velleman, *The Possibility of Practical Reason* (Ann Arbor: Scholarly Publishing Office, University of Michigan Library, 2009), p. 200.

[27] Raimo Tuomela, *The Philosophy of Sociality: The Shared Point of View* (Oxford: Oxford University Press, 2007).

goal and, consequently, the other members of the group. In we-mode groups, there is a collective acceptance by the group members to achieve a certain end for the common good. This also entails that group members possess certain rights and duties relative to the other members.[28] There is no such agreement in I-mode groups, just as there are no rights and duties that exist between those groups' members.

Tuomela uses what he terms the "Collectivity Condition," defined as "the idea of the group members necessarily 'standing or falling together' concerning group-relevant activities and items," to distinguish formally between I-mode groups and we-mode groups.[29] It is possessed only by we-mode groups. "The Collectivity Conditions," he writes, "gives us a reason to say that the depersonalization that occurs in social groups is part of the basic structure of group life (in its we-mode content) and thus is not a mere contingent feature of groups."[30] Tuomela refers to the Collectivity Condition as a "cornerstone" of his account because it underlies all we-mode thinking and therefore is critical to understanding collective action in general.[31] In order to understand collective action, one must realize that there is a categorical difference between people engaged in an activity "for the group" and those acting for their own self-interest. This distinction allows Tuomela to acknowledge a difference between business corporations (generally I-mode groups) and groups such as churches or universities (maybe) that are organized for a common (shared) purpose (generally we-mode groups). Here is a more formal explanation of the we-mode:

> A group member thinks or acts in the we-mode if and only if he is (i) 'we-committed' (participates in the collective commitment) to a thought (the mental state and its content) or, respectively, to an action that is (ii) collectively accepted in the group as the group's thought or action and that is (iii) for the group's "use" and accordingly gives the group members a group reason for their thinking and acting.[32]

It should also be noted that we-mode groups rely on reflexive acceptance of the group's ethos: "Necessarily (in a conceptual or quasi-conceptual sense), the members collectively accept (with collective commitment) E as g's ethos if and only if (it is correctly assertible for them that) E is g's ethos."[33] Thus, the membership of an individual in a group relies upon the group-as-such and the group relies upon the individual "believing in" the group. This reflexivity shows the importance of acknowledging the group as distinct from the individual. In his article "The We-Mode and the I-mode," Tuomela articulates the reason for drawing a distinction between we-mode groups and I-mode groups:

[28] Raimo Tuomela, *The Philosophy of Social Practices: A Collective Acceptance View* (Cambridge: Cambridge University Press, 2002), p. 200.

[29] Tuomela, *The Philosophy of Sociality*, p. 28.

[30] *Id.* at 10.

[31] *Id.* at 189.

[32] *Id.* at 9.

[33] *Id.* at 20.

Normative group beliefs and goals, and the like, are based on some operative members acting for the group and creating its views and goals, and the like. The operative members act as members of the group and for the group, being collectively committed to what they accept for the group. Thus, what they do is in the we-mode ... *We-mode attitudes are causally real, and they obviously may affect the person's actions in ways differing from the causal impact of their relevant I-mode attitudes.* The social world abounds with cases like this. Normative group properties are accordingly needed for the correct description and the explanation of social life, and this gives a necessity argument of the constitutive kind of the need of we-mode thinking and acting in many central contexts.[34]

Basically, I take Tuomela to be arguing that as members of a group acting in a we-mode, it is impossible to reduce the individual's actions to the I-mode because there is a functional difference between a person acting with a group goal in mind as opposed to a private goal. To reduce we-mode to I-mode would be to miss the true reason for the individual's actions and how the group functions according to the Collectivity Condition.[35]

This is a powerful point for the institutionalist debate surrounding the freedom of the church given that anti-institutionalists are sometimes susceptible to grounding First Amendment rights on the individual's freedom of conscience (or speech). By incorporating Tuomela's approach, one is able to differentiate between (a) groups in which members view themselves principally as individuals in I-mode groups, and (b) groups in which members view themselves as a part of a larger whole, we-mode group. With this distinction, one is able to argue that these two types of groups should be treated differently according to their purpose. For Tuomela, one is able to consider we-mode groups as a "quasi-person" to which one can attribute mental states.[36] Thus, we-mode groups should be viewed with some level of autonomy in the law.

Tuomela succinctly describes his theory of institutions:

Social institutions are regarded as special collectively social practices (recurrent actions as group members) that are normatively governed – in part by constitutive norms. At bottom, institutions are group-level phenomena accountable in terms of the we-mode. However, in actual life, institutional activities normally also include lots of I-mode activities that accordingly can be said to have colonized the realm of we-mode institutional action. The special institutional status (including a conceptual, social, normative component) is central to a social institution.[37]

Tuomela considers the church (churches) to be such a social institution.[38] As such, the church as an institution tends to foster democratic civil society

[34] Raimo Tuomela, "The We-Mode and the I-Mode," in *Socializing Metaphysics: The Nature of Social Reality*, ed. Frederick F. Schmitt (Lanham: Rowman & Littlefield Publishers, 2003), pp. 93, 111 (emphasis added).

[35] Tuomela, *The Philosophy of Sociality*, pp. 28, 189.

[36] *Id.* at 20.

[37] *Id.* at 9.

[38] *Id.* at 192.

because its members share the we-belief that there are certain activities that are not under the control of the state. Accordingly, the church is an area where different ideas about human purposes – liberty, fulfillment, and so on – are able to form. This is only one version of an argument in favor of freedom of the church using Tuomela's theory of institutions, and there are likely many others.

Similarly, Christian List and Philip Pettit's work on group agency may help provide an argument for viewing the collective as a whole as opposed to a collection of individuals:

> Given the talk of group agents is not readily translatable into individualistic terms, and given that it supports a distinct way of understanding and relations to the social world, we can think of such entities as autonomous realities. Although their agency depends on the organization and behavior of individual members, as individualism requires, they display patterns of collective behavior that will be lost on us if we keep our gaze fixed at the individual level. And to lose sight of those patterns is to lose an important source of guidance as participants in the social world.[39]

As List and Pettit point out, one way of understanding group agency is what they call the "authorization" view: "group agents exist when a collection of people each authorize an independent voice as speaking for them in this or that domain, committing themselves to be bound by it just as an individual is bound by what he or she affirms or promises."[40] This is the view of group agency at work in many liberal accounts, for it was the view first articulated by Hobbes and later refined in some respects (most especially regarding majoritarianism) by Locke. But as List and Pettit argue, "If a group agent is to display the rationality that agency requires, its attitudes cannot be a majoritarian or other equally simple function of the attitude of its members. The group agent has to establish and evolve a mind that is not just a majoritarian or similar reflection of its members' minds; in effect, it has to develop a mind of its own. This gives rise to the kind of autonomy that we ascribe to group agents."[41]

In combination, one can take Tuomela's argument for the differentiation between I-mode groups and we-mode groups to show that the church is a unique, we-mode institution that has existed as a counterbalance to the state (evinced by using List and Petit's group agency theory to view the church's role in relation to the state) and should be granted a particular institutional status in order to foster its role in civil society.

More basically and in a historical perspective, my suspicion is that there is a struggle here between accounts of individuals and groups in the state that marks the birth of liberalism in Hobbes and in his influence in Anglophone liberal political theory. Notwithstanding a renewed interest in Hobbes on civil

[39] Christian List and Philip Pettit, *Group Agency: The Possibility, Design, and Status of Corporate Agents*, (Oxford: Oxford University Press, 2011), p. 6.

[40] *Id.* at 7.

[41] *Id.* at 8.

association and religion,[42] relatively little effort has been made to bring the fruits of that scholarship to bear on contemporary discussions in law and legal theory.[43] "[T]he sovereign, in every commonwealth, is the absolute representative of all the subjects," wrote Hobbes at the birth of the modern state, "and therefore no other can be representative of any part of them, but so far forth as he shall give leave."[44] As summarized by Pettit, multitudes for Hobbes "are an aggregate or heap of agents" and a "dissolute number of individual persons."[45] Hobbes provides an especially influential account of group personality that constitutes an important tradition within liberalism and partly shapes the current debate over freedom of the church.

The sources for this Hobbesian view include the most extensive discussion of groups in Chapter XXII ("Of Systems Subject, Political and Private") as well as the remarks toward the end of Chapter XXIX ("Of Those Things that Weaken a Commonwealth") in which Hobbes notes the problem of "the great number of corporations, which are as it were many lesser commonwealths in the bowels of a greater, like worms in the entrails of a natural man."[46] Finally, on account of the neglect of Part III ("Of a Christian Commonwealth") and Part IV ("Of the Kingdom of Darkness") of *Leviathan*,[47] many standard interpretations of Hobbes miss the fact that Part III includes the longest – by far – chapter in the book, which is Chapter XLII ("Of Power Ecclesiastical"). It is in that chapter that Hobbes engages at length with the figure who is, to my knowledge, the contemporary of Hobbes's most frequently cited in *Leviathan*, Cardinal Robert Bellarmine, precisely on the question of the authority of religious corporations (primarily the Roman Catholic Church).

At least one counter-tradition to Hobbes on group personality in Anglophone liberal political theory is represented by the English pluralists (primarily the legal historian F.W. Maitland and the historian of political theory John Neville Figgis) who provide an account of political authority, the history of common law principles of incorporation, and the place of churches and other corporate bodies in the modern state that seeks to undermine the Hobbesian view of

42 See, e.g., Michael Oakeshott, *Hobbes on Civil Association* (Indianapolis: Liberty Fund, 1975); Jean Hampton, *Hobbes and the Social Contract Tradition* (Cambridge: Cambridge University Press, 1986); Aloysius P. Martinich, *The Two Gods of Leviathan: Thomas Hobbes on Religion and Politics* (Cambridge: Cambridge University Press, 1992); and Philip Pettit, *Made with Words: Hobbes on Language, Mind, and Politics* (Princeton: Princeton University Press, 2008).

43 Writing before much of the recent revival of interest in Hobbes, John Rawls could say in *A Theory of Justice* simply that Hobbes "raises special problems." John Rawls, *A Theory of Justice* (Cambridge: Harvard University Press, 1971), p. 11.

44 Thomas Hobbes, *Leviathan*, ed. and trans., Edwin Curley (Indianapolis: Hackett Publishing Company, 1994), p. xxii.

45 Pettit, *Made with Words*, p. 72.

46 Hobbes, *Leviathan*, p. 218.

47 See Don Herzog, *Happy Slaves: A Critique of Consent Theory* (Chicago: University of Chicago Press, 1989), p. 73 ("Notoriously, the standard account of Hobbes doesn't even mention the second half of the book.").

sovereignty and individualism.[48] "If the law allows men to form permanently organised groups," wrote Maitland, "those groups will be for common opinion right-and-duty-bearing units."[49] Figgis argued that Hobbes's theory of sovereignty was a "venerable superstition" (insofar as Hobbes's account of sovereignty denied that groups could exist except by concession of the state) and that it was "as a series of groups that our social life presents itself, all having some of the qualities of public law and most of them showing clear signs of a life of their own, inherent and not derived from the concession of the State."[50]

For this purpose, the most important of these English pluralists was John Neville Figgis (1866–1919), an Anglican clergyman who spent much of his adult life as a member of the Community of the Resurrection, an Anglican monastic community in West Yorkshire. Figgis studied under the Liberal (in both the partisan and theoretical sense) Catholic historian and politician Lord Action at Cambridge, and Figgis was the initial editor of many of Acton's writings. It was through F. W. Maitland's work, however, that Figgis became interested in the question of corporations and their relation to the state. In early work – primarily his 1896 book, *The Divine Right of Kings* and lectures on the history of political theory published in 1907 as *Political Thought from Gerson to Grotius: 1414–1625* – Figgis was not concerned primarily with the question of group personality. The controversy over the Scottish Free Church case in 1904 in which the House of Lords decided in favor of a minority rump in the Scottish church (later reversed by Parliament), however, led to Figgis's work on the place of churches in the state.[51]

As Figgis posed the question in *Churches in the Modern State*:

> Does the Church exist by some inward living force, with powers of self-development like a person; or is he a mere aggregate, a fortuitous concourse of ecclesiastical atoms, treated it may be as one for purposes of convenience, but with no real claim to a mind or will of her own, except so far as the civil power sees good to invest her for the nonce with a fiction of unity?[52]

For his part, Figgis does not think that churches should be treated differently than other forms of association life: "Since, as a fact, religious bodies are only

[48] A notable exception is David Runciman, *Pluralism and the Personality of the State* (Cambridge: Cambridge University Press, 1997).

[49] Frederic W. Maitland, "Moral Personality and Legal Personality," in *State, Trust, and Corporation*, ed. David Runciman and Magnus Ryan (Cambridge: Cambridge University Press, 2003), p. 68. Russell Hittinger draws out the implications of Maitland's view for accounts of sovereignty and authority in "Society, Subsidiarity, and Authority in Catholic Social Thought," in *Civilizing Authority: Society, State, and Church*, ed. Patrick McKinley Brennan (Lanham: Lexington Books, 2007).

[50] John Neville Figgis, *Churches in the Modern State*, 2nd edition (Ann Arbor: University of Michigan Library, 1914), p. 224.

[51] Kenneth R. Ross, *Church and Creed in Scotland: The Free Church Case 1900–1904 and its Origins* (Edinburgh: Rutherford House, 1988).

[52] Figgis, *Churches in the Modern State*, p. 40.

one class of a number of other societies," he writes, "all laying claim to this inherent life, it is clear that the question concerns not merely ecclesiastical privilege, but the whole complex structure of civil society and the nature of political unions."[53] For Figgis, the state can set out requirements for the recognition of societies, "[b]ut all this does not and need not imply that corporate personality is the gift of the sovereign, a mere name to be granted or withheld at its pleasure."[54]

As summarized by David Runciman, Figgis's central concept in *Churches in the Modern State* was the *communitas communitatum*. "By it," writes Runciman, "Figgis understood a society made up of self-formed and self-governing associations, each of which co-existed in a broader framework, itself capable of generating a sense of community. This broader community was the state, but although broader, it did not condition the lives of those lesser groups that it contained."[55] The freedom of the church can be defended and understood best as an example of Figgis's *communitas communitatum*, a challenge to Hobbesian accounts of state sovereignty and liberal individualism. The state cannot interfere with the church in certain respects not because the *state* has granted an exemption from an otherwise generally applicable law. Rather, the state simply has no jurisdiction over such claims. It is not because the state has, in Hobbes's words, "given leave" to groups to be autonomous from the state. Religious corporations are, instead, free and autonomous (quite literally in the sense of self-norming or self-legislating) groups within the state.

Of course, the challenge is to deflect the counter-argument that the reach of state sovereignty extends (in these cases) "all the way down" through groups to individuals. So the task for those who defend Figgis's pluralism and its relevance to the freedom of the church is to weaken the hold of a certain Hobbesian picture of sovereignty that holds us in its grip – even among the many who reject various implications of Hobbes. Figgis and the English pluralists argued against the Hobbesian state by asserting that groups are *real* and that they possess *real* personality. "What we actually see in the world," Figgis claimed, "is not on the one hand the State, and on the other a mass of unrelated individuals; but a vast complex of gathered unions, in which alone we find individuals."[56]

[53] *Id.* at 41.

[54] *Id.* Indeed, Figgis argues that denial of real personality to groups would be tyrannical:

> It is, in a word, a real life and personality which those bodies are forced to claim, which we believe they possess by the nature of the case, and not by the arbitrary grant of the sovereign. To deny this real life is to be false to the facts of social existence, and is of the same nature as that denial of human personality which we call slavery, and is always in its nature unjust and tyrannical.

[55] David Runciman, *Pluralism and Personality of the State* (Cambridge: Cambridge University Press, 2005), p. 144.

[56] Figgis, *Churches in the Modern State*, p. 70.

What has this to do with freedom of the church? Skeptics about freedom of the church often seem to assume that there are only individuals – individual intentions, plans of life, desires, and so forth. Groups – where they exist – just are aggregations of individuals. By contrast, those who advocate the freedom of the church assume that it is possible to form *real* groups – right and duty-bearing entities, in the phrase of Maitland's, that have legal (not natural) personality.

My concluding and important point here is to call attention to the atomism that divides proponents and skeptics of the freedom of church. I borrow the term from Charles Taylor, who writes that "Atomism represents a view about human nature and the human condition which (among other things) makes a doctrine of the primacy of rights plausible; or to put it negatively, it is a view in the absence of which this doctrine is suspect to the point of being virtually untenable."[57] We have a difficult time imaging our political life based on any other set of assumptions about persons and their communities. As Taylor goes on to argue:

> It is clear that we can only join this issue [over atomism] by opening up questions about the nature of man. But it is also clear that the two sides are not on the same footing in relationship to these questions. Atomists are more comfortable standing with the intuitions of common sense about the rights of individuals and are not at all keen to open these wider issues. And in this they derive support in those philosophical traditions which come to us from the seventeenth century and which started with the postulation of an extensionless subject, epistemologically a *tabula rasa* and politically a presuppositionless bearer of rights. It is not an accident that these epistemological and political doctrines are often found in the writings of the same founding figures.[58]

Taylor is referring, of course, to Locke, who makes frequent appearances in the literature expressing skepticism about the freedom of the church. Lockean epistemology shapes the intuition about what constitutes justified belief, Lockean tolerance renders voluntary membership the dominant ecclesiological understanding, and Locke's atomism about human subjectivity makes accounting for groups and social institutions seem like metaphysical nonsense.

SEXUAL MORALITY

There are, as it happens, real groups that believe God has taught authoritatively about a range of moral matters: killing in wartime, care for the poor and marginalized, the organization of civil society … and sex. Most religious believers would likely say it is not the first (or even the second or third) thing to be said about their faith, but nonetheless many hold that the church is an authoritative teacher of sexual morality. In *The Triumph of the Therapeutic*,

[57] Charles Taylor, "Atomism," *Philosophical Papers*, Volume 2: *Philosophy and the Human Sciences* (Cambridge: Cambridge University Press, 1985), pp. 187, 189.

[58] Taylor, *Atomism*, p. 210

Phillip Rieff called attention to this link between sexual morality and Christian corporate identity:

Historically, the rejection of sexual individualism (which divorces pleasure and procreation) was the consensual matrix of Christian culture. It was never the last line drawn. On the contrary, beyond that first restriction there were drawn others, establishing the Christian corporate identity within which the individual was to organize the range of his experience. Individuality was hedged round by the discipline of sexuality, challenging those rapidly fluctuating imperatives established in Rome's remissive culture, from which a new order of deprivations was intended to release the faithful Christian believer.[59]

My point here is a limited but important one: freedom of the church is especially controversial today on account of broader arguments in our culture about sexuality and because those arguments about sexuality are especially important (to a greater or lesser degree) to religious institutions. For religious believers – who, of course, hold a wide range of views themselves on sexual morality – part of the debate turns on whether it is even possible for a religious institution to teach authoritatively about marriage, child-bearing, and other sexual matters. But because such teachings of the churches are now widely rejected, these questions have become more pressing.

The case law surrounding group autonomy and institutional religious freedom bear out the importance of sex and gender. Consider the modern (post-1970) line of freedom of association cases, which have usually been about matters of sex and gender: *Roberts* v. *Jaycees*,[60] *Hurley* v. *Irish-American Gay, Lesbian, and Bisexual Group of Boston*,[61] *Boy Scouts* v. *Dale*,[62] and *Christian Legal Society* v. *Martinez*.[63] Although the Supreme Court's ministerial exception case, *Hosanna-Tabor* v. *EEOC*,[64] raised a claim of disability discrimination, other ministerial exception cases in the courts of appeal had routinely confronted allegations of gender discrimination.[65]

Traditional Christian views on sexuality pose challenges on at least two fronts. First, traditional accounts often hold to a view affirming a natural differentiation of the sexes and the biological significance of gender, with profound (though diminishing and perhaps reconcilable) implications for gender equality and sex. As argued at length by Alexander Pruss in his recent book on Christian sexual ethics, the theological commitments (particularly the doctrine of creation) of Christianity entail the significance of nature and natural

[59] Philip Rieff, *The Triumph of the Therapeutic: Uses of Faith after Freud* (New York: Harper and Row, 1966), p. 17.

[60] *Roberts* v. *United States Jaycees*, 468 U.S. 609 (1984).

[61] *Hurley* v. *Irish-American Gay, Lesbian, and Bisexual Group of Boston*, 515 U.S. 557 (1995).

[62] *Boy Scouts of America* v. *Dale*, 530 U.S. 640 (2000).

[63] *Christian Legal Society* v. *Martinez*, 130 S. Ct. 2971 (2010).

[64] *Lutheran Church & School* v. *EEOC*, 132 S. Ct. 694 (2012).

[65] See, e.g., *EEOC* v. *Catholic University of America*, 83 F.3d 455 (D.C. Cir. 1996) (dismissing gender discrimination claim brought by canon law professor denied tenure).

desire: "A *natural* biological striving in a human being is always valuable in itself (though it may be contextually inappropriate), since it is the normal functioning of a creature made in the image and likeness of God."[66] Second, churches are among the most well-organized and persistent opponents of permissive views on a range of matters related to sex and reproduction, with abortion, the recent Health and Human Services (HHS) contraceptive mandate, access to artificial reproduction, and same-sex marriage being the most pertinent examples.

One's position in these debates will vary depending on whether one embraces (in Nancy Rosenblum's phrase) "the logic of congruence" between public and private ordering. As Rosenblum and Robert Post put it in their introduction to *Civil Society and Government*

> Advocates of congruence fear that the multiplication of intermediate institutions does not mediate but balkanizes public life. They are apprehensive that plural associations and groups amplify self-interest, encourage arrant interest-group politics, exaggerate cultural egocentrism, and defy government. What is needed, in their view, is a strong assertion of public values and policies designed to loosen the hold of particular affiliations, so that members will be empowered to look beyond their groups and to identify themselves as members of the larger political community. The "logic of congruence" envisions civil society as reflecting common values and practices "all the way down."[67]

According to this logic of congruence, all groups (emphatically including the churches – the most recalcitrant holdouts) should be shaped by the state's views of gender equality and sex.

This is complicated by several further considerations, including the problem of "internalities" – dissenting employees, students, and others subject (properly or not, depending on one's view) to an institutions' moral claims when, for example, a Catholic university refuses to cover artificial contraception in its health plan. Religious believers themselves are also sometimes in a conflicted position – agreeing with, say, legal norms of gender equality in most employment settings but not within churches when it comes to the hiring decisions for ministers.

Underlying this is the difficulty of differentiating applications of justice to particular settings. When accounts of sexual morality and justice more generally aspire to universalistic application, it becomes more difficult to permit dissent and differentiation within the legal order on such matters. As noted by Jacob Levy, institutional considerations have been in disfavor among political theorists for a generation, but his topic there (federalism) applies as well to subsidiary institutions in civil society such as the church: "[T]he dominant mood in political philosophy since the early 1970s has been one of disdain

[66] Alexander Pruss, *One Body: An Essay in Christian Sexual Ethics* (Notre Dame: University of Notre Dame Press, 2012), p. 141 (emphasis in original).

[67] Nancy L. Rosenblum and Robert C. Post, "Introduction," in *Civil Society and Government*, ed. Nancy L. Rosenblum and Robert C. Post (Princeton: Princeton University Press, 2001).

for questions of institutional design."[68] As Levy argues, this is in large part because "[i]n this post-1971 intellectual landscape [since the publication of John Rawls's *A Theory of Justice*, it has sometimes been suggested, or causally assumed, that liberalism is synonymous with moral universalism applied to politics."[69]

In such a climate, the secular debate over sexual morality inevitably comes to shape religion itself. The order of intelligibility internal to the church is revelation-redemption-liturgy and worship-doctrine-moral teaching, while the external view is tempted to turn that order on its head by emphasizing first the moral and political force of ecclesial arguments. In the contemporary debate over the freedom of the church, most of the discussion proceeds in the reverse order of these topics, that is, we begin with debate over a moral (frequently sexual) issue, then ask later whether there are institutional rights of exemption from otherwise generally applicable legal requirements. For skeptics of the freedom of the church, it seems that because we *can* argue in our accepted terms of discourse about whether, say, employers should provide contraceptive benefits to their employees or whether gay and lesbian couples should be accorded rights to marry, that is what we *do* argue about. Whether groups are real or merely aggregations of individuals or whether God exists and has spoken authoritatively to religious communities – well, that is just too difficult because such views are not subject to reasonable debate.

By contrast, those who advocate for the freedom of the church *begin* with a theological claim about God and his calling together a people, and only *then* (and much later) start worrying about what this means for, say, sexuality and a host of other "applied" topics. And so even the order in which we argue about the freedom of the church and the premises lurking behind the arguments of its advocates and its skeptics is itself a site of disagreement.

This focus on sexuality distorts the discussion over the freedom of the church because this interminable debate over these moral questions is already such a prominent feature of public life, and the church (and its legal status) becomes yet another site of such debate. The debate frequently becomes a distraction of a kind, and churches come to be understood – both by those internal and external to them – as little more than advocacy organizations that primarily engage in advocacy in the public sphere and just happen to do other things. The Catholic Church comes to be seen as little more than a pro-life advocacy organization that just happens to operate large institutions such as hospitals, universities, and social service agencies – as if the National Rifle Association happened by historical accident to operate a chain of restaurants.

These disagreements come to distort the idea of the freedom of the church in at least two ways. First, because both sides in the discussion are sometimes

[68] Jacob T. Levy, "Federalism, Liberalism, and the Separation of Loyalties," *Am. Political Science Rev.* 101 (2007), 459, 463.

[69] *Id.*

at pains not to address the substantive moral questions in play, the discussion of the freedom of the church comes to be a poor substitute for those questions. My hypothesis is that participants in these debates (at least sometimes) *really* disagree about such moral questions, but flee to the seemingly safer and more abstract debate over the First Amendment as a way around confronting the moral questions, perhaps because such questions seem intractable to the participants. But a second consideration cuts the other direction, that is, the place of certain moral teachings – particularly moral teachings on sexuality – in the life of churches comes to take on a misplaced priority and thereby distorts, for both believers and non-believers alike, the very idea of what a church is for.

What I have sought to do here is to suggest that the rejection of the freedom of the church (as a legal category) rests upon premises just as contestable as the endorsement of freedom of the church. The legal doctrine of the freedom of the church is shaped amid a complicated set of historical constitutional practices, but also amid a set of philosophical and theological views about God, groups, and sexual morality. I do not pretend here to have any ready resolution to the debate, but, as in so many discussions, achieving clarity about the competing premises doing the work in a set of arguments is sometimes sufficient work unto the day.

7

Our fractured attitude towards corporate conscience

Brett G. Scharffs

I. INTRODUCTION

A. CVS

On February 5, 2014, the nation's largest pharmacy, CVS Caremark, announced it would stop selling cigarettes and other tobacco products at its more than 7,600 stores. Calling the decision "simply the right thing to do for the good of our customers and our company," CVS President and CEO Larry J. Merlo explained, "The sale of tobacco products is inconsistent with our purpose – helping people on their path to better health."[1]

In many ways this was a courageous decision. CVS estimated it would lose about $2 billion in annual revenue ($1.5 billion from lost tobacco sales and $500 million in sales of other products to tobacco customers).[2] The company's stock fell 3.2% in premarket trading on the day of the announcement.[3] CVS anticipated this would result in a loss of 17 cents in earnings per share.[4] Customers would be inconvenienced, and those who previously came in to CVS to buy cigarettes together with other products could be expected to take

[1] "Message from Larry Merlo, President and CEO," CVS Pharmacy, (February. 5, 2014), http://info.cvscaremark.com/cvs-insights/cvs-quits.

[2] Sam Ro, "Here's How Much CVS Will Lose When It Stops Selling Cigarettes," *Business Insider*, February 5, 2014, accessed August 18, 2015, www.businessinsider.com/the-cost-of-not-selling-tobacco-to-cvs-2014-2. ("In fiscal 2012, CVS had $123 billion in net sales and earned $3.03 per share from continuing operations.")

[3] Vincent Trivett, "Pre-Market: Twitter, Yelp Earnings on Tap; Private-Sector Job Creation Eases," *Minyanville*, February 5, 2014, accessed August 18, 2015, www.minyanville.com/business-news/markets/articles/Pre-Market253A-Twitter-Yelp-Earnings-on/2/5/2014/id/53650.

[4] Profit is defined as income (typically money from consumers) minus the cost of production (wages, cost of renting and building buildings, and cost of goods sold).

their business elsewhere. If sales were to decline significantly, employees would lose their jobs.[5]

A critic might accuse the company of harming their three most important constituencies – customers, employees, and shareholders.[6] Nevertheless, our instinctive reaction – certainly mine – is to praise CVS, not condemn it.[7] The company placed its core values – "helping people on their path to better health" – ahead of the bottom line. Principle trumped profits.[8]

The company's decision was met with almost universal praise, including from the highest levels of the US government. Within minutes of the announcement, President Obama complimented CVS for "setting a powerful example" and said the company's decision "will help advance [his] administration's efforts to reduce tobacco-related deaths, cancer, and heart disease, as well as bring down health care costs."[9] On the day of the announcement, US Department of Health and Human Services Secretary Kathleen Sebelius issued a statement lauding CVS for its "leadership in helping to make the next generation tobacco-free."[10] Noting the high costs exacted by tobacco in lost lives and resources, Secretary Sebelius stated that she had already "called on all sectors of the United States – from businesses to local and state governments to the faith community – to join in the Obama Administration's sustained effort to make the next generation tobacco-free."[11] Notice the breadth of Secretary Sebelius' appeal – to businesses, to all levels of government, and to religious groups.

5 CVS makes $126 billion annually and employs over 200,000 employees. "2013 Annual Report, CVS Caremark," CVS Caremark, accessed May 25, 2016, http://investors.cvshealth.com/~/media/Files/C/CVS-IR-v3/reports/cvs-ar-2013.pdf; "About us," CVS Caremark, accessed May 25, 2016, http://cvshealth.com/about. Thus, a $2 billion loss in revenue could translate to about 3,000 lost jobs.

6 Brian Powell, "Fox Freaks Out over CVS Ending Sales of Tobacco," *Media Matters*, February 5, 2014, accessed August 18, 2015, http://mediamatters.org/blog/2014/02/05/fox-freaks-out-over-cvs-ending-sales-of-tobacco/197947; Eli Langer, "CVS Fights Back Against Critics of Tobacco Move," *CNBC*, February 5, 2014, accessed August 18, 2015, www.cnbc.com/id/101392069.

7 "26 Leading Health Groups Call on Drug Stores and Other Retailers to Follow CVS's Example and End Tobacco Sales," *Press Release*, February 26, 2014, http://www.prnewswire.com/news-releases/26-leading-health-groups-call-on-drug-stores-and-other-retailers-to-follow-cvss-example-and-end-tobacco-sales-247256541.html, accessed May 25, 2016.

8 In the long term, the decision may facilitate profits. "Smoking cessation is a growth business, while tobacco use simply isn't. The $2 billion in revenue wasn't going to stay at that level for much longer …." Ed Morrissey, "CVS to stop selling tobacco products," *HotAir*, February 5, 2014, accessed August 18, 2015, http://hotair.com/archives/2014/02/05/cvs-to-stop-selling-tobacco-products/.

9 Aaron Blake, "Obama praises CVS's decision to stop selling cigarettes," *The Washington Post*, February 5, 2014, accessed August 18, 2015, www.washingtonpost.com/blogs/post-politics/wp/2014/02/05/obama-praises-cvss-decision-to-stop-selling-cigarettes/.

10 "Statement by Health and Human Services Secretary Kathleen Sebelius on CVS Tobacco Announcement," Department of Health and Human Services, Press Release, February 5, 2014, accessed August 18, 2015, www.hhs.gov/news/press/2014pres/02/20140205a.html.

11 *Ibid.* ("As we know from the recently released 50th Anniversary Surgeon General Report on smoking and health, nearly 500,000 Americans die each year due to smoking, and smoking

B. The birth control mandate

Almost exactly two years earlier, on January 20, 2012, the Obama administration ignited a firestorm of controversy when it announced regulations implementing a health insurance mandate requiring virtually all employers to include coverage of contraception, sterilization, and abortion inducing drugs.[12] This was part of the administrative enactment of the Affordable Care Act, more commonly known as Obamacare.[13]

The mandate included an exemption for certain religious employers, but only those that met four requirements: first, their primary purpose had to be the inculcation of religious values; second, they were required primarily to employ only those of their faith; third, they could primarily serve only those of their faith; and fourth, they had to qualify as a church per se for tax purposes.[14]

costs us $289 billion annually. Each day, more than 3,200 youth under age 18 in the United States try their first cigarette and more than 700 kids under age 18 become daily smokers. If we fail to reverse course, 5.6 million children alive today will die prematurely due to smoking. This is unacceptable.")

[12] The announcement (available at www.hhs.gov/news/press/2012pres/01/20120120a.html) by Kathleen Sebelius, President Obama's Secretary of Health and Human Services, came as a rejection of appeals, mainly from Roman Catholic bishops, to modify the existing contraceptive provisions of the Affordable Care Act (ACA) to create a broader exemption for religious groups. In lieu of those concessions, non-exempt religious organizations were given a one year grace period to comply with the existing mandate. Robert Pear, "Obama Reaffirms Insurers Must Cover Contraception," *The New York Times*, January 20, 2012, accessed August 18, 2015, www.nytimes.com/2012/01/21/health/policy/administration-rules-insurers-must-cover-contraceptives.html. Although many critics (including more than 500 academics and religious figures who signed the February 14, 2012 open letter, "Unacceptable," infra n. 27) say abortifacients are covered, the HHS website explicitly says they are NOT. The opposing sides' definition of "abortifacient" probably differs.

[13] The ACA states, "A group health plan and a health insurance issuer offering group or individual health insurance coverage shall, at a minimum provide coverage for and shall not impose any cost sharing requirements for ... with respect to women, such additional preventive care and screenings not described in paragraph (1) as provided for in comprehensive guidelines supported by the Health Resources and Services Administration for purposes of this paragraph." Patient Protection and Affordable Care Act, 42 U.S.C. § 300gg – 13, Sec. 2713(a)(4). The HRSA's guidelines require health care plans to include, "[a]ll Food and Drug Administration approved contraceptive methods, sterilization procedures, and patient education and counseling for all women with reproductive capacity." "Women's Preventive Services: Required Health Plan Coverage Guidelines," US Department of Health and Human Services: HRSA, June 13, 2012, accessed August 18, 2015, www.hrsa.gov/womensguidelines/.

[14] The Mandate "provide[s] HRSA additional discretion to exempt certain religious employers from the Guidelines where contraceptive services are concerned ... [F]or purposes of this policy, a religious employer is one that: (1) has the inculcation of religious values as its purpose; (2) primarily employs persons who share its religious tenets; (3) primarily serves persons who share its religious tenets; and (4) is a non-profit organization under section 6033(a)(1) and section 6033(a)(3)(A)(i) or (iii) of the Code. Section 6033(a)(3)(A)(i) and (iii) refer to churches, their integrated auxiliaries, and conventions or associations of churches, as well as to the exclusively religious activities of any religious order." "Group Health Plans and Health Insurance Issuers Relating to Coverage of Preventive Services under Patient Protection and Affordable Health

This exemption was extremely narrow. On this definition, church-owned hospitals, charitable service organizations and most religious schools would not qualify for the exemption.[15] Indeed, critics argued that Jesus Christ's own ministry would not qualify, since he ministered to believers as well as non-believers.[16]

The Catholic Church immediately objected, and over the following few weeks a cascade of public opposition from many who care about religious liberty began to gather force.[17] Critics argued that the mandate was a grievous violation of religious liberty – a requirement for Catholic and other religious institutions to pay to cover medical services that violate core doctrines of their respective faiths.[18] Supporters of the mandate responded that this was a matter of equal access to women's health, and opposition to the mandate was denounced as part of a broader "war on women" promulgated by religious conservatives.[19]

Care Act: Amendment," *Federal Register* Vol. 76, Num. 149, February 15, 2012, accessed August 18, 2015, www.regulations.gov/#!documentDetail;D=IRS-2010-0017-1015.

[15] Robert Pear, "Obama Reaffirms Insurers Must Cover Contraception," *The New York Times*, January 20, 2012, accessed August 18, 2015, www.nytimes.com/2012/01/21/health/policy/administration-rules-insurers-must-cover-contraceptives.html.

[16] "Under such inexplicably narrow criteria ... even the ministry of Jesus and the early Christian Church would not qualify as 'religious,' because they did not confine their ministry to their co-religionists or engage only in a preaching ministry. In effect, the exemption is directly at odds with the parable of the Good Samaritan, in which Jesus teaches concern and assistance for those in need, regardless of faith differences ... [T]he government has no business engaging in religious gerrymanders, whereby some churches are 'in' and others are 'out' for regulatory purposes based on who their teaching calls them to serve, how they constitute their workforce, or whether they engage in 'hard-nosed proselytizing.' "

USCCB: Office of the General Counsel, "United States Conference of Catholic Bishops Nationwide Bulletin Insert," August 31, 2011, pg. 9, accessed August 18, 2015, www.usccb.org/about/general-counsel/rulemaking/upload/comments-to-hhs-on-preventive-services-2011-08-2.pdf.

[17] "Facing vocal opposition from religious leaders and an escalating political fight, the White House sought on Tuesday to ease mounting objections to the contraceptive rule ... [T]he growing uproar surrounding [the rule] ... showed that social issues still resonate strongly on the political stage. With Congressional Republicans coming out in opposition to the administration stance, the contraception fight was threatening to erupt into a major political confrontation." Helene Cooper and Katharine Q. Seelye, "Obama Tries to Ease Ire on Health Insurance Contraception Rule," *The New York Times*, February 7, 2012, accessed August 18, 2015, www.nytimes.com/2012/02/08/health/policy/obama-addresses-ire-on-health-insurance-contraception-rule.html?ref=us.

[18] *e.g.*, Richard W. Garnett, "Column: HHS Mandate Still Undermines Religious Freedom," *USA Today*, February 15, 2012, accessed August 18, 2015, http://usatoday30.usatoday.com/news/opinion/forum/story/2012-02-15/obama-contraceptive-mandate-compromise-bishops/53103138/1.

[19] "The U.S. Conference of Catholic Bishops' decision to reject the White House compromise on birth control access in health insurance is further evidence that their concern is not religious liberty, but playing politics with women's lives ... The Bishops' cloaking their anti-women's sexuality view in religious liberty arguments is nothing more than their trying to do with health insurance reform what they have not been able to do from the pulpit: deny women access to modern contraceptives." Rev. Debra Haffner, "Column: Stop Playing Politics with Women's

The argument about access was mostly a red herring, since contraceptive, sterilization, and abortion services are widely available, with heavy subsidies from federal programs.[20] Thus, the controversy was more about who would pay – the government, or private institutions, including religious employers.[21]

Access to Contraception," *Erin Burnett OutFront*, June 13, 2012, accessed August 18, 2015, http://outfront.blogs.cnn.com/2012/02/14/column-stop-playing-politics-with-womens-access-to-contraception/.

"Let's admit what this debate is really and what Republicans really want to take away from American women. It is contraception," Sen. Charles E. Schumer (D-N.Y.) outrageously claimed while opposing the Blunt amendment. Sen. Frank R. Lautenberg (D-N.J.) said the GOP was yearning to return to "the Dark Ages … when women were property that you could easily control, trade even, if you wanted to." The Obama campaign insists that "if Mitt Romney and a few Republican senators get their way, employers could be making women's healthcare decisions for them" and require that women seek a permission slip to obtain birth control." Jonah Goldberg, "Birth control agitprop," *The Los Angeles Times*, March 6, 2012, accessed August 18, 2015, http://articles.latimes.com/2012/mar/06/opinion/la-oe-goldberg-contraception-20120306.

20 "Health and Human Services itself touts community health centers, public clinics and hospitals as some of the available alternatives; doctors and pharmacies are others. Many of the entities, with Planned Parenthood being the most prominent, already furnish free contraceptives. The government could have the rest of these providers make contraceptive services available free and then compensate them directly. A mandate on employers who object for religious reasons is among the most restrictive means the government could have chosen to increase access." David B. Rivkin, Jr. and Edward Whelan, "Birth-Control Mandate: Unconstitutional and Illegal," *The Wall Street Journal*, February 15, 2012, accessed August 18, 2015, http://online.wsj.com/article/SB10001424052970204795304577223003824714664.html.

"'The government knows that [most] employer-based insurance plans already cover these services,' Hannah Smith, senior counsel at the Becket Fund for Religious Liberty, tells me. 'So it's not about expanding contraceptive access. It's about forcing religious-based organizations to provide this against their beliefs.' Indeed, the Guttmacher Institute found that in 2010, 'nine in 10 employer-based insurance plans cover[ed] a full range of prescription contraceptives.'" Kirsten Powers, "Obama's Baffling Catholic Decision: Birth Control Trumps Religious Freedom," *The Daily Beast*, February 7, 2012, accessed August 18, 2015, www.thedailybeast.com/articles/2012/02/07/birth-control-trumps-religious-freedom-in-obama-s-catholic-decision.html.

"Advocates for the contraceptive mandate claim that there is a need for women to have an increased access to contraception. However it is not widely publicized that the US government is already providing roughly $2 billion for domestic family planning. Most health plans cover such services, so this mandate is aimed at only marginally increasing the vast access to contraception that already exists, primarily by forcing those who oppose such coverage to carry it." Jeanne Monahan, Contraception Mandate a Profound Violation of Religious Freedom, U.S. News, (February 9, 2012), www.usnews.com/debate-club/should-catholic-and-other-religious-institutions-have-to-cover-birth-control/the-uproar-over-obamas-choice-has-to-do-with-more-than-contraception.

21 "If you are too poor in America to pay for your own contraceptives, the government already pays for them for you. As Rich Lowry writes in his February 17 column, "a vast government apparatus exists to provide poor women access to contraceptives, from Medicaid and community health centers to Title X. There are roughly 4,500 Title X-funded clinics around the country. They are required to provide free birth control to the poor and subsidized birth control to people with incomes between 100 percent and 250 percent of poverty." This assistance for the poor is not at issue today. No one is calling for an end to such public assistance … What is at issue … is whether the government has the power to force a religious institution to pay for contraceptives and even abortion inducing drugs for its employees, when the use of contraceptives and drugs is contrary to the institution's religious beliefs." Peter Ferrara, *Bringing Rationality to the Rush Limbaugh/*

In the face of vocal and building opposition, on February 10, 2012, President Obama announced a "compromise" – religious employers would not be required to cover contraception, sterilization, and abortifacients; instead, their insurance plans would.[22]

This compromise was immediately denounced by many of the original critics of the contraceptive mandate as a distinction without a difference, since it would be the religious employers who would have to pay the insurance companies.[23] For example, an open letter signed by over 500 scholars and religious

Contraception Controversy, FORBES, (March 8, 2012, 11:00 PM"), www.forbes.com/sites/peter-ferrara/2012/03/08/bringing-rationality-to-the-rush-limbaughcontraception-controversy/.

[22] "Now, after the many genuine concerns that have been raised over the last few weeks … we've reached a decision on how to move forward … [I]f a woman's employer is a charity or a hospital that has a religious objection to providing contraceptive services as part of their health plan, the insurance company – not the hospital, not the charity – will be required to reach out and offer the woman contraceptive care free of charge … The result will be that religious organizations won't have to pay for [or] provide these services directly." *Remarks by the President on Preventive Care, Feb. 10, 2012* (June 13, 2012, 3:00 PM), www.whitehouse.gov/the-press-office/2012/02/10/remarks-president-preventive-care.

[23] "President Barack Obama's birth control 'accommodation' … was nothing but an accounting trick that still forces Catholic (and other religious) institutions to provide medical insurance that guarantees free birth control, tubal ligation and morning-after abortifacients – all of which violate church doctrine on the sanctity of life." Charles Krauthammer, *Overreach: Obamacare vs. the Constitution*, THE WASHINGTON POST (June 13, 2012, 2:00 PM), www.washingtonpost.com/opinions/charles-krauthammer-overreach--obamacare-vs-the-constitution/2012/02/16/gIQAmupcIR_story.html.

"That's the compromise. Religious organizations will no longer be required to violate their faith directly…just indirectly." Matthew Clark, *What President Obama's 'Accommodation' of Religious Liberty Accomplished*, AMERICAN CENTER FOR LAW AND JUSTICE (June 13, 2012, 2:00 PM), http://aclj.org/obamacare/president-obama-accommodation-religious-liberty-accomplished.

"[W]here does [the money to pay for contraception] come from, if not from [religious institutions] and not the [patient]? Insurance companies won't be making donations. Drug makers will still charge for the pill. Doctors will still bill for reproductive treatment. The reality, as with all mandated benefits, is that these costs will be borne eventually [by the religious institutions] via higher premiums …. [They] will still pay for birth control, even if it is nominally carried by a third-party corporation. This cut-out may appease a few of the Administration's critics, especially on the Catholic left – but only if they want to be deceived again, having lobbied for the Affordable Care Act that created the problem in the first place. The faithful for whom birth control is a matter of religious conviction haven't been accommodated at all. They'll merely have to keep two sets of accounting books … One major problem will be how the rule applies to large organizations that self-insure. Arrangements in which an employer pays for care directly and uses insurers to manage benefits and process claims (not to take on insurance risk) account for the majority of the private market. In these cases there isn't even a free lunch to pretend exists." *Immaculate Contraception*, THE WALL STREET JOURNAL (February 13, 2012), http://online.wsj.com/article/SB10001424052970203646004577215150068215494.html.

"Administration officials said that final rules for 'self-insured employers' would be issued after the November elections but before August 1, 2013, when a transition period is scheduled to end … The new Obama policy leaves two big questions unanswered: Who will provide the money to pay the claims for contraceptive drugs and devices? Who will pay the fees normally paid by the employer?" Robert Pear, U.S. Clarifies Policy on Birth Control for Religious Groups, THE NEW YORK TIMES (March 16, 2012),

leaders (including Harvard Law Professor Mary Ann Glendon, Catholic University President John Garvey, and Princeton philosopher Robert P. George) asserted, "This so-called 'accommodation' changes nothing of moral substance and fails to remove the assault on religious liberty and the rights of conscience which gave rise to the controversy."[24]

Nearly one hundred lawsuits have been filed challenging the contraceptive mandate, by both nonprofits who were dissatisfied with the accommodation,

www.nytimes.com/2012/03/17/health/policy/obama-administration-says-birth-control-mandate-applies-to-religious-groups-that-insure-themselves.html.

"Officials said they have concluded that for technical legal reasons the law's reach does not extend to 'self-insured' student plans, meaning those for which a college or university collects premiums directly from students, then uses the pool to pay for their health care ... [T]he Obama administration suggested various proposals for how it should deal with self-insuring employers that object to the birth control rule on religious grounds ... One idea is to require administrators to draw on revenue from other businesses they often also engage in – running disease management or drug benefit programs for instance. Another is to grant them rebates from a special re-insurance fund that all administrators must pay into under a separate provision of the health-care law. The final option is for the federal government to incentivize private, multi-state health insurance plans to step in with birth control coverage in cases where an employer refuses to do so." N.C. Aizenman, *Birth Control Rule Won't Apply to All Student Plans at Colleges*, White House Says, THE WASHINGTON POST (March 16, 2012), www.washingtonpost.com/national/health-science/white-house-fleshes-out-exemptions-to-birth-control-rule/2012/03/16/gIQAoLB5GS_story.html. Despite its problems, various religious groups endorsed the compromise, including Catholic Charities USA, Catholics United, and others. See Jennifer Palmieri, *What They Are Saying: Preventive Health Care and Religious Institutions* WHITE HOUSE (February 12, 2012), www.whitehouse.gov/blog/2012/02/12/what-they-are-saying-preventive-health-care-and-religious-institutions.

24 The letter reads more fully: "This so-called 'accommodation' changes nothing of moral substance *and fails to remove the assault on religious liberty and the rights of conscience which gave rise to the controversy. It is certainly no compromise. The reason for the original bipartisan uproar was the administration's insistence that religious employers, be they institutions or individuals, provide insurance that covered services they regard as gravely immoral and unjust. Under the new rule, the government still coerces religious institutions and individuals to purchase insurance policies that include the very same services.* It is no answer to respond that the religious employers are not 'paying' for this aspect of the insurance coverage. For one thing, it is unrealistic to suggest that insurance companies will not pass the costs of these additional services on to the purchasers. More importantly, abortion-drugs, sterilizations, and contraceptives are a necessary feature of the policy purchased by the religious institution or believing individual. They will only be made available to those who are insured under such policy, by virtue of the terms of the policy. It is morally obtuse for the administration to suggest (as it does) that this is a meaningful accommodation of religious liberty because the insurance company will be the one to inform the employee that she is entitled to the embryo-destroying "five day after pill" pursuant to the insurance contract purchased by the religious employer. It does not matter who explains the terms of the policy purchased by the religiously affiliated or observant employer. What matters is what services the policy covers. The simple fact is that the Obama administration is compelling religious people and institutions who are employers to purchase a health insurance contract that provides abortion-inducing drugs, contraception, and sterilization. This is a grave violation of religious freedom and cannot stand. It is an insult to the intelligence of Catholics, Protestants, Eastern Orthodox Christians, Jews, Muslims, and other people of faith and conscience to imagine that they will accept as assault on their religious liberty if only it is covered up by a cheap accounting trick." *Unacceptable* (open letter) (February 14, 2012) (emphasis added), www.becket-fund.org/wp-content/uploads/2012/02/Unacceptable2-14-7am1.pdf.

and for-profit businesses that were not covered by the accommodation.[25] One suit was filed by the Little Sisters of the Poor, an international Roman Catholic congregation of religious sisters that operates thirty homes in the United States, where "the elderly and dying are treated as if they were Jesus himself and cared for with love and dignity until God calls them home."[26]

Another suit was brought by Hobby Lobby, a company with a strong Christian identity in its ownership and self-understanding. Founded in 1972 by David Green, the Oklahoma City-based Hobby Lobby is a privately held chain of arts and crafts stores with more than 550 stores nationwide, more than 22,000 employees, and over $3 billion in sales.[27] The company is a closely held family business that strives to abide by Christian principles, including donating 10% of its profits to charitable activities and closing its stores on Sunday.[28] In many ways, Hobby Lobby is an extremely employee-friendly workplace, with starting salaries of $14 per hour (which is 80% more than the minimum wage) and a comprehensive self-insured health plan, including a health care and wellness clinic at its headquarters with no co-pays.[29]

In its lawsuit challenging the contraception mandate, Hobby Lobby asserted that the "Green family's religious beliefs forbade them from participating in, providing access to, paying for, training others to engage in, or otherwise supporting abortion-causing drugs and devices."[30]

[25] As of May 2014, there were some 96 lawsuits challenging the contraception mandate. HHS Information Central, THE BECKET FUND FOR RELIGIOUS LIBERTY, www.becketfund.org/hhsinformationcentral/, (last visited May 6, 2014).

[26] Case page, Little Sisters of the Poor, THE BECKET FUND FOR RELIGIOUS LIBERTY, www.becketfund.org/littlesisters/. The Becket Fund, a religious liberty advocacy law firm, brought suit on behalf of the Little Sisters of the Poor, "seeking to uphold their right to carry out their vows of obedience in their service to the poor." The Becket Fund explained, "Although the government does allow exemptions for church and church-type entities from the HHS Mandate for religious reasons, this accommodation does nothing for the Little Sisters. Because the government refuses to classify them as a 'religious employer,' the Little Sisters are required to hire a third party to provide these objectionable services to their employees, and thus are still forced to participate in the government's scheme. Believing that every human person has God-given worth, the Little Sisters cannot provide contraceptive, abortion, and sterilization services that go against their religious beliefs." *Ibid.* In January, 2014, the Little Sisters of the Poor received an injunction from the Supreme Court protecting them from the application of the HHS Mandate while their case is before the Tenth Circuit Court of Appeals.

[27] FORBES, Hobby Lobby Stores, www.forbes.com/companies/hobby-lobby-stores/, (last visited February 5, 2013).

[28] HOBBY LOBBY press release, *Hobby Lobby marks 40 years of helping families celebrate life*, www.hobbylobby.com/assets/pdf/40years/40years.pdf, (last visited May 19, 2014; no longer available).

[29] Complaint, Hobby Lobby *v.* Sebelius, 2012 WL 4009450 (W.D.Okla.) (Filed September 12, 2012); Leonardo Blair, *Hobby Lobby Raises Minimum Wage to $14 for Full-Time Employees*, CHRISTIAN POST, April 18, 2013, www.christianpost.com/news/hobby-lobby-raises-minimum-wage-to-14-for-full-time-employees-94233/.

[30] Complaint, Hobby Lobby *v.* Sebelius, 2012 WL 4009450 (W.D.Okla.) (Filed September 12, 2012).

Lori Windham, senior counsel at the Becket Fund for Religious Liberty, which represented Hobby Lobby in the lawsuit, explained the company's position: "Washington politicians cannot force families to abandon their faith just to earn a living. Every American, including family business owners like the Greens, should be free to live and do business according to their religious beliefs."[31]

Some opponents to providing an exemption for businesses such as Hobby Lobby roundly ridiculed the notion that a for-profit business can have a conscience at all. For example, one representative op-ed opposed to Hobby Lobby's position stated in its headline "Religious Freedom is for People, Not Corporations."[32] Indeed, during the 2012 presidential campaign, eventual Republican nominee Mitt Romney (who, like President Obama, is a graduate of Harvard Law School) was derided for voicing the black letter law view that corporations are persons.[33] The very idea that a corporation is a person and that, like individuals, a corporation could have conscientious scruples became the punch line of jokes by TV comedians.[34]

II. WHY THE DIFFERENCE?

The contrasting experiences of CVS on the one hand and Hobby Lobby on the other hand create an interesting puzzle. CVS was widely praised (including by President Obama and HHS Secretary Kathleen Sebelius) for its conscientious concern for health, whereas Hobby Lobby found itself before the Supreme Court trying to defend its rights of conscience, with the self-same Secretary Sebelius arguing that corporations have no free exercise rights or even free exercise interests (rights and interests that are of a paradigmatic conscientious character).[35] This seems rather bizarre – one company was praised for acting in accord with its conscience, and the other was criticized for having the temerity to claim that it has a conscience. What is going on here?

[31] Becket Fund, *Hobby Lobby sues over HHS Mandate*, press release, (September 12, 2012), www.becketfund.org/hobbylobbysueshhs/.

[32] Elizabeth B. Wydra, *Religious Freedom is for People, Not Corporations* CNN, (November 26, 2013), www.cnn.com/2013/11/26/opinion/wydra-supreme-court-obamacare/index.html. ("From the nation's founding until today, the Constitution's protection of religious liberty has been seen as a personal right, inextricably linked to the human capacity to express devotion to a God and act on the basis of reason and conscience.")

[33] Phillip Rucker, *Mitt Romney Says Corporations are People at Iowa State Fair*, WASHINGTON POST, (August 11, 2011), www.washingtonpost.com/politics/mitt-romney-says-corporations-are-people/2011/08/11/gIQABwZ38I_story.html.

[34] Geneva Sands, *Colbert super-PAC jokes that Romney is 'serial killer' of corporations*, THE HILL, (January 16, 2012), http://thehill.com/video/campaign/204299-colbert-super-pac-accuses-romney-of-being-a-serial-killer-.

[35] By the time the case was decided, Sylvia Burwell had replaced Secretary Sebelius as Secretary of HHS, so the case was decided as Burwell *v.* Hobby Lobby Stores, Inc. 573 U.S. (2014).

A. The government's arguments in Hobby Lobby

In the Hobby Lobby case, Secretary Sebelius did not just take the position that Hobby Lobby's free exercise rights were outweighed by a strong government interest in providing contraceptive care to women; rather, the government took the position that Hobby Lobby had no free exercise interests or rights at all.[36] In the government's view, the case did not present a situation where the conscientious interests of Hobby Lobby needed to be balanced against the government's interests; rather, the government denied that a company has any free exercise interests at all.

The technical threshold issue in the Hobby Lobby case was whether the contraception mandate imposed a substantial burden on the free exercise rights of either Hobby Lobby, as a company, or upon the Greens, as the owners. The Obama administration took the position that the answer to both questions is, 'No.'

1. Substantial burden on free exercise?

Does the contraception mandate represent a substantial burden on religious exercise?

Secretary Sebelius proffered three arguments to support the contention that free exercise rights and interests were not implicated in the Hobby Lobby case. First, she maintained, Hobby Lobby is a for-profit company and such companies have no free exercise rights or interests.[37] Second, she argued, recognizing such rights and interests would violate basic principles of corporations having an identity separate from their owners.[38] Third, she urged that the Greens' free exercise interests were not implicated, because the mandate applied not to them personally, but only to their company.[39] The Supreme Court rejected each of these arguments.

A. FOR-PROFIT CORPORATION In the Hobby Lobby case, the US government took the position that, because it is a for-profit corporation, Hobby Lobby has no free exercise rights or interests at all. According to Secretary Sebelius, the claims of Hobby Lobby fail because it is a for-profit corporation that is not a person exercising religion under the Free Exercise Clause or the Religious Freedom Restoration Act.[40] For-profit businesses, Secretary

[36] Sebelius *v.* Hobby Lobby, brief for Petitioner Kathleen Sebelius, et. al., 2014 WL 173486 (U.S. 2014), 15–18.

[37] *Ibid.* at 15–20. "The claims of the respondent for-profit corporations fail at the threshold because they are not persons exercising religion within the meaning of RFRA."

[38] *Ibid.* at 25–26. "Nothing in RFRA purports to reject the bedrock principle that a corporation is legally distinct from its owners."

[39] *Ibid.* "There is thus no basis on which to impute the individual-respondents' religious beliefs to the corporate-respondents."

[40] *Ibid.* at 15. "The claims of the respondent for-profit corporations fail at the threshold because they are not persons exercising religion within the meaning of RFRA."

Sebelius argued, should be concerned with making a profit rather than pursuing conscience-based missions. Free exercise rights, in the Secretary's view, are limited to individuals and religious non-profit institutions. "For profit corporations 'are different from religious non-profits in that they use labor *to make a profit*, rather than to perpetuate a religious values-based mission.' "[41] When corporations enter the marketplace, they subject themselves to legislation designed to protect health, safety, and welfare of their employees.[42]

The Court rejected the argument that Hobby Lobby was not a "person" within the meaning of the Religious Freedom Restoration Act (RFRA). RFRA, the court noted, provides protection to "persons," a term that was not defined in the act. Looking to the Dictionary Act, the Court noted that the definition of the word person includes corporations as a possible meaning. The Court further found that there was nothing in RFRA that "suggests a congressional intent do depart from the Dictionary Act definition ..."[43] The Court also noted that it has previously entertained RFRA and free exercise claims brought by nonprofit corporations, and that "HHS concedes that a nonprofit corporation can be a 'person' within the meaning of RFRA." Thus, the Court concluded that "this concession effectively dispatches any argument that the term 'person' as used in RFRA does not reach the closely held corporations involved in these cases." The court added, "No known understanding of term 'person' includes *some* but not all corporations."[44]

B. SEPARATE CORPORATE ENTITY The second reason the government gave for not recognizing Hobby Lobby's religious freedom interests has to do with the structure of the corporation as a separate entity from its owners. Secretary Sebelius argued that granting corporations religious rights would "disregard fundamental tenets of American corporation law."[45] A corporation is a "distinct legal entity, with legal rights, obligations, powers, and privileges different from those of the natural individuals who created it, who own it, or whom it employs."[46] The government continued, "Few norms are more deeply ingrained into the fabric of American law than the principle that 'a corporation and its stockholders are deemed separate entities.' "[47] Based upon the idea that a corporation is legally distinct from its owners, the government concludes, "There is thus no basis on which to impute the individual respondents' religious beliefs

41 Hobby Lobby, Brief for Petitioner, at 19, quoting Gilardi *v.* United States Department of Health and Human Services, 733 F.3d 1208, 1242 (D.C. Cir. 2013) (Edwards, J., concurring in part and dissenting in part), petition for cert. pending. No. 13–567 (filed November 5, 2013).

42 Hobby Lobby, Brief for Petitioner, at 19.

43 Slip op at 19, 573 U.S. ___ (2014).

44 *Ibid.*, slip op at 19–20.

45 Brief of Petitioner Kathleen Sebelius, Sebelius *v.* Hobby Lobby Stores, Inc., at 23.

46 *Ibid.* at 23, quoting Cedric Kushner Promotions, Ltd. *v.* King, 533 U.S. 158, 163 (2001).

47 *Ibid.* at 23, quoting New Colonial Ice Co. *v.* Helvering, 292 U.S. 435, 442 (1934).

to the corporate respondents."[48] According to this argument a corporation, unlike a natural person, cannot exercise religion.

The government's argument misrepresented the significance of separate corporate legal existence. The point of separate entities is not to prevent corporations from having views or commitments (including moral or religious commitments) "imputed" to them. How else could a corporation get its values and priorities, if not from its owners and managers? Rather, the corporate form provides a mechanism for shielding owners from personal liability for the debts and obligations of the corporation – a mechanism designed to encourage entrepreneurship and risk-taking. To say that the beliefs of owners must not be "imputed" to corporations is clearly incorrect.[49] Separation for liability purposes does not require separation for all purposes. Businesses worldwide are expected to concern themselves with matters of conscience, including their impact on the environment, social justice, and a wide range of morally significant issues.[50]

The court rejected this argument as well. "While it is certainly true that a central objective of for-profit corporations is to make money, modern corporate law does not require for-profit corporations to pursue profit at the expense of everything else, and many do not do so. For profit corporations, with ownership approval, support a wide variety of charitable causes, and it is not at all uncommon for such corporations to further humanitarian and other altruistic objectives."[51]

C. NO VIOLATION OF THE GREENS' FREE EXERCISE RIGHTS On the other hand, the government argues that the Greens' free exercise rights are not violated, because the HHS Mandate applies only to the corporation, not to them as individuals: "Federal law does not require *the Greens* to provide health insurance, particular health benefits, or any other form of compensation to the corporation's employees. The Greens do not personally employ the 13,000 individuals who work for Hobby Lobby: the corporation does."[52]

[48] *Ibid.* at 25.

[49] This paragraph is based on the Brief of 9 Academic Institutions and 27 Comparative Law and Religion Scholars in Support of Hobby Lobby and Conestoga Wood, Sebelius *v.* Hobby Lobby Stores, Inc., 2014 WL 334444 (U.S.), 3.

[50] *Ibid.* "Decisions by foreign and international tribunals reinforce the principle that government should not require collective religious rights to be checked at the gate before entering the for-profit world. The requirements of ethos organizations – both religious and secular – are widely recognized and are consistently granted exemptions from otherwise applicable laws. But the principle is broader: a corporation's eligibility for religious freedom protections turns not on status as a for-profit or non-profit corporation, but on commitment to convictions that fall within the ambit of religious freedom rights. As borne out by international experience, corporations holding such convictions need and deserve protections if full religious freedom is to be achieved in society."

[51] Slip op at 23.

[52] Brief of Petitioner Kathleen Sebelius, at 27.

RFRA does not make this distinction, but rather broadly protects "any" religious exercise.[53] To argue that forcing a company to do something does not have implications for its owners would mean that the government could force a company owned by those who conscientiously object to military service to channel all their production into the building of weapons of war. The government could force a Jewish butcher who does business as a corporation (but not as a partnership or sole proprietorship) to process pork, or force any business to provide abortion coverage or assisted suicide coverage in their health plans. In sum, it is a view that projects a statist authority far beyond anything we have come to view as acceptable in our pluralistic liberal democracy with its commitment to individual rights and freedoms.

The court rejects the "dramatic consequences" of this argument, noting that, "According to HHS … if these merchants chose to incorporate their businesses … they would forfeit all RFRA (and free exercise) rights. HHS would put these merchants to a difficult choice: either give up the right to seek judicial protection of their religious liberty or forgo the benefits, available to their competitors, of operating as corporations."[54]

As the International Center for Law and Religion Studies (ICLRS) noted in a brief on behalf of a number of international academic institutions and international law scholars:

> The Government's argument has a 'heads we win, tails you lose' quality, arguing on the one hand that the RFRA rights of the owners of the corporation are not violated because it is only their businesses (and not they) that are subject to the contraceptive mandate, but contending on the other hand that the businesses do not have any free exercise rights, because they are separate legal entities, impervious to the convictions of their owners. In fact, restrictions on collective expression of religion by for-profit corporations substantially burden the free exercise rights of both corporations and owners.[55]

The doctrine of the corporate veil was intended to liberate corporate enterprise, not to hobble religion in the commercial sector.

2. *Deep underlying question*

Lurking beneath the surface of the technical question of whether a corporation is a "person" for purposes of the RFRA lies a more fundamental question about the character and status of corporations. Is a corporation the sort of thing about which we can meaningfully speak of having a conscience? The question does not need to be considered metaphysically or even ontologically; the real question is rather more pedestrian: what kinds of rights and duties do we want and expect corporations to have?

[53] Brief of Respondent Hobby Lobby, Sebelius *v.* Hobby Lobby Stores, Inc., 2014 WL 546899 (U.S.) 17.

[54] Slip op at 17.

[55] Brief of 9 Academic Institutions, at 4.

Do we want them to act conscientiously (as Secretary Sebelius praised CVS for doing when it announced its decision not to sell tobacco products), or do we want to refrain from "imputing" moral values of owners and managers to corporations, treating them simply as market vehicles that should concern themselves only with pursuing profits (as Secretary Sebelius said Hobby Lobby should do)?

B. Apple, the green energy company

A recent event at Apple, Inc. sheds light on the tension between corporate conscience and the pursuit of profits. At a shareholder meeting in February 2014, Apple Chief Executive Tim Cook rebuked what the press described as "right-wing" investors who criticized Cook for spending large amounts of corporate money on green energy initiatives that wasted firm profits.[56] The investors unsuccessfully pressed a shareholder proposal that would have forced the company to disclose information about its green energy programs.[57] As reported in *The Independent*,

> Responding to calls from the National Centre for Public Policy Research (NCPPR), a conservative think tank and investor, for Apple to refrain from putting money in green energy projects that were not profitable, [Cook] shot back that Apple did "a lot of things for reasons besides profit motive." The chief executive added: "We want to leave the world better than we found it."

Cook exhibited a rare flash of anger when he addressed the NCPPR representative directly: "If you want me to do things only for ROI [return on investment] reasons, you should get out of this stock."[58]

The same article noted that, "Since taking the helm at Apple in 2011, Cook has made notable improvements to the company's use of renewable energy, increasing the use of solar, wind and geothermal resources used to power Apple's offices from around a quarter of its total energy use to more than 75 per cent." The article also noted that Apple under Cook has given millions of dollars in charity "in contrast to his predecessor [Steve] Jobs, who reportedly once told colleagues that giving money to charity was a waste of time."[59]

NCPPR responded with a press release titled, "Tim Cook to Apple Investors: Drop Dead." The Press Release stated: "Here's the bottom line: Apple is as obsessed with the theory of so-called climate change as its board member

[56] Loulla-Mae Eleftheriou-Smith, *Apple's Tim Cook: Business isn't just about making profit*, INDEPENDENT, (March 2, 2014), www.independent.co.uk/life-style/gadgets-and-tech/news/apples-tim-cook-business-isnt-just-about-making-a-profit-9163931.html.

[57] For the text of the proposal, see the SEC filing prepared in advance of the board meeting, Apple Corp., Definitive Proxy Statement, (Form 14-K), http://investor.apple.com/secfiling.cfm?filingID=1193125-14-8074&CIK=320193.

[58] Eleftheriou-Smith, *supra* note 56.

[59] *Ibid.*

Al Gore is … The company's CEO fervently wants investors who care more about return on investments than reducing CO_2 emissions to no longer invest in Apple. Maybe they should take him up on that advice."[60]

What went unnoticed by most observers is that the type of claim Tim Cook was making on behalf of Apple is very similar to the claim being made by Hobby Lobby.[61]

C. Corporate Social Responsibility (CSR)

But what about the broader claim that it is ridiculous to think of a business as something that can have a "conscience" or a "moral point of view" – the idea that religious freedom is for people, not corporations?

Although some have reflexively derided the suggestion that a corporation is a person and that a business can exercise conscience, this view is directly contradicted by liberal orthodoxy concerning corporate social responsibility. For decades, social progressives have been arguing that corporations should be allowed (or even encouraged or expected) to pursue social ends that might detract from the general rule of profit maximization.[62]

Corporate social responsibility or CSR (tellingly, sometimes called "corporate conscience" or "corporate citizenship") calls for businesses to engage in self-regulation and positive actions that transcend the maximization of shareholder profit.[63] Corporations are urged to go beyond the letter of the law (beyond mere compliance), and to abide by the spirit of the law, emerging international norms, ethical standards, or codes of conduct.[64] CSR urges

[60] The National Center for Public Policy Research, press release, "Tim Cook to Apple Investors: Drop Dead" (February 28, 2014), www.nationalcenter.org/PR-Apple_Tim_Cook_Climate_022814.html.

[61] An exception is Eric Schulzke, writing in the *Deseret News*, who drew a comparison between Hobby Lobby's conscientious concerns and those of Apple. Eric Schulzke, *Apple joins Hobby Lobby values corporate causes before profits*, Deseret News National Edition, (March 3, 2014), http://national.deseretnews.com/article/1086/Apple-joins-Hobby-Lobby-values-corporate-causes-before-profits.html.

[62] See, e.g., Simon B. Brooks, *CSR and the StraightJacket of Economic Rationality*, 30 *Intl. J.L. & Soc. Policy* 11 (2010); Antonio Argandoña and Heidi von Weltzien Hoivik, *Corporate Social Responsibility: One Size Does Not Fit All. Collecting Evidence from Europe*, 89 *Journal of Business Ethics* 221; Jonathan P. Doh and Terrence R. Guay, Corporate Social Responsibility, Public Policy, and NGO Activism in Europe and the United States: An Institutional-Stakeholder Perspective 43 *Journal of Management Studies* 47 (2006); see generally Corporate Social Responsibility and Alcohol (Marcus Grant and Joyce O'Connor eds., 2005).

[63] See Antonio Argandoña and Heidi von Weltzien Hoivik, *Corporate Social Responsibility: One Size Does Not Fit All. Collecting Evidence from Europe*, 89 *Journal of Business Ethics* 221 at 223, examining "responsibility" as a non-legal term.

[64] See Jonathan P. Doh and Terrence R. Guay, "Corporate Social Responsibility, Public Policy, and NGO Activism in Europe and the United States: An Institutional-Stakeholder Perspective," 43 *Journal of Management Studies* 47 (2006). "Corporate social responsibility (CSR) – actions taken by the firm intended to further social goods beyond the direct interests of the firm and that which is required by law."

corporations to consider how corporate policies and actions impact the environment, employees, consumers, and communities, all of whom are regarded (in addition to shareholders) as stakeholders.[65]

CSR is defended in two ways: the first is that it is an admissible exception to the rule that corporations should seek to maximize shareholder value; the second is an argument that pursuing responsible corporate behavior will actually enhance long-term profitability.[66] In either case, corporations are urged to act "responsibly," to behave "ethically," to embrace "corporate conscience," and be good "citizens." Note that moral responsibility, conscience, and citizenship are all concepts that we might say apply exclusively to natural persons.

Consider just a sampling of the types of social conscience concerns that companies promote.

- Coca Cola devotes millions of dollars to the protection and preservation of polar bears and the arctic environment.[67]
- Patagonia expresses concern for the environment and pays more for goose down that is harvested in ways that protects "sound animal welfare."[68]
- The Body Shop processes cosmetics in ways that protect animal life.[69]

[65] See Antonio Argandoña and Heidi von Weltzien Hoivik, *Corporate Social Responsibility: One Size Does Not Fit All. Collecting Evidence from Europe*, 89 *Journal of Business Ethics* 221 at 225. "[S]ociety can act as a wake-up call to the conscience of the owners, managers, and employees, confronting them with the firm's responsibilities. "

[66] *Ibid.* at 230. "Companies cannot disregard them: even when they say that their only goal is maximizing profits, they are formulating a statement about their responsibility toward stakeholders and society, though very limited. CSR is an integral part of a firm's strategy and its competitiveness and must continue to be highly diversified, even firm specific, in order to be successful."; Joshua Daniel Margolis and James Patrick Walsh, People and Profits?: the search for a link between a company's social and financial performance 8–10 (2001).

[67] *WWF and the Coca Cola Company Team Up to Protect Polar Bears*, World Wildlife Foundation, accessed 28 April, 2016, http://worldwildlife.org/projects/wwf-and-the-coca-cola-company-team-up-to-protect-polar-bears. "In addition to our freshwater conservation efforts, WWF and the Coca-Cola Company joined forces to help protect the polar bear and its habitat. Building upon Coca-Cola's Support since 2007 of WWF's polar bear conservation efforts, we launched the Arctic Home Campaign in North American during the 2011 holiday season to raise widespread awareness and funds for these efforts."

[68] Press Release, *Patagonia Announces Move to 100% Traceable Down*, Patagonia (November 6, 2013), http://www.prnewswire.com/news-releases/patagonia-announces-move-to-100-traceable-down-230851261.html. "Patagonia Inc., the outdoor apparel company, is proud to announce the company's move to 100% Traceable Down across its entire collection of down-insulated products, starting in the Fall 2014 season. Patagonia Traceable Down is sourced from birds that have been neither force-fed for *foi gras* production nor plucked for their feathers and down during their lifetime. Six years in the making, Patagonia's Traceable Down standard provides a robust assurance of sound animal welfare."

[69] The Body Shop, *Animal Protection Principles*, http://www.bodyshopinfo.com/assets/aat_principles.pdf (last visited May 6, 2014). "The Body Shop believes that no animals should be harmed for the purposes of producing cosmetic and toiletry products. Against animal testing. We are opposed to the use of animal testing for cosmetics purposes and have taken an active

- Ben and Jerry's promotes a variety of liberal social causes such as fair trade, which it says "is about making sure people get their fair share of the pie. The whole concept of fair trade goes to the heart of our values and the sense of right and wrong. Nobody wants to buy something that was made by exploiting somebody else."[70]

The list could go on and on. It is not that all of these companies have to prioritize the same social values. But as a society and through our legal system, we encourage them to act in socially responsible ways, and reward them for doing so.

Efforts to encourage social responsibility take place at the international, national, and local level, both by government and non-government entities. For example, as the ICLRS brief put it, "the United Nations encourages corporate conscience through the UN Global Compact, particularly in the areas of human rights, labor, the environment, and anti-corruption."[71] The Compact's first two principles call upon businesses to "respect the protection of internationally proclaimed human rights" and "make sure that they are not complicit in human rights abuses."[72] International non-government organizations such as the International Organization for Standardization (ISO) create definitive international business management standards, which explain that corporate social conscience is an integral part of business.[73]

Corporate conscience is a standard feature of transnational corporations. In its annual international survey of corporate social responsibility, KPMG noted

role in changing legislation, inspiring industry practice, and supporting research for alternatives. We will continue to lead the way by demonstrating the highest monitoring standards and clear customer communications. We do not test our cosmetic products or ingredients on animals, nor will we commission others to do so. We never have and we never will. We will lead by example, showing that innovative products, consumer safety and animal protection can go hand in hand."

[70] Ben And Jerry's, "Our Values" (last visited May 1, 2014), www.benjerry.com/values/. "Our Social Mission compels us to use our Company in innovative ways to make the world a better place," seeking to "improve the quality of life locally, nationally and internationally." The company strives to "minimize our negative impact on the environment," to "show a deep respect for human beings inside and outside our company," to "seek and support nonviolent ways to achieve peace and justice," to "create economic opportunities for those who have been denied them and to advance new models of economic justice that are sustainable and replicable," and "support sustainable and safe methods of food production that reduce environmental degradation, maintain the productivity of the land over time, and support the economic viability of family farms and rural communities."

[71] Brief of 9 Academic Institutions and 27 Comparative Law and Religion Scholars in Support of Hobby Lobby and Conestoga Wood, Sebelius *v.* Hobby Lobby Stores, Inc., 2014 WL 334444 (U.S.) 26.

[72] See *Ibid.*, citing UNITED NATIONS, *The Ten Principles*, available at www.unglobalcompact.org/what-is-gc/mission/principles.

[73] *Ibid.* at 27, citing Int'l Org. for Standardization, Discovering ISO 26000 (2010), 2; Schematic Overview of ISO 2600, available at www.iso.org/iso/discovering_iso_26000.pdf; see also lists of codes at www.business-humanrights.org/Categories/Principles.

that 93% of the 250 largest companies in the world report on their corporate responsibility activities. Of the 100 largest companies in 34 countries, 71% of publicly traded companies conduct corporate social responsibility reporting. In the United States, 86% of companies report on corporate responsibility.[74]

1. Charitable activities and contributions

As argued in the ICLRS Brief,

> In the United States, virtually all states have permissive statutes that allow corporations to give to charity even when this does not benefit the corporation. Even prior to the existence of state corporate philanthropy laws, the New Jersey Supreme Court rejected a shareholder's suit challenging a company's decision to donate to Princeton University, reasoning that as the nation's wealth has shifted into corporate hands, citizens have reasonably "turned to corporations to assume the modern obligations of good citizenship in the same manner as humans do."[75]

2. Tax exemptions

The ICLRS brief also discussed tax exemptions as an example of conscience. "The US federal government also fosters corporate conscience: corporations may deduct up to 10% of their taxable income for charitable contributions, and do not require a business purpose for the contribution. It has established numerous programs that permit for-profit organizations to obtain federal grants for charitable activities."[76]

To put it starkly: There is something unsettling (perhaps pernicious) in the reality that corporations should be encouraged to act conscientiously with respect to the protection of sea life, but are ridiculed as being out of bounds when their conscience is the religiously-motivated protection of human life.

It is important to note that if you are an employee of these businesses, you have no choice whether corporate profits will be used to pay you more or to support environmental or social causes with which you may disagree; if you are a customer of these businesses, you have no choice whether the dollar you spend on ice cream or shampoo will be used in part to support social or political causes with which you may disagree. Of course, you can work elsewhere, or buy a different brand of ice cream or shampoo, but these options are not viewed as providing an adequate reason for allowing Hobby Lobby to exercise its sense of corporate responsibility by not subsidizing what it views as morally intolerable.[77]

[74] *Ibid.* at 28, citing KPMG, KPMG International Survey Of Corporate Responsibility Reporting 2013, 10.

[75] *Ibid.* at 32, citing A.P. Smith Mfg. Co. *v.* Barlow, 13 N.J. 145, 98 A.2d 581 (1953).

[76] *Ibid.* at 32–33, citing examples.

[77] Brief for Petitioner Kathleen Sebelius at 57. "Congress set certain minimum, privately-enforceable standards for those private plans in order to advance the statute's public-health and employee- and policy-holder-protection goals."

In contemporary America we find ourselves perilously close to a conventional wisdom that views certain forms of conscience as something to be respected when exercised by corporations, but religiously-motivated conscience is derided as not just illegitimate but nonsensical. The hypocrisy is barely noticed.

D. Hobby Lobby seeks an exemption (unlike CVS and Apple)

Perhaps I will be accused of ignoring an important distinction. A defender of CVS – or Apple or Patagonia or Ben and Jerry's – might argue that these situations are very different, since Hobby Lobby is seeking an exemption from a federal law, whereas these other companies are simply exercising corporate conscience within existing laws.

But this distinction is a little too convenient, for several reasons. The first is that Apple and CVS do not need to seek an exemption, because (unlike Hobby Lobby) the Obama Administration, sympathetic to their causes, has not adopted regulations seeking to force them to act contrary to their conscience.

More importantly, whenever a corporation acts in ways that do not seek to maximize shareholder profit, in a very real sense they are taking advantage of an exception to the general rule that corporations exist to make money for their owners.

Recall that in the Hobby Lobby case, the government took the position that Hobby Lobby should stick to making money and not concern itself with unborn human life.[78] The government took the position that it is wrong to consider Hobby Lobby as an entity that can exercise conscience, since it is a corporation with a legal existence separate from their owners. They further argued that the owners' free exercise interests were not implicated because it is just the business, and not the owners qua owners, that was subject to the contraceptive mandate.[79]

The government's position in Hobby Lobby was sweeping – it was that a corporation is not a person with conscientious interests, that it should be concerned with making money rather than matters of conscience, and that the interests of owners are divorced from those of the corporation because of the separate legal status of the corporation. But if this is true, then it should be no

[78] *Ibid.* at 33. "Likewise, a proffered burden may be deemed not substantial in cases where the nature of applicable legal regimes and societal expectations necessarily impose objective outer limits on when an individual can insist on modification of, or heightened justifications for, governmental programs that may offend his beliefs. Under these principles, respondents have not alleged a substantial burden as a matter of law."

[79] *Ibid.* at 27. "Federal law does not require the Greens to provide health insurance, particular health benefits, or any other form of compensation to the corporations' employees. The Greens do not personally employ the 13,000 individuals who work for Hobby Lobby; the corporation does."

less true for these other companies – like CVS or Apple – that pursue other conscience-based policies.

To say Hobby Lobby is a "person" under RFRA, to say corporations can operate as "good citizens" and shoulder social responsibility, to say business owners can be expected to be respectful of human rights and other important social values, does not mean they will win a claim for an exemption from general and neutral laws. Rather it means that if their free exercise interests are substantially burdened, then the government needs to show that it has a compelling state interest in imposing the burden and that there is no less restrictive means of accomplishing that interest.

Perhaps the reason the government was so eager to deny that Hobby Lobby had free exercise interests at all was because it realized that arguments for the existence of a compelling government interest justifying the contraceptive mandate and claiming that the contraceptive mandate is the least restrictive means of accomplishing that interest, were exceptionally weak.

Let me try to explain.

1. *Experiencing a free exercise burden does not create an entitlement to an exemption*

If Hobby Lobby (or the Greens) had suffered a substantial burden of their free exercise rights, this would trigger balancing under the compelling state interest test. Under this standard, the government can justify the burden by showing that it was necessitated by a weighty interest, and that there was no less restrictive a means of achieving that interest.[80]

A. COMPELLING STATE INTEREST The argument that there was a compelling state interest justifying the contraceptive mandate is weak. By its terms, the mandate does not apply to employers with fifty or fewer employees, which means it does not apply to approximately 90% of employers and about 50% of all employees.[81] In addition, in February 2014, Obama announced that he

[80] There is a wide consensus that the religious party does not automatically win under the "strict scrutiny" standard. For example, many civil rights laws are thought to be narrowly tailored to meet a compelling government interest. See, e.g., Douglas Laycock, *Imaginary Contradictions: A Reply to Professor Oleske*, 67 VAND. L. REV. EN BANC 89 (2014).

[81] WHITE HOUSE, *The Affordable Care Act Increases Choice and Saving Money for Small Businesses*, available at www.whitehouse.gov/files/documents/health_reform_for_small_businesses.pdf, (last visited May 3, 2014). "The law specifically exempts all firms that have fewer than 50 employees – 96 percent of all firms in the United States or 5.8 million out of 6 million total firms – from any employer responsibility requirements. These 5.8 million firms employ nearly 34 million workers. More than 96 percent of firms with 50 or more employees already offer health insurance to their workers. Less than 0.2 percent of all firms (about 10,000 out of 6 million) may face employer responsibility requirements. Many firms that do not currently offer coverage will be more likely to do so because of lower premiums and wider choices in the Exchange."

would delay the implementation of Obamacare for employers with between 50 and 100 employees for another year, until 2016.[82] If the mandate satisfied a compelling interest, why did the government allow so many exceptions?[83] It is odd to claim that there is a state interest so strong that we must force Hobby Lobby to offer these services in violation of sincerely and strongly held religious beliefs, when there is not enough of a compelling state interest to apply this law to 90% of all employers. Instead of being a compelling interest, the contraception mandate seems primarily to be a cost-shifting mechanism, moving the expense of providing contraceptives from individuals and the government to private businesses.[84]

The Court sidesteps this issue, concluding, "We find it unnecessary" to adjudicate the question of compelling interest, since it was clear that the government had not adopted the least restrictive means of furthering that interest.[85]

B. LEAST RESTRICTIVE MEANS The argument that there is no less restrictive means of accomplishing the government's interest would appear to be even weaker, since there are a wide range of alternative ways the government could provide contraceptives to women who work at the small handful of companies that object to providing contraceptive or abortifacient drugs.[86]

- For example, the government could provide contraceptives to these employees through public clinics, or programs such as Planned Parenthood that

[82] Alex Wayne, *Small Businesses Get Further Delay for Obamacare Coverage*, BLOOMBERG (February 11, 2014), www.bloomberg.com/news/2014-02-10/small-businesses-get-further-delay-for-obamacare-coverage.html.

[83] See Brief for National Association of Evangelicals, *Sebelius* v. *Hobby Lobby Stores, Inc.*, 2014 WL 325703 (U.S.), 20 (U.S., 2014). "Second, the cost of emergency contraception is not large. And until January 1, 2013, there was no Federal entitlement vested in the employees to have preventive reproductive health care including emergency contraception. It makes no sense to claim that something that did not exist until January 1, 2013, is suddenly compelling. Common sense tells us it is not." Indeed, Congress intended to give latitude to the Department of Health and Human Services to provide an exemption. See Brief for Petitioner, *Conestoga Wood Specialties Corp.* v. *Sebelius*, 2014 WL 173487 (U.S.), 44 (U.S., 2014). "Through the 'comprehensive' authority Congress gave Respondents to create religious exemptions, churches and their integrated auxiliaries are exempt from the Mandate's scope."

[84] See Brief for National Association of Evangelicals, *Sebelius* v. *Hobby Lobby Stores, Inc.*, 2014 WL 325703 (U.S.), 20 (U.S., 2014), heading titled "There Is No Compelling Interest in Preventing the Cost of Contraceptives from Being Shifted to Employees."

[85] Slip op at 40.

[86] If the government could reasonably set up a program that would rectify a liberty infringement, the infringement is not the "least restrictive means" of accomplishing a compelling government interest. *United States* v. *Alvarez*, 132 S. Ct. 2537, 2551 (2012) (plurality opinion). "[H]owever, at least one less speech-restrictive means by which the Government could likely protect the integrity of the military awards system. A Government-created database could list Congressional Medal of Honor winners. Were a database accessible through the Internet, it would be easy to verify and expose false claims."

receive large amounts of government funding.[87] For those who do not live near a clinic, internet-based systems and mail delivery could be used.
- Or the government could provide a tax credit to women who work for employers with religious objections to providing the drugs in question.[88] They could make the certification themselves, and it could be checked in the way that other fraudulent claims are checked by the IRS.
- Or the government could provide such employees vouchers that they could use to obtain contraceptives.[89]
- Or the government could reimburse pharmacies that provide contraceptives to people who work for employers who have a religious objection to providing coverage.[90]

The Court concluded that HHS has not demonstrated that it has utilized the least restrictive means for accomplishing the government's interest, because "HHS itself has demonstrated that it has at its disposal an approach that is less restrictive than requiring employers to fund contraceptive methods that violate their religious beliefs."[91] The Court noted that HHS "has already established an accommodation for nonprofit organizations with religious objections."[92]

What I am suggesting is that the reason the government took such an absolute stand against the idea that Hobby Lobby had any free exercise interests was because the arguments that there is a compelling state interest behind the contraceptive mandate and that it represents the least restrictive means are so weak. The government's best option was to try to head the religious freedom claim off at the pass, denying that corporations have any rights or interests relating to religion at all. The problem is that this is directly contradicted by the government's own behavior, encouraging companies to act conscientiously

[87] See, e.g., 42 C.F.R. § 59.5(a)(1), authorizing grants to "[p]rovide a broad range of acceptable and effective medically approved family planning methods … and services" through Title X of the Public Health Service Act.

[88] See Brief of the Knights of Columbus, *Sebelius* v. *Hobby Lobby Stores, Inc.*, 2014 WL 333883 (U.S.) 25 n.4 (U.S., 2014), "Given the breadth of the government's authority to tax and spend and its existing vast involvement in the provision of health care services, the government could just as easily address its interests through social welfare programs, the provision of tax credits, and so forth." (citation omitted).

[89] A voucher is a set of funding which is designed to replace the money given to an organization and instead to give it to the individual (or, perhaps more common, the individual's designee) in order to fund a desired service in a different way. For example, parents can receive a voucher to go towards tuition for a charter school for their children, and the public school where the child would normally go would not get the corresponding funding normally associated with that child.

[90] See *Korte* v. *Sebelius*, 735 F.3d 654, 686 (7th Cir. 2013). "The government can provide a 'public option' for contraception insurance; it can give tax incentives to contraception suppliers to provide these medications and services at no cost to consumers; it can give tax incentives to consumers of contraception and sterilization services. No doubt there are other options."

[91] Slip op. at 43.

[92] *Ibid.*

and praising them for doing so when their values reflect the government's own priorities.

III. WHY ARE WE HERE?

In the remainder of this chapter, I will briefly survey what I perceive to be four underlying causes of our inconsistent attitudes towards corporate conscience. These are first, the concept of public reason, which has come to dominate our thinking about public discourse; second, the conceit of general and neutral laws and the idea that such provisions are sufficient to protect religious freedom; third, changing views about religion as a social institution; and fourth, our habit of thinking of vindicating religious freedom as a matter of granting an exemption. I will then conclude with three modest suggestions of ways to correct or bring greater balance to our thinking about corporate conscience.

A. Public reason and conscience

A broader context helps us reflect better upon the status of claims of conscience in our public discourse. I believe we are at a moment of crisis for the idea of conscience. To a significant extent this can be traced to philosophical debates about public reason as a model for legitimate public discourse.

Public reason theorists – whether John Rawls, Immanuel Kant, or Thomas Hobbes – all begin the same way: distinguishing between public reason (which they view as being politically and morally legitimate) and private reason (which is politically and perhaps morally illegitimate).[93] Public reason theorists argue that in the public forum, public reason is acceptable and this is reason which should appeal to any rational person regardless of their deep philosophical or religious commitments. Private reason, in contrast, is an unacceptable form of discourse in the public realm.[94]

There is something appealing about public reason, in that it encourages us to speak to each other in mutually meaningful ways, to seek common principles

[93] Rawls, POLITICAL LIBERALISM (2d ed. 2013); THOMAS HOBBES, LEVIATHAN, ch. XIII; IMMANUEL KANT, WHAT IS ENLIGHTENMENT? (1787).

[94] RAWLS, POLITICAL LIBERALISM,at 213–47. See, *e.g.*, *ibid.* at 223–24: "It is essential that a liberal political conception include, besides its principles of justice, guidelines of inquiry that specify ways of reasoning and criteria for the kinds of information relevant for political questions. Without such guidelines, substantive principles cannot be applied and this leaves the political conception incomplete and fragmentary." and *Ibid.* at 236: "The [Supreme Court] justices cannot, of course, invoke their own personal morality, nor the ideas and virtues of morality generally. Those they must view as irrelevant. Equally, they cannot invoke their or other people's religious or philosophical views. Nor can they cite political values without restriction. Rather, they must appeal to the political values they think belong to the most reasonable understanding of the public conception and its political values of justice and public reason."

that everyone can accept, and to not impose our own personal and religious views on others.[95]

What does this have to do with conscience? Conscience is a prototypical private reason. Often it is not even accurate to characterize it as an argument. When conscience speaks to us, the metaphors we use are things like "inner light,"[96] "still small voice,"[97] "having a feeling,"[98] or "whisperings."[99] However, the dictates of conscience, which sometimes come to us and are felt quite powerfully, are not necessarily things we articulate through public reason and they are not necessarily things that we wish to impose on others. But we do want to be able to live our lives in peace and safety and with enough space where our private convictions of conscience can be lived and respected.[100]

Claims of conscience are by their nature often private rather than public. When Martin Luther stood before Emperor Charles V's Diet of Worms in 1521, Luther is reported to have said: "... my conscience is captive to the Word of God. Thus I cannot and will not recant, because acting against one's conscience is neither safe nor sound. God help me. Amen."[101] In some accounts, Luther is attributed with the famous words, "I cannot do otherwise, here I stand, may God help me."[102] Whether he uttered precisely those words or not, the implication is clear. Luther believed his views were based upon a correct interpretation of scripture, which he viewed as being more authoritative than the word of the Pope or the Church's councils (that day's equivalent of public reason).

The point is that since claims of conscience are by their very nature often private, by definition they are illegitimate in the eyes of public reason. As public reason comes to dominate our way of thinking about acceptable public discourse, conscience is imperiled.

95 Public reason creates an environment where in a pluralistic society, there can be clear communications about public issues. Non-religious reasons for opposing abortion, for instance, have proved a powerful influence on the debate on abortion. Proposed ultrasound laws focus on the nature of the fetus' growth. While offensive to some, showing a mother a picture of her womb and child is hardly religious in nature. Thus, public reason can provide an incentive to focus on the best arguments outside of religion.

96 *Cf.* John 8:12. "Then spake Jesus again unto them, saying, I am the light of the world: he that followeth me shall not walk in darkness, but shall have the light of life."

97 1 Kings 19:12.

98 See 1 Nephi 17:45 (Latter-day Saint scripture). People deprived of conscience were "past feeling."

99 This metaphor is used in many different faiths. See, e.g., Marcie Mcnuitt WHISPERINGS OF THE SPIRIT (2010); Helaman 5:46 (Latter-day Saint scripture).

100 See, e.g., YANN MARTEL, THE LIFE OF PI 297 (2001). "Love is hard to believe, ask any lover. Life is hard to believe, ask any scientist. God is hard to believe, ask any believer. What's your problem with hard to believe?" See also *Ibid.* at 298. "Reason is the very best tool kit.... But be excessively reasonable and you risk throwing out the universe with the bathwater."

101 Michael G. Baylor, *Action and Person: Conscience in Late Scholasticism and the Young Luther*, in 20 *STUDIES IN MEDIEVAL AND REFORMATION THOUGHT* 1, 1 (Heiko A. Oberman et al. eds., 1977).

102 *Ibid.*

1. Hobbes

In understanding the trajectory of the role of public reason in political discourse, and the prospects for claims of conscience surviving in a political culture in which public reason is the dominant conception of acceptable political and legal reasoning, it is helpful to understand something about the genesis of the idea of public reason and the stark clarity with which its implications for conscience were originally understood.

The concept of public reason was not invented by Rawls, or even Immanuel Kant (to whom it is often traced).[103] It was Thomas Hobbes, writing a hundred years before Kant, in *Leviathan*, who introduced the idea, albeit in a form that might make contemporary liberals shudder. As Kant did a century later, public reason was contrasted by Hobbes with "private reason," which was identified with claims of conscience. For Hobbes, public reason was the will of the sovereign (and nothing more); it was the reason given by the King or Parliament (representing the public), as opposed to reasons given by subjects (private reasons). In Hobbes's understanding of the justification of the state, in agreeing to be subject to the absolute sovereign, subjects exercised their will to have their "private judgments" substituted by the sovereign's "public judgments."[104]

In Hobbes's understanding of the state, individuals agreed to be governed by the sovereign as a way of escaping the state of nature (the "war of all against all"), where life, in his memorable description, is "solitary, poor, nasty, brutish, and short."[105] Following the dictates of the omnicompetent sovereign, for Hobbes, vindicated conscience, since the individual had already consented to submit to political authority.[106] Thus, Hobbes insisted that "people who made

[103] Rawls traces the lineage of the idea of public reason to Kant, noting that the idea "is suggested by Kant's distinction between public and private reason in WHAT IS ENLIGHTENMENT? (1784), although his distinction is different from the one used here." POLITICAL LIBERALISM, at 213 n. 2. Rawls also cites the contemporary Kantian, Onora O'Neill. *Ibid.*

[104] See THOMAS HOBBES, LEVIATHAN, ch. XIII. "And reason suggesteth convenient articles of peace upon which men may be drawn to agreement."

[105] *Ibid.* Hobbes argues that even those who don't consent to be ruled by the sovereign are under obligation to be so ruled, due to the consent of the majority.

> "Because the major part has by consenting voices declared a sovereign, he that dissented must now consent with the rest – that is, be contented to avow all the actions he shall do – or lese justly be destroyed by the rest. For if he voluntarily entered into the congregation of them that were assembled, he sufficiently declared thereby his will, and therefore tacitly covenanted, to stand to what the major part should ordain; and therefore, if he refuse to stand thereto or make protestation against any of their decrees, he does contrary to his covenant, and therefore unjustly. And whether he be of the congregation or not, and whether his consent be asked or not, he must either submit to their decrees or be left in the condition of war he was in before, wherein he might without injustice be destroyed by any man whatsoever." *Ibid.*t ch. XVIII.

[106] Columbia University Professor Herbert W. Schneider, in his introduction to LEVIATHAN describes Hobbes's "representative theory of absolute authority" as follows: "Hobbes's myth of 'Leviathan,' of the artificial creation of a social organism or collective person, is his way of escaping the traditional assumption that authority always comes from above. According to this theory, an authority is an agent or person authorized, the legal bearer of another's person.

conscientious objections to the king's laws were in fact disobeying their own conscience, since they had agreed to take his judgment and law ('the public conscience') as their own."[107]

As Professor Bryan Garsten explains, "a person who followed the laws in a Hobbesian commonwealth was by definition acting according to the dictates of conscience, since he had transferred the right of determining 'the public conscience' to the sovereign: [in the words of Hobbes,] 'The law is the public Conscience.'"[108] As Hobbes put it:

> The conscience being nothing else but a man's settled judgment and opinion, when he hath once transferred his right of judging to another, that which shall be commanded, is no less his judgment, than the judgment of that other; so that in obedience to laws, a man doth still according to his conscience, but not his private conscience. And whatsoever is done contrary to private conscience, is then a sin, when the laws have left him to his own liberty, and never else.[109]

For Hobbes, it was no sin to act contrary to conscience, provided this was at the direction of the sovereign. Ceding conscience to the sovereign in matters of public importance also shields individuals from the preaching and prophesizing of those who claim to speak on behalf of God.

As Garsten explains in his masterful book, *Saving Persuasion: A Defense of Rhetoric and Judgment*:

> We have seen that when Hobbes devised his understanding of representation, he was asking citizens to disregard not only their own judgments and dictates of conscience but also, and perhaps more importantly, those judgments supplied to them by preachers and prophesiers. He asked citizens to protect themselves from the influence of these orators by chaining their ears to the lips of the sovereign, whose words he called the 'public conscience' and, in Chapter 37 of Leviathan, the 'public reason.' For the sake of peace,

The unity of a commonwealth is created when a group of men covenant to appoint a single 'body' or will as the common bearer of the person of each. Thus a government becomes the representative or authoritative person of all the members of the 'body politic' and in virtue of having such unity of authorized will or person the commonwealth establishes sovereignty." LEVIATHAN, Editor's Introduction at xii (Bobbs Merrill, 1958). A social contract substitute for understanding sovereignty as divine right, "it was his attempt to justify absolutism by 'natural justice.'" *Ibid.*

107 BRYAN GARSTEN, SAVING PERSUASION: A DEFENSE OF RHETORIC AND JUDGMENT (2009), 180. Hobbes does favor some protection for conscience, by distinguishing sharply between beliefs and actions, and saying that the sovereign's laws should govern (with limited exceptions) actions and not beliefs. He traces to Aristotle, Cicero and other heathens the mistake of

> extend[ing] the power of the law, which is the rule of actions only, to the very thoughts and consciences of men by examination and *inquisition* of what they hold, notwithstanding the conformity of their speech and actions. By which men are either punished for answering the truth of their thoughts or constrained to answer an untruth for fear of punishment. HOBBES, LEVIATHAN, at Sec. 17.

108 Garsten, at 43.

109 *Ibid.*, n. 75.

he argued, 'the Private Reason must submit to the Publique.' Public reason was thus created as a means of avoiding controversy by providing an external source of unified judgment. It sought to avoid the political tumult that resulted when each citizen was left to judge for himself and thus made prey to the influence of orators.[110]

2. *Rawls*

We would expect a Rawlsian liberal to object strongly to their understanding of public reason being linked with Hobbes's sovereign Leviathan. Indeed, Rawls expressly denies that "aristocratic and autocratic regimes" exhibit public reason, because in such regimes it is "rulers" that consider the public good, if it is considered at all.[111] Declares Rawls,

> Public reason is characteristic of a democratic people: it is the reason of its citizens, of those sharing the status of equal citizenship. The subject of their reason is the good of the public: what the political conception of justice requires of society's base structure of institutions, and the purposes and ends they are to serve.[112]

It is not that Rawls's and Hobbes's conceptions of public reason are the same; it is rather that they share an important structural similarity. In a Rawlsian world, public reason is no longer identified with the will of the sovereign (whom Hobbes says rational people – out of fear, hope, and reason – will have agreed to obey).[113] Rather, public reason is identified with the will of properly enlightened democratic majorities who are governed by correct principles of public reason (in other words, of good liberals striving to achieve the public good in a properly structured democracy).

But for the conscientious objector, the result is precisely the same: their claims of conscience are illegitimate, at least to the extent their claims rely upon "private" reasons (including comprehensive conceptions of the good, such as religious conceptions) rather than "public" reasons.

A. RAWLS ON CONSCIENCE So what does Rawls have to say about conscience? In his chapter on public reason, Rawls discusses liberty of conscience, but primarily as a protection of individuals from overbearing churches. Says Rawls,

> In a democratic society nonpublic power, as seen, for example, in the authority of churches over their members, is freely accepted. In the case of ecclesiastical power, since apostasy and heresy are not legal offenses, those who are no longer able to recognize a church's authority may cease being members without running afoul of state power.[114]

[110] GARSTEN, SAVING PERSUASION, at 177.
[111] RAWLS, POLITICAL LIBERALISM, at 213.
[112] *Ibid.*
[113] HOBBES, LEVIATHAN, at ch. XIII.
[114] RAWLS, POLITICAL LIBERALISM, at 221.

Thus, liberty of conscience protects individuals from churches; the state does not lend its authority to the punishment of apostasy or heresy. As Rawls explains in a footnote, "In this case we think of liberty of conscience as protecting the individual against the church."[115]

But for Rawls, there are no analogous rights of freedom of conscience from the authority of the state short of renouncing one's citizenship. As Rawls explains, in contrast with religious groups, where you can evade the institution's authority, by withdrawing, "the government's authority cannot be evaded except by leaving the territory over which it governs, and not always then."[116] Read that again; this is breathtaking.

According to Rawls, if the state insists on forcing us to act in violation of our conscience, we really have only one option – we can emigrate (and even that may not put us beyond the reach of the state's jurisdiction).

We do not, says Rawls, accept the government's authority in the same way we accept the authority of a church. "Nevertheless, we may over the course of life come freely to accept, as the outcome of reflective thought and reasoned judgment, the ideals, principles, and standards that specify our basic rights and liberties, and effectively guide and moderate the political power to which we are subject."[117] In other words, not unlike Hobbes's subject, a citizen in a Rawlsian liberal state, may come to accept the dictates of public reason as something they "freely accept."

3. *The Public Reason Two-Step*

Consider the basic form of reasoning that might fail to protect conscience: first, coercive legislation should be based upon public reasons; second, private reasons (such as religious convictions) do not count as public reasons and can therefore be discounted. This is what we might call the "public reason two-step."

Where does a strong commitment to public reason lead? If I am right, then we have reason to worry that it may lead to the Liberal Leviathan – the tyranny not of Hobbes's imperial sovereign, but the tyranny of imperious majorities (or

[115] *Ibid.*, n. 8. Rawls goes on to explain, "This is an example of the protection that basic rights and liberties secure for individuals generally. But equally, liberty of conscience and other liberties such as freedom of association protect churches from the intrusions of government and from other powerful associations. Both associations and individuals need protection, and so do families need protection from associations and government, as do the individual members of families from other family members (wives from their husbands, children from their parents). It is incorrect to say that liberalism focuses solely on the rights of individuals; rather, the rights it recognizes are to protect associations, smaller groups, and individuals, all from one another in an appropriate balance specified by its guiding principles of justice."

[116] Rawls, Political Liberalism, at 222.

[117] Rawls, Political Liberalism, at 222. This is not so unlike Hobbes's argument about why we accept the will of the sovereign (public reason) as having priority over our own personal judgments of right and wrong (private reason). For Rawls, if we belong to a liberal political community, we will accept its judgments as binding on us.

perhaps overbearing judges),[118] confident (even self-righteous) in the reasonableness of their own views, and with every reason (in their minds) to disparage and disregard claims of conscience by those who would dissent – such claims of conscience being ipso facto "unreasonable" because they do not satisfy the conditions of public reason.

B. General and neutral laws

This leads to a second feature of our predicament. The goal of public reason is general and neutral laws – but as we have seen from the flag salute cases,[119] to the prohibition of wearing yarmulkes in the military,[120] to the prohibition of religious use of the hallucinogenic drug peyote by the Native American Church,[121] general and neutral laws need not give weight to claims of conscience.

When Justice Scalia said in *Employment Division* v. *Smith*[122] that the Free Exercise Clause only requires that laws that burden religion be general and neutral, the analytical spotlight is trained only on the government's reasons and behavior; claims of conscience are not merely outweighed, they are given no weight whatsoever.

Similarly, the government in the contraceptive mandate case argued that the contraceptive mandate was a general and neutral law.[123] As such, according to the view of Secretary Sebelius and the Obama administration, the religious claims of Hobby Lobby did not need to be considered at all. They are not just outweighed, they are given no weight whatsoever.

118 Justice Scalia begins his dissent in Windsor (the Defense of Marriage Act case) with a withering critique of judicial arrogance and power-mongering. "This case is about power in several respects. It is about the power of our people to govern themselves, and the power of this Court to pronounce the law. Today's opinion aggrandizes the latter, with the predictable consequence of diminishing the former. We have no power to decide this case. And even if we did, we have no power under the Constitution to invalidate this democratically adopted legislation. The court's errors on both points springs for from the same diseased root: an exalted conception of the role of this institution [the Supreme Court] in America." *United States* v. *Windsor*, 133 S. Ct. 2675, 2698 (2013) (Scalia, J., dissenting).

119 When first asked to rule on whether it was unconstitutional to require Jehovah's Witnesses to salute the flag, the Court ruled that requirement was constitutional. *Minersville Sch. Dist.* v. *Gobitis*, 310 U.S. 586 (1940). However, the ruling was overturned just three years later: *W. Virginia State Bd. of Educ.* v. *Barnette*, 319 U.S. 624, 63 S. Ct. 1178, 87 L. Ed. 1628 (1943).

120 The Supreme Court ruled the opposite in *Goldman* v. *Weinberger*, 475 U.S. 503 (1986). However, Congress overruled the ruling by creating a statutory exemption. See 10 U.S.C. § 774 (2012).

121 *Employment Div., Dep't of Human Res. of Oregon* v. *Smith*, 494 U.S. 872 (1990).

122 *Ibid.*

123 See Brief for Kathleen Sebelius, *Conestoga Wood Specialties Corporation* v. *Sebelius*, 2014 WL 546900 (U.S.), 15 (U.S.,2014) (Conestaga Wood is a case argued in parallel with Hobby Lobby, focusing on the Free Exercise Clause arguments).

If free exercise is not violated whenever religion is burdened by general and neutral laws, the protection of free exercise approaches the vanishing point. Not only can the HHS mandate be characterized as a general and neutral law, so could a law requiring all company health care plans to pay for abortions, or to pay for assisted suicide.[124]

C. Status of religion

A third cause of our fractured attitudes towards corporate conscience can be traced to changing attitudes about religion as a social institution. When he was president of the University of Utah, in April 2011 Michael Young gave a speech at the LDS International Society at a Management Society conference at Brigham Young University.[125] In that address, President Young identified a spectrum of social attitudes concerning religion, and expressed concern that views in the United States are drifting disconcertingly along this spectrum.

1. Religion is good

At one end of the spectrum is the idea that "religion is unique, good, important, or even necessary in a just society."[126] This is the view that was often expressed at the time of the founding and is exemplified by President George Washington's farewell address.[127] It is the view codified in the First Amendment, which does treat religion as something that deserves special recognition and protection.[128]

2. Religion is ordinary: equally good

Next along the spectrum is the view that "religion is actually not special. These arguments do not deny the goodness of religion, but they claim religions do not hold a monopoly on virtuous conduct, and that is absolutely true. They go on

[124] See Transcript of Oral Argument, *Sebelius*, v. *Hobby Lobby*; and *Conestoga Wood* v. *Sebelius*, 2014 WL 1219115 (U.S.), 75 (U.S.Oral.Arg., 2014).

[125] Michael K. Young, *Erosion of Religious Freedom: Impact on Churches*, in THE INTERNATIONAL SOCIETY: 22ND ANNUAL CONFERENCE 2, (April 4, 2011), http://ldsinternationalsociety.org/wp-content/uploads/2014/10/22nd.pdf.

[126] *Ibid.* at 4.

[127] Washington's farewell address said: "Of all the dispositions and habits which lead to political prosperity, religion and morality are indispensable supports. In vain would that man claim the tribute of patriotism, who should labor to subvert these great pillars of human happiness, these firmest props of the duties of men and citizens.... And let us with caution indulge the supposition that morality can be maintained without religion. Whatever may be conceded to the influence of refined education on minds of peculiar structure, reason and experience both forbid us to expect that national morality can prevail in exclusion of religious principle."

[128] U.S. Const., amend. I: "Congress shall make no law respecting an establishment of religion, or prohibiting the free exercise thereof". But see also Mark V. Tushnet, *Questioning the Value of Accommodating Religion*, in Stephen L. Feldman, LAW AND RELIGION: A CRITICAL ANTHOLOGY 249–50 (claiming that providing religious accommodations in and of themselves threaten religion); BRIAN LEITER, WHY TOLERATE RELIGION? (2012).

to say that, therefore, all good and moral organizations should be recognized and treated equal."[129] In this view, religions are like other good organizations such as the Humane Society and Mothers Against Drunk Driving. "There is a moral equivalency and an institutional equivalency between all these, and religions really deserve no more protection than those organizations deserve, no less but no more."[130]

3. *Religion is a private affair*

Next is the view that religion is a private affair "and should be entirely excluded from the public square."[131] The underlying idea here is that religious fervor can produce dangerous results.[132] Religious people, in this view, should stick to helping victims of hurricanes and stay out of politics.[133] This is an important shift, "because it suggests that religions and religious-motivated dialogue and religious-moved people not only do not deserve special treatment, but they should be disadvantaged in the public square. They normally should not have a favored place in our constitutional order, but they should not even be afforded the free speech protections every other citizen in our nation is guaranteed."[134]

4. *Religion as suspect or harmful*

Further along the spectrum is the view that "religion has a negative impact on society."[135] This view is very suspicious of religion in the public sphere. As one law professor put it, "Religious participation in the political process can produce dangerous results: fervent beliefs fueled by suppressed fear are easily transformed into movements of intolerance, repression, hate, and persecution. There are, in short, substantial reasons for exercising caution with respect to religious involvement in the public square."[136]

With respect to corporate conscience, the concern is that religiously motivated conscience will be treated with more suspicion than other motives. For example, I wonder what the response would have been if the owners of CVS had said, "we are going to stop selling tobacco products because we are conscientious Mormons or Seventh Day Adventists, and we have health codes that forbid the use of tobacco."[137] Would that be greeted with the same sort of

[129] Young, *supra note* 125, at 5.
[130] *Ibid.* at 4.
[131] *Ibid.* at 5.
[132] *Ibid.* Young uses statements made regarding the Proposition 8 campaign to illustrate that some wish churches not to be in the public square at all; others wish churches to be involved in causes that are universally lauded – donations to Hurricane victims.
[133] *Ibid.*
[134] *Ibid.* at 5–6.
[135] *Ibid.* at 6.
[136] William P. Marshall, *The Other Side of Religion*, 44 HASTINGS L.J. 843, 859 (1993).
[137] The Word of Wisdom is a code of health forbidding tobacco in scripture of The Church of Jesus Christ of Latter-day Saints. See Doctrine and Covenants Section 89. It is unclear whether members of the church would be under any obligation to avoid providing tobacco products in

positive response? Now, continue with me in this thought experiment. Imagine that we lived in a time where the tobacco lobby from the southern states was very powerful and they were worried about other companies following the example of CVS and worried about the implications for the life and well-being of tobacco farmers in the south and they manage to pass a law saying that all stores must sell lawful, legal tobacco products. Stay with me long enough to imagine that we lived in a world where that legislation could pass. Let me ask this, would CVS get an exemption from the legislature? I think they might, based upon the health reasons that they just gave. But would a religiously motivated employer be given an exemption? I think the answer is much more likely to be, no. I think it's strange that we would be so open minded to claims of conscience of one sort but so close minded to claims of conscience of the other sort.

D. Exemptions, rather than vindication of freedom

A fourth cause of our confusion about corporate conscience comes from our deeply ingrained habit of thinking about vindicating religious freedom as a matter of granting an exemption. Our free exercise jurisprudence is distorted by thinking primarily in terms of exemptions. When businesses such as Apple are permitted to forgo profits to pursue green energy initiatives, when Coca Cola diverts profits to protecting Polar Bears, when Patagonia is mindful of geese, or when Ben and Jerry's utilizes higher-priced suppliers, we do not think we are granting them an exemption.

But when Hobby Lobby seeks to vindicate its conscience, not only does the legal and political system refuse to accommodate them through legislation or regulation, Courts treat their claims as a request for a special exemption or exception to a general rule. We allow exceptions frequently. All of these companies are taking advantage of exceptions to the rule that corporations should maximize shareholder profit. But we don't even think of this as an exception. But when a religious accommodation is sought, this is characterized completely differently. It is an extraordinary request. It is styled as a desire to evade the law. It is styled as discrimination.

In our modern way of thinking, claims of conscience are usually viewed as providing a conflict between equality and freedom. Some rule, such as a

the way I describe. On the one hand, the Word of Wisdom is only a sin for those under covenant to keep the commandments. On the other hand, some leaders of the Church teach that church members should avoid selling products with serious societal consequences, such as alcohol or pornography. See Lynn G. Robbins, *Making a Living and a Life*, BYU-IDAHO SPEECHES, available at www2.byui.edu/Presentations/Transcripts/Devotionals/2010_10_12_Robbins.htm, noting that a grocer might sell coffee and tea in good conscience, but that "[s]ome products and services may be detrimental to the individual while others damage the community. Coffee and tea, for example, would be products that have individual consequences. Alcohol and pornography, however, have proven to also have community consequences."

draft of all able-bodied men, is applied in a general and neutral way (that is the equality dimension), and those opposed to military service on religious or other conscientious grounds claim that they should be exempted (or free) from the requirement.

The usual view of an accommodation of conscience is that it involves granting an *exception* to a rule that would otherwise apply equally to everyone. Freedom to follow one's conscience is viewed as a compromise of a general rule that ideally should be applied in an evenhanded manner. Viewing an accommodation this way has hardened into habit.[138] An accommodation of religion is almost always styled as an exemption or exception to a general rule.[139] We think of accommodations of religious conscience as involving special claims for an exception to a rule that is general in its applicability and that otherwise treats everyone equally. Thus, for example, when we grant a conscientious objector an exemption to military service, we view this as a special dispensation.[140] An accommodation involves a compromise of a general principle, an adaptation to a special request, an adjustment to unusual needs or sensitivities.

This same way of thinking is reflected in contexts other than military service. We speak of "exemptions" for requirements to participate in patriotic observances such as reciting the Pledge of Allegiance in school.[141] Jewish servicemen in the Air Force are granted an exemption from the uniform policy forbidding non-regulation headgear.[142] A medical resident who opposes participating in performing an abortion is (sometimes, but only sometimes) given an exception.[143]

[138] See, e.g., Kent Greenawalt, *Establishment Clause Limits on Free Exercise Accommodations*, 110 W. VA. L. REV. 343 (2007).

[139] The White House, Fact Sheet: *Women's Preventive Services and Religious Institutions*, www.whitehouse.gov/the-press-office/2012/02/10/fact-sheet-women-s-preventive-services-and-religious-institutions. The original HHS mandate exception "accommodates religious liberty;" See generally Robin Fretwell Wilson, *The Calculus of Accommodation: Contraception, Abortion, Same-Sex Marriage, and Other Clashes Between Religion and the State*, 53 B.C. L. Rev. 1417 (2012), characterizing a variety of exemptions as "accommodations."

[140] *United States* v. *Seeger*, 380 U.S. 163, 175 (1965). "Congress ... set about providing an exemption from armed service."

[141] For a 50-state survey of such laws and their exceptions, see FIRST AMENDMENT CENTER, "Pledge of Allegiance statutes, state by state." www.firstamendmentcenter.org/pledge-of-allegiance-statutes-state-by-state.

[142] 10 U.S.C. § 774 (2012).

[143] See Eric Schulze, *Pro-life Health Professionals in Conflict Between Conscience and Career* DESERET NEWS NATIONAL EDITION, (March 17, 2012), www.deseretnews.com/article/765560407/Abortion-creates-conflict-for-pro-life-medical-workers.html?pg=all, noting both "the Accreditation Council for Graduate Medical Education (ACGME) ruled in 1995 that, with limited exceptions, OB/GYN residency programs must include abortion training or lose accreditation" and that "Vanderbilt University's nursing program began requiring program applicants to pledge that they would participate in abortions," but abandoned that following threats of legal action.

But "exceptions" are commonplace in the law. Indeed they are an ordinary feature of sensitive laws that take account of differences. Minimum wage laws contain exceptions;[144] tax laws contain exceptions;[145] criminal laws contain exceptions.[146] But for some reason, when an exception is made for religion, this is treated as a special sort of problem, when in reality making exceptions is part of the ordinary process of designing rules that are properly nuanced and take account of contextual factors.

IV. CONCLUSION

A. Pluralism

We should celebrate CVS, Apple, Coca Cola, Patagonia and The Body Shop and Ben and Jerry's for their commitment to conscience and to thinking beyond the bottom line. It is not important that we agree with all of the causes pursued by these companies, or that their causes are equally valuable in our eyes.

But we should celebrate, not condemn, Hobby Lobby as well. Their rights of conscience are burdened when they are subject to the powerful state that seeks to compel them to act in ways that violate their deeply held religious beliefs. The burden to religion is obvious. The correct question is whether (1) the government has a compelling state interest in coercing Hobby Lobby and the Greens to obey the law in spite of their religious objections, and (2) whether there is a less restrictive means of accomplishing that end.

B. Monolithic secularism

What does it mean to live in an increasingly secular state? I believe there is a titanic struggle being waged over what a secular state should look like, and what its attitude towards religion, and claims of conscience more broadly, should be.

144 See Fair Labor Standards Act Advisor, *Exceptions*, United States Department of Labor, www.dol.gov/elaws/esa/flsa/screen75.asp. "Some employees are exempt from the overtime pay provisions, some from both the minimum wage and overtime pay provisions and some from the child labor provisions of the Fair Labor Standards Act (FLSA)."; *ibid.*, exempting "Babysitters on a casual basis," "Companions for the elderly," "Federal criminal investigators," "Homeworkers making wreaths," "Newspaper delivery[persons]," "Newspaper employees of limited circulation newspapers," and "Switchboard operators."

145 Tax exemptions go under many names, e.g., "credits" and "deductions." See generally Internal Revenue Service, Form 1040 (2013), available at www.irs.gov/pub/irs-pdf/f1040.pdf, giving tax exemptions such as the "child tax credit," "residential energy credits," "retirement savings contribution credit," "American opportunity credit," "standard deduction [depending on number of dependents]," "credit for federal tax on fuels," "educator expenses," "moving expenses," "IRA deductions," "domestic production activities deduction."

146 See, e.g., Martin D. Schwartz, *The Spousal Exception for Criminal Rape Prosecution*, 7 *Vt. L. Rev.* 33 (1982).

It is somewhat of an oversimplification, but two general attitudes can be identified – what is often called "secularity" and "secularism." Both secularity and secularism are linked to the general historical process of secularization, but as I use the terms, they have significantly different meanings and practical implications.[147]

[147] The distinction, of course, is not original to me. For other discussions of the difference between secularity and secularism see, e.g., Fr. Evaldo Xavier Gomes, *Church-State Relations from a Catholic Perspective: General Consideration on Nicolas Sarkozy's new Concept of Laïcité Positive*, 48 J. CATH. LEGAL STUD. (2009), p. 201, setting forth a Catholic perspective on the distinction between secularity and secularism, in which secularity is "one of the attributes of the state in the eyes of the Church" and secularism is "characterized by a negative conception of separation between Church and state, in which the Church is persecuted or denied basic rights." Gomez goes on to say, "[a]ccording to the Catholic conception, secularity is understood as a healthy cooperation between Church and state. In this sense, the Church and state are not opposed to each other; both are in the service of human beings, so between them there must be dialogue, cooperation, and solidarity." *Ibid.* at 211. Le-ann Thio, *Constitutional Accommodation of the Rights of Ethnic and Religious Minorities in Plural Democracies: Lessons and Cautionary Tales From South-East Asia*, 22 PACE INT'L L. REV. 43, addressing accommodation of racial and religious minorities in society and asserting that "attention needs to be paid both to constitutional and non-constitutional solutions, to ensure the protection of the identity and culture of minorities," and warning that "[f]orcible assimilation and repressive measures against minority groups, utilizing the 'tools of coercion' ... will only exacerbate conflict and thwart the forging of a durable peace."

Thio, in discussing the challenges of fostering a national identity among minority groups and tribes offers secularity as a helpful solution but rejects secularism as problematic, using Islamic revivalism and demands for legal systems based on Sharia as an example: "Secularism itself as a constitutional principle is a useful ordering device for state-religion relations insofar as it does not adopt the form of a substantive, anti-theistic ideology which is hostile towards religious belief. Rather than descend into a form of secular fundamentalism, the principle of secularity operates as a framework under which disparate religious groups may peacefully co-exist. This requires that religious (and non-religious) groups are treated equally under the law, that is, the state is to adopt a neutral posture towards religious groups." *Ibid.* at 73–74. See also András Sajó, *Preliminaries to a concept of Constitutional Secularism*, 6 INT'L J. CONST. L. (2008), 605, advocating a "robust notion of secularism" characterized by a "duty of public reason giving in law" that "denies the acceptability of divine reasons" and "precludes any source of law but the secular" to combat what he calls "strong religion," which aspires "to control or reclaim the public square." Sajó's definition of the term "secularism" as "legal arrangements that [do] not follow considerations based on the transcendental or the sacred" may be closer to what I mean by 'secularity' than 'secularism'. As Sajó uses the term, 'secularism' takes no specific position regarding religion, but rather focuses on the concept of public reason, the idea that in politics and law reasons should be translated, or at least translatable into public reason, reasons that are accessible to all citizens. As is often the case, the devil is in the definitions. *Ibid.* at 607–08. He acknowledges that "secularism is a somewhat unfortunate term for use in constitutional theory" because as a term it is "overloaded," referring to different although related concepts in different languages and in different academic disciplines. *Ibid.* at 608. See also András Sajó, *Constitutionalism and Secularism: The Need for Public Reason*, 30 *Cardozo L. Rev.* (2009); Lorenzo Zucca, *The Crisis of the Secular State – A Reply to Professor Sajó*, 7 INT'L J. CONST. L. (2009); András Sajó, *The Crisis That Was Not There: Notes on a Reply*, 7 INT'L J. CONST. L. (2009). An early formulation of this distinction is found in DAVID MARTIN, NOTES TOWARDS A GENERAL THEORY OF SECULARIZATION (1969), revised as ON SECULARIZATION: TOWARDS A REVISED GENERAL THEORY (2005), at 85 et seq. (distinguishing "secularity" from "principled secularism").

By "secularity" I mean an approach to religion–state relations that avoids identification of the state with any particular religion or ideology (including secularism itself) and that endeavors to provide a neutral framework capable of accommodating a broad range of religions and beliefs.[148] By "secularism," in contrast, I mean an ideological position that is committed to promoting a secular order.[149]

Secularity is a more modest concept, committed to creating what might be called a broad realm of "constitutional space"[150] in which competing conceptions of the good (some religious, some not) may be worked out in theory and lived in practice by their proponents, adherents, and critics. Secularism, in contrast, is itself a positive ideology that the state may be committed to promoting, an ideology that may manifest itself as opposition to religiously based or religiously motivated reasons by political actors. This ideology may also be manifest in hostility to religion in public life, and an insistence that religious manifestations, reasons, or even beliefs be relegated to an ever-shrinking sphere of private life. From this ideology, you even see an aggressive proselytizing atheism, or what has been called "secular fundamentalism."[151]

In most modern liberal democratic legal systems, there are proponents of both secularity and secularism. Constitutional and other legal texts addressing religion–state issues can often be interpreted as supporting one or the other of these views and, in fact, some of the key debates involving freedom of religion and belief turn on the difference between these two approaches. Historically, French *laïcité* is closer to secularism, while American separationism is closer to secularity. But there are debates in both societies about how strictly secular the state (and more broadly, the public realm) should be. This tension between two conceptions of the secular runs through much of religion–state theory in contemporary settings.

C. George Washington on accommodation

One way of framing the issue is about how we will think about religious accommodations. I have noted that we tend to think of them as exemptions to

[148] See Brett G. Scharffs, *Four Views of the Citadel: The Consequential Distinctions between Secularity and Secularism*, 6 *Religion and Human Rights* 109, 110 (2011). See also *ibid.* at 109 (calling "secularity" a "fundamental component of liberal pluralism and a bastion against religious extremism").

[149] *Ibid.* at 110. See also *ibid.* at 109, calling secularism "a misguided, even dangerous ideology that may degenerate into its own dystopian fundamentalism."

[150] I would like to thank Carolyn Evans of Melbourne University School of Law for drawing my attention to the concept of "constitutional space."

[151] See Paul F. Campos, *Secular Fundamentalism*, 94 *Colum. L. Rev.* 1814 (1994), arguing that Rawls's central concept in Political Liberalism of "public reason" is empty, "and that Rawls's analysis of political issues amounts to little more than the shamanistic incantation of the word 'reasonable.'" According to Campos, Rawls employs the concept of "reasonableness" in the same way that "God" is invoked in dogmatic religious argument. *Ibid.* at 1817.

general and neutral rules. We are reluctant to give such exemptions, because we want everyone to be treated equally.

But there is another, much more appealing way of thinking about accommodation. It is suggested by George Washington and his reaction to the Quakers' conscientious objection to military service. Twenty years before the American Revolution, George Washington was commander of all Virginia forces in the French and Indian War. Six Quakers were drafted into the Virginia militia and sent to Winchester to fight with Washington, but they refused to take up arms. Washington was perplexed with this first encounter with Quaker pacifism. After consulting with the British colonial administrator in colonial Virginia, Washington responded in the conventional way: He imprisoned the dissenters, fed them prisoner's rations, and released them when the conflict had passed.[152]

But by the end of the Revolutionary War, Washington had developed a friendly and supportive attitude towards the Quakers in spite of their conscientious objection to military service, their perceived pro-British attitudes, and their perceived troublemaking on the sensitive slavery issue. In a letter to the Annual Meeting of Quakers written in 1789, shortly after being elected President, Washington described Quakers as "exemplary and useful citizens" and maintained that the "conscientious scruples of all men should be treated *with great delicacy and tenderness*."[153]

We tend to think of accommodating religion (including religious conscience) as primarily a matter of making exceptions. But in saying that "conscientious scruples" should be treated with "great delicacy and tenderness" Washington evokes a very different meaning of the word "accommodation."

The genius of Washington's formulation is that an accommodation does not have to be viewed as a regrettable exception or unfortunate compromise. The word has a very different meaning when we provide accommodation, a haven or place of abode, to a traveler or wayfarer.[154] Here, providing accommodation has the connotation of creating a safe place, a place of protection, peacefulness, and rest:[155] a place where a weary traveler can sleep safely, let down their guard, all while being in a position of vulnerability. The traveler may be a stranger or foreigner; their habits and customs may be different. Providing accommodation protects and shelters.[156]

[152] Paul F. Boller, Jr., *George Washington and the Quakers*, in *The Bulletin of Friends Historical Association No.* 2, 49, 69–70 (Autumn 1960).

[153] *Ibid.* at 78, citing Library of Congress, *Papers of George Washington* 52 (No. 333).

[154] See *Merriam Webster's Collegiate Dictionary*, 11th Ed. (2003) 8, citing accommodation first as "something supplied for convenience, or to satisfy a need as (a) lodging, food and services or traveling space and related services." Another definition points to it as a "reconciliation of differences," a stark contrast to an "exception." *Black's Law Dictionary* (9th Ed.) (2004): "a convenience provided by someone, Esp. lodging and food."

[155] See *Ibid.* A "Public Accommodation" such as a hotel is something accessible to all, not an "exception" for few.

[156] *Webster's*, see note 154.

Contrast what we might call an ethic of rights (where an accommodation is an exception or exemption) with an ethic of hospitality (where an accommodation is a safe place of shelter and refuge).[157] The stranger or minority seeking accommodation is in a very real way asking us whether there is room for them in our inn.

These two different senses of accommodation suggest a very different underlying attitude, or even theoretical justification, for accommodation. The first approach – viewing an accommodation as an exception or a compromise – reflects a rights-based attitude. The second approach – viewing providing accommodation as providing a safe place of protection – reflects a hospitality-based attitude.

In another letter written at the time of his election as president, Washington wrote to a Jewish congregation in Newport, Rhode Island. This letter has been described as "his most beautifully enduring statement on religious toleration, showing that he had no notion of foisting a Christian state on the nation."[158]

Wrote Washington:

> All possess alike liberty of conscience and immunities of citizenship. It is now no more that toleration is spoken of, as if it was by the indulgence of one class of people that another enjoyed the exercise of their inherent natural rights. For happily the government of the United States, which gives to bigotry no sanction, to persecution no assistance, requires only that they who live under its protection should demean themselves as good citizens.[159]

In his public statements, Washington occasionally invoked or quoted scripture. The passage most frequently cited by Washington is from the Hebrew Bible book of Micah.[160] In his letter to the Jewish congregation in Newport, Washington writes, invoking Micah 4:4: "Every one shall sit in safety under his vine and fig tree and there shall be none to make him afraid."[161]

Notice again the ethic of hospitality, rather than an ethic of rights. The purpose of protecting religious freedom is not just a matter of vindicating rights, it is to allow every person to have a safe place, a place to rest in the shade and nourishment of his own vine and fig tree, to live without fear.

157 For a sample of the literature on this, see Getrud Nunner-Winkler, *Two Moralities? A critical discussion of an Ethic of Care and an Ethic of Responsibility*, in AN ETHIC OF CARE. FEMINIST AND INTERDISCIPLINARY PERSPECTIVES (Mary Jeanne Larrabee ed., 1992).

158 RON CHENROW, WASHINGTON: A LIFE 632 (2010).

159 *Washington's Letter to the Hebrew Congregation*. Available in full form at *The Papers of George Washington*, 6 presidential series, July–November 1790, at 284 (Mark A. Mastromarino ed., 1996); see also RON CHENROW, WASHINGTON: A LIFE 632 (2010).

160 The address to the Hebrew Congregation at Newport "concludes utilizing the President's most often quoted verse of Scripture. (Washington quotes from the Bible with more frequency than is generally recognized)." PETER R. HENRIQUES, REALISTIC VISIONARY: A PORTRAIT OF GEORGE WASHINGTON (2006), 185.

161 "Letter to the Hebrew Congregation," in *Papers*, 284.

Washington often cited the broader passage in Micah 4:1–4, which speaks of many nations going to the house of the Lord established in the top of the mountains. Micah speaks of a time when swords will be beaten into plowshares, and spears into pruning hooks: "nation shall not lift up a sword against nation, neither shall they learn war any more." Then in Micah 4:4, it says: "But they shall sit every man under his vine and under his fig tree; and none shall make them afraid: for the mouth of the Lord of hosts hath spoken it." Thus, Washington's statement about treating claims of conscience with great delicacy and tenderness should be read within the broader context of Micah's vision of the last days. Washington, like others, saw the American experiment as a step in the fulfillment of Micah's prophecy.[162]

I don't want to make Washington out as a deep religious thinker; in truth, he was a deeply practical man, and did not consider himself to be a theoretician or intellectual. Indeed, a little handbook of maxims called *The Rules of Civility* has been cited as one of the three most important books that Washington tried to live by.[163] The final maxim in that book is, "Labour to keep alive in your Breast that Little Spark of Celestial fire Called Conscience."[164] I think it is safe to say that creating space for human beings to respond and live true to their conscience was one of Washington's most important guiding principles.

For Washington, religious freedom was one of the leading accomplishments of the American Revolution. In a letter to George Mason he wrote, "No man's sentiment are more opposed to any kind of restraint upon religious principles than mine are."[165] He cautioned his soldiers, "While we are contending for our own Liberty, we should be very cautious of violating the Rights of Conscience in others, even considering that God alone is the Judge of the Hearts of Men, and to him only in this Case, they are answerable."[166]

[162] See generally Daniel L. Dreisbach, *The 'Vine and Fig Tree' in George Washington's Letters: Reflections on a Biblical Motif in the Literature of the American Founding Era*, 299 *Anglican and Episcopal History* 76, no.3 (September 2007).

[163] Henriques, Realistic Visionary, at 181.

[164] *Ibid.*

[165] Quoted in Henriques, Realistic Visionary, at 184; see also Founders Online, National Archives, *From George Washington to George Mason* (October 3, 1785), http://founders.archives.gov/documents/Washington/04-03-02-0260.

Henriques says: "During the debate over ratifying the Constitution, Baptists were concerned that the separation of state and church might be compromised. Washington made his position crystal clear: 'If I could have entertained the slightest apprehension that the Constitution framed in the convention, where I had the honor to preside, might possible endanger the religious rights of any religious society, certainly I would never have placed my signature to it; and, if I could now conceive that the general government might ever be administered as to render liberty of conscience insecure, I beg you will be persuaded that no one would be more zealous than myself to establish effectual barriers against the horrors of spiritual tyranny, and every species of religious persecution.' "

Henriques, Realistic Visionary, at 184.

[166] Cited in Henriques, at 185; see also *The Writings of George Washington from the Original Manuscript Sources, 1745–1799*, ed. John C. Fitzpatrick (Washington DC: US Government Print,1931–1944)

Washington's insights have remarkable contemporary salience. Accommodating conscience on Washington's view is not a matter of making an exception to a general and neutral law. Accommodating religion is not a matter of defining the scope of a right as much as it is adopting a mindset of hospitality. As he so beautifully puts it, "the conscientious scruples of all men should be treated with great delicacy and tenderness."

8

Religious freedom in the world today

Roger Scruton

Controversy surrounds the First Amendment to the American Constitution, and will continue for as long as the United States exists. Just what is forbidden and what permitted by the "no establishment" clause? Historically speaking the need for the clause is easy to understand: the Union brought together a great number of communities, most of which adhered to some form of Christian worship, but many of which were adamant that it was their own form, and not the form practiced by their rivals, which was the right one. To attempt to impose a single established church on all the states would have led to the breakdown of the Union. At the federal level, therefore, the Government of the United States was to show no favoritism in religious affairs. That relatively weak interpretation of the 'no establishment' clause is, it seems to me, all that historical hermeneutics authorize. But it is not how the clause is interpreted today by the secularists, who argue that it authorizes a kind of fumigation of all public institutions – including public schools, law-courts, state universities and colleges – in order to extirpate the religious bug. The assumption seems to be that there can be religious *freedom* only where there is an enforced *absence* of religion from the state.

This radical secularist approach leads very quickly to a paradox. If there really is religious freedom, then it ought to be possible for each citizen to conduct his life as his faith requires. But religious people may believe that they are under a duty to bear witness to their faith. Teachers, advisors, and legislators cannot act as though their religious beliefs had no bearing on what they say and do. They can of course endeavor to make room for disagreement, and this at least the 'no establishment' clause requires. But they cannot act as though the voice of religion were silenced as soon as they enter the classroom, the law-court or the debating chamber. To take the secularist path to religious freedom is therefore to oppress religion, not to free it.

When the Founding Fathers, under the influence of James Madison, inserted the 'no establishment' clause into the Constitution, it was not because they wished people to cease acknowledging their religion in public life.[1] The Founders were either Christians or, like Jefferson, fellow-travellers of the Faith, who did not wish Christianity to vanish from the prominent place in public life that it had enjoyed since the first colonial settlements. They were also acutely aware of the religious oppressions of Europe, from which their ancestors had fled to the New World in order to freely practice their faith. The Founders wanted to separate state from church, not to exclude faith from public life. And they wanted free churches, answerable to their congregations and not to law-makers. The Established Church of England was to them repugnant less as an attempt to impose Christianity than as a symbol of royal power and its intrusion into every sphere of social life. Moreover the 'no establishment' clause was meant as a limitation on the powers of *Congress*, and not on the powers of the individual States. The Founders surely did not intend the clause to authorize Congress to intrude on the State of Massachusetts, for example, which at the time had an absolute ban against Roman Catholicism – a ban which the Federal Government made no effort to lift.

Today's radical secularists interpret the 'no establishment' clause in another way entirely. It has been regarded as a violation of the 'no establishment' clause that a court should display the Ten Commandments, or that public schools should begin the day with prayers. As I suggested above, such decisions do not convey a desire to protect religious freedom, so much as a desire to deprive religion of the place that it naturally demands in the public life of a nation whose people remain, in their own understanding at least, firmly within the faith traditions rooted in the Judeo-Christian Bible. Nobody was forcing children to take part in the public prayers at school, or forcing anyone to genuflect before the Ten Commandments in the courtroom. Yet there are currents of opinion in America which not only take offense at school prayers and doctrinal icons, but which believe that it is part of the spirit of democratic freedom to forbid them. Religion, for such people, is not just a private affair: it is something to be *privatised*, to be confined within the home like some habit that, however innocuous in itself, becomes offensive when displayed in public.

But this brings me to what, I think, is the crucial issue posed by religious freedom in the world today, which is the extent to which the religions of the world can actually be reconciled with the secular rule of law and the freedoms, including the freedom of religion, that we take for granted. Christians are under an obligation to bear witness to their faith, but this does not mean inflicting their faith on others or forcibly requiring others to submit to it. As the founder of the Christian faith himself showed, you bear witness not through triumphing over your rivals but through submitting to their judgment. And the Greek

[1] See Seamus Hasson, "Religious Freedom and the American Inheritance," in Roger Scruton, ed., *Liberty and Civilisation: The Western Inheritance* (New York: Encounter Books, 2009).

word used for the concept of witness, so understood – *marturein* – is now used to denote those who have been put to death or tormented for the sake of their faith. The Christian faith, as it understands itself today, does not demand that we silence its critics, or even that we forbid them to practice their faith.

The contrast with Islam is a vivid one. Although the Muslim must also bear witness to his faith, and does so by repeating the *shahadah*, or witness statement, that there is no God but Allah and Muhammad is his prophet, the real *shahîd* or martyr is not just someone who suffers for his faith, but someone who makes a dent in the world of unbelievers, maybe taking as many of them with him into the afterlife as he can. Is it really possible for a religion that sees itself in that way to adjust to the demands of religious freedom?

In order to answer that question we should look again at history, and in particular at the history of Islam. Islamic civilization defines itself in terms not of freedom but of submission. *Islam*, *salm*, and *salaam* – submission, peace, and safety – all derive from the verb *salima*, whose primary meaning is to be secure, unharmed, or blameless, but which has a derived form meaning to surrender. The *muslim* is the one who has surrendered, submitted, and so obtained security. In that complex etymological knot is tied a vision of society and its rewards far different from anything that has prevailed in modern Europe and America.

Western civilization, like Islam, grew from a common religious belief and a sacred text, and, like Islam, originated in a religious movement among Semitic people – though people living (during the critical years) under an imperial yoke, for whom submission was already a day-to-day reality – though submission to a secular government, rather than to a religious creed. Western civilization has left behind its religious belief and its sacred text, to place its trust not in religious certainties but in open discussion, trial and error, and a ubiquitous habit of self-criticism. But the odd thing is that, while Islamic civilization is riven by conflict, Western civilization seems to have a built-in tendency to equilibrium. Freedoms that Western citizens take for granted are all but unheard of in Islamic countries, and while no Western citizens are fleeing from the West, 70% of the world's refugees are Muslims fleeing from places where their religion is the official doctrine. Moreover, those refugees are all fleeing to the West, recognizing no other place as able to grant the opportunities, freedoms, and personal safety that they despair of finding at home.

Equally odd, however, is the fact that, having arrived in the West, many of these Muslim refugees begin to conceive a hatred of the society by which they find themselves surrounded, and to take revenge against it for some fault so heinous that they can conceive of nothing less than final destruction as the fitting punishment. Odder still is the fact that those Muslims who settle down, integrate, and acquire some kind of loyalty to Western institutions and customs often produce children who, despite being brought up in the West, identify themselves in opposition to it – an opposition so fierce as again to verge on the desire for annihilation.

A superficial response to these disturbing facts is to put the blame on Islam – to argue, with an undeniable degree of plausibility – that Islam is a medieval fossil, unadapted to modern conditions, and unable to adjust to the enormous social, economic, and demographic changes that have shaken our planet. But then "modern conditions" are precisely those conditions that result from the global outreach of Western technology, Western institutions, and Western conceptions of political freedom. Why blame Islam for rejecting them, when they, in their turn, involve a rejection of the idea on which Islam is founded – the idea of God's immutable will, revealed once and for all to his Prophet, in the form of an unbreachable and unchangeable code of law?

In *The West and the Rest* I explored the vision of society and political order that lies at the heart of "Western civilization." And I tried to show how the apparent conflict with Islam is fed by the decay of that vision, and the loss of the political loyalty on which it depends. I argued that we should look back to the very beginnings of Western civilization in the Greek city state, in order to understand the deep *spiritual* reality behind the eventual emergence of the secular rule of law.

The action of Sophocles' *Antigone* hinges on the conflict between political order, represented and upheld by Creon, and religious duty, represented in the person of Antigone. The first is public, involving the whole community; the second is private, involving Antigone alone. Hence, the conflict cannot be resolved. Public interest has no bearing on Antigone's decision to bury her dead brother, while the duty laid by divine command on Antigone cannot possibly be a reason for Creon to jeopardize the state.

A similar conflict informs the *Oresteia* of Aeschylus, in which a succession of religious murders, beginning with Agamemnon's ritual sacrifice of his daughter, lead at last to the terrifying persecution of Orestes by the furies. The gods demand the murders; the gods also punish them. Religion binds the house of Atreus, but in dilemmas that it does not resolve. Resolution comes at last only when judgment is handed over to the city, personified in Athena. In the political order, we are led to understand, justice replaces vengeance, and negotiated solutions abolish absolute commands. The message of the *Oresteia* resounds down the centuries of Western civilization: it is through politics, not religion, that peace is secured. Vengeance is mine, saith the Lord; but justice, says the city, is mine.

The Greek tragedians wrote at the beginning of Western civilization. But their world is continuous with our world. Their law is the law of the city, in which political decisions are arrived at by discussion, participation, and dissent. It was in the context of the Greek city-state that political philosophy began, and the great questions of justice, authority, and the constitution are discussed by Plato and Aristotle in terms that are current today.

However, two great institutions intervene between the modern world and its premonition in ancient Greece: Roman law, conceived as a universal jurisdiction, and Christianity, conceived as a universal church. St Paul was a Roman citizen, versed in the law, who shaped the early church through the legal idea of the *universitas* or corporation. The Pauline church was designed, not as a sovereign body, but as a universal citizen, entitled to the protection of the secular and imperial powers but with no claim to displace those powers as the source of legal order. This corresponds to Christ's own vision; in his parable of the tribute money, Caesar's public jurisdiction is tacitly contrasted with the inner authority of religion, governing the person-to-person relationship between the individual and God: "Render therefore unto Caesar the things which are Caesar's; and unto God the things that are God's" (Matthew 22:30). And Christ's vision contrasts radically with the vision set before us in the Koran and the Sunnah, according to which sovereignty rests with God and his Prophet, and legal order is founded in divine command.

The Christian separation of religious and secular authority recalls Aeschylus's solution to the dilemmas thrust upon mortals by the gods. This Christian approach was developed by St Augustine in *The City of God* and endorsed by the fifth-century *Pastoral Rule* of St Gregory, which imposed the duty of civil obedience on the clergy. The fifth-century Pope Gelasius I made the separation of church and state into doctrinal orthodoxy, arguing that God granted "two swords" for earthly government: that of the Church for the government of men's souls, and that of the imperial power for the regulation of temporal affairs. This idea persists in the medieval distinction between *regnum* and *sacerdotium*, and was enshrined in the uneasy coexistence of Emperor and Pope on the two "universal" thrones of medieval Europe. Much wise and subtle argument was expended by medieval thinkers on the distinction between the two sources of authority in human affairs, with the early fourteenth-century thinker Marsilio of Padua expressing what was to become the accepted Western view of the matter in his *Defensor Pacis*. According to Marsilio it is the state and not the church that guarantees the civil peace, and reason, not revelation, to which appeal must be made in all matters of temporal jurisdiction.

Throughout the course of Christian civilization, we find a recognition that conflicts must be resolved and social order maintained by political rather than religious jurisdiction. The separation of church and state was from the beginning an accepted doctrine of the church. Indeed, this separation *created* the church, which emerged from the Dark Ages as a legal subject, with rights, privileges, and a domestic jurisdiction of its own.

No similar institution exists in Islamic countries. There is no legal entity called "The Mosque" to set beside the various Western churches. Nor is there any human institution whose role it is to confer "holy orders" on its members. Those Muslims who have religious authority – the '*ulema*' ("those with knowledge") – possess it directly from God. Islam has never incorporated itself as a legal person or a subject institution, a fact which has had enormous political repercussions. In its original form, Islam aimed at government; it had no interest in creating a subject institution under an independent sovereign power. In short, Islam does not recognize the political as a separate source of authority and law from the religious. Law and authority both come from God, and social order arises from a collective submission to God's will.

Freedom of conscience, as we have understood it in the West, requires secular government. But what makes secular law legitimate? That question is the starting point of Western political philosophy, and is now mired in academic controversy. But, to cut an interminable story indecently short, the consensus among modern thinkers is that the law is made legitimate by the consent of those who must obey it. This consent is shown in two ways: by a real or implied "social contract," whereby each person agrees with every other to the principles of government; and by a political process through which each person participates in the making and enacting of the law. The right and duty of participation is what we mean, or ought to mean, by "citizenship," and the distinction between political and religious communities can be summed up in the view that political communities are composed of citizens, religious communities of subjects – of those who have 'submitted'. And if we want a simple definition of the West as it is today, it would be wise to take the concept of citizenship as our starting point. That is what the millions of migrants are roaming the world in search of: an order that confers security and freedom in exchange for consent.

The problem is, that although that is what people want, it does not make them happy. Something is missing from a life based purely on consent, and on the polite accommodation with your neighbors – something of which Muslims retain a powerful image through the words of the Koran. This missing thing goes by many names: sense, meaning, purpose, faith, submission. People need freedom; but they also need the goal for which they can renounce it. That is the thought contained in the word 'Islam': the willing submission, from which there is no return. But this particular act of submission may mean renouncing not your freedom only, but also the very idea of citizenship. It may involve retreating from the open dialogue on which the secular order depends into "the shade of the Koran," as Sayyid Qutb put it, in a disturbing book that has been an inspiration to the Muslim Brotherhood ever since. Citizenship is precisely not a form of brotherhood, of the kind for which so many Islamists yearn: it is a relation among strangers, a collective apartness, in which all fulfillment and all meaning are confined to the private sphere. To have created this form of renewable loneliness is the great achievement of Western civilization, and of course my way of describing it raises the question whether that achievement is worth defending, and if so how.

My answer is that yes, it is worth defending, but only if we recognize the truth that the present conflict with Islamism makes vivid to us: the truth that citizenship is not enough, and that it will endure only if it is associated with meanings to which the rising generation can attach its hopes and its search for identity. This, it seems to me, is the position that we have reached. The secular rule of law grants freedom of speech and freedom of religion; it upholds the right of opposition and implants discussion, disagreement, and compromise in the heart of the legislative order. Islam, by contrast, is suspicious of those freedoms, and demands submission to a single religious law as its price. In the recent conflict in Egypt, the posters waved by Morsi's supporters from the Muslim Brotherhood did not advocate democracy or human rights; they declared that "all of us are with the shar'iah." They were announcing a religious unity, and an adherence to a religious law, from which a considerable number of Egyptians are excluded, either by their faith or by their adherence to the secular state. This search for unity is contained in the very word "brotherhood" – *ikhwân*. To repeat what seems to me to be the fundamental point: Citizenship is a relation among strangers: it binds people in a web of obligations, in which difference and diversity are part of the deal. Brotherhood is a relation among family members: it binds people in a relation of mutual commitment, in which identity and uniformity are the meaning and the goal.

I don't think we can see the actions of the Boston bombers in any other terms. They had come with their family to the United States in search of that precious thing that their homeland did not provide: citizenship, the participation in a secular form of government which offers no consolation, but only the freedom to seek it. And because they did not find consolation, they decided to reject the surrounding political order and to throw in their lot with a religion that (in their eyes) permitted them to kill and maim those whom it judges to be outside the fold. It is when confronting such examples that the radical secularists of our time seem to have such a powerful case. The natural response is to say that religious freedom is all very well, provided religion is regarded as a private practice, which does not lay down laws for the public sphere, and which yields to the secular law whenever there is a conflict between them. If your religion seeks to override the secular law, or advocates activities that the secular law judges to be criminal, then your religion becomes a threat to the political order. It is not merely that it cannot be adopted as an established religion in America. It is that it is at odds with the very freedom that it exploits.

Does this mean that freedom of religion cannot be extended to Muslims? No, but it does mean that Muslims must renounce important traditional components of their faith, if they are to enjoy the protection of a state which guarantees their freedom. It is a general assumption of secular government in the Western tradition that those who claim a right must also confer it, and that the religious freedoms that Muslims claim in the *Dar al-harb* ought to be acknowledge and conferred in the *Dar al-islam* if our governments are to be placed under an obligation to grant them. This means that the aspiration to live in brotherhood, under the shar'iah, is one that Muslims have to drop, if they wish to enjoy the rights and the privileges of citizenship. For the shar'iah does not permit the secular law to prevail over what it calls the Will of God, nor does it recognize the equal right of all to practice and testify to the faith that guides them. But can Muslims drop the aspiration for the pure life governed by the Will of God alone, and still remain *muslimoun*? For many of them that doesn't make sense.

There is another freedom that comes into play when considering the place of Islam in the modern state, and that is the freedom to criticize. Few assaults on free speech in Western democracies have been as vehement as that now carried out in the name of Islam by its European adherents, who often regard public criticism of their faith as an intolerable offense, and may seek by threats and demonstrations to silence it. In September 2006, Robert Redeker, a French schoolteacher, published an article in *Le Figaro* arguing that Christians, when incited to violence in the name of their religion, can find no authority for this in the life and words of Christ, as recorded in the gospel, while Muslims, incited to violence in the name of *their* religion, can find plenty of support for their passions in the Koran. Although true, this statement was found to be offensive by a section of Muslim opinion, nor did Mr Redeker mince his words.[2] Mr Redeker received credible death-threats against himself and his family, and he and they now live in hiding under police protection. Europeans look with mounting dismay on a creed that they dare not criticize, and which demands more and more space to affirm itself while yielding less and less space to its critics. It is now increasingly rare for public discussion of Islam and its stance to proceed with the open-minded concern for truth that is necessary if the discussion is to get us anywhere. Of course, mockery of another's faith is not guaranteed by freedom of speech – since mockery is a form of abuse. But it is not mockery, only, that Muslims seek to forbid: it is criticism, including the plain assertion of uncomfortable truths, such as those asserted by M. Redeker. Christians by contrast, and Mormons in particular, have to put up not only with endless criticism, often ignorant criticism, of their beliefs, but also ridicule of a kind that is sometimes hard to bear. But Christ's injunction to turn the other cheek has always come to mind in the midst of their persecutions, and on the whole they bow down and acquiesce in the secular order.

Freedom to criticize a religion is not a part of religious freedom; but it is one of the freedoms from which religious freedom grows. If you are allowed to criticize and even to mock Christianity, as many do, but forbidden to mock or criticize Islam, then the two faiths do not compete on equal terms. This does not mean that non-Muslims are losing their religious freedom. But the reluctance of our legislatures to take action against Islamist belligerence – to create the criminal offenses necessary to prevent the intimidation of critics and opponents – is a sign that freedom is gradually slipping down the political agenda, with appeasement taking its place.

It should be clear therefore that the question of religious freedom is not only of great urgency in the world today, but also of great complexity, asking us to clarify just where freedom lies in our scheme of values. I wish to conclude,

[2] See Christian Delacampagne, "The Redeker Affair," *Commentary* (2007) www.commentarymagazine.com/articles/the-redeker-affair/.

therefore, by exploring the conditions that have contributed to the freedom of religion that we have enjoyed in the West, and inquiring as to whether they could be reproduced elsewhere.

Christ, called upon to explain the law and how we must adhere to it, said the following: "Love the Lord thy God with all thy heart, and with all thy mind, and with all thy soul and with all thy strength; and love thy neighbour as thyself. On these two commandments hang all the law and the prophets." In reducing the commandments to these two, he was following a long-standing rabbinical tradition, which we can see at work also in the Torah, notably in the book of Leviticus, and in the teachings of Christ's contemporary, Rabbi Hillel. Christ's statement of the law was to be adopted as orthodoxy by his followers, who therefore saw the old law of prohibitions as a *deduction* from two more fundamental commandments, which do not take the form of prohibitions but of duties, and which enjoin nothing concrete in the world of human affairs. The two duties command us to look on the world with a view to loving what we find, and must be obeyed inwardly before they can be translated into deeds. Exactly what deeds will follow cannot be demonstrated a priori, as Christ went on to show with the parable of the Good Samaritan. Approaching the world in the posture commanded by Christ you are already open to legal innovation. Indeed, the law becomes just one among many instruments whereby we take charge of our lives and attempt to fill our hearts with the love of God, and our world with the love of our neighbor.

The story of the good Samaritan, offered in answer to the question "who is my neighbour?," tells us that "love of neighbour," while a religious duty, does not require the imposition of religious conformity, and is not a form of brotherhood. It is already shaped according to the requirements of citizenship. You love your neighbor by administering to his needs in adversity, regardless of whether he belongs to you through family, faith, or ethnic identity. On this understanding, the laws that govern us do not require the kind of collective submission that the Islamists long for, and the secular order can take charge of the mutual dealings on which we all depend for survival. Religious freedom can exist, within the Christian conception, as a religious duty – a form of respect for the neighbor as someone *other* than me. And I sense that there is a deep point to be made here, concerning the nature of Christianity. The Christian religion involves a recognition of the Other, as other than me, and for this reason has been able to adapt to the world of politics, the goal of which is to create a community of people who acknowledge each other as other, and consent nevertheless to be governed by a single system of law.

It seems to me, therefore, that religious freedom, as we have enjoyed it, is itself a legacy of the religions that have enjoyed precedence in the Western world – the Judaeo-Christian faiths for which the stranger and the brother have an equal claim. When those faiths decline, as they have been declining during our times, there remains only the shell of the political order that grew from them. And people hunger for the spiritual life which that shell protected. It seems to me that Christianity provided that life; Islam cannot, in its present form, provide it, since it presses against the shell of secular law, and threatens always to replace it with another kind of law entirely – a law directed *against* the otherness of others, rather than a law designed to protect them.

9

The first of all freedoms is liberty of conscience

Michael Novak

INTRODUCTION

Liberty of conscience, and particularly religious liberty, is called the first liberty because all other human rights reach the level of inalienability from it. At least that is the way in which Thomas Jefferson, James Madison, John Adams, Benjamin Franklin, and other founders argued for natural rights. The reasoning of the founders about natural rights began with their grasp of our self-evident *duty of gratitude to and worship of* a Power infinitely greater than ourselves. If we have so primordial a *duty*, we must have a *right* to fulfill it. In fulfilling this right, no earthly power dare interfere. Humans have a natural right to fulfill this most primary of all duties. Furthermore, no one else can perform our duties to the Creator for us. Our duty and our right to fulfill it are inalienable. So too with all other natural rights.

The crux of the original American argument for religious liberty is found in three documents of the founding period: the Virginia Declaration of Rights (1776), the Virginia Bill for Establishing Religious Freedom (enacted in 1786), and James Madison's Memorial and Remonstrance against Religious Assessments (1785).

The Virginia Declaration of Rights defines religion as "the duty which we owe to our Creator, and the manner of discharging it." This was the definition used throughout the founding period, codified in Webster's dictionary in 1828. This definition was held to be self-evident. For anyone who understands herself as a creature, it is self-evident that she owes her Creator at least gratitude; and then, upon contemplating the immensity of his creation, the worship due to a being of a higher, indeed altogether other, order. Furthermore, this duty "can be directed only by reason and conviction, not by force or violence."

Thomas Jefferson adds two further notes to this conception. The first is this: "Almighty God hath created the mind free, and manifested his Supreme will that free it shall remain." And second, human persons exercise this freedom, not by caprice, but only by a personal understanding and reasoned grasp of the facts presented to them. As the opening line of the Bill notes: "the opinions and belief of men depend not on their own will, but follow involuntarily the evidence proposed to their minds."

As James Madison makes clear in his Remonstrance, the right to fulfill one's duty of gratitude and worship is not only self-evident, but "inalienable," and in two senses. First, it is inalienable because this duty "must be left to the conviction and conscience of every man." For "the opinions of men, depending only on the evidence contemplated by their own minds, cannot follow the dictates of other men." Thus, this duty inheres singly in each person, and cannot be shucked off onto any other, not mother nor father nor other loved one, nor any other human being whatsoever. It is inescapably a personal responsibility.

Second, it is inalienable precisely insofar as it is a duty written into human nature, prior to the conventions and obligations of civil society. Madison writes: "This duty is precedent, both in order of time and in degree of obligation, to the claims of Civil Society. Before any man can be considered as a member of Civil Society, he must be considered as a subject of the Governour of the Universe." This duty to God cannot be interfered with by any lesser authority. Even to attempt to do so would be an abuse both of the Creator and of the individual.

To summarize, our natural rights are properties of our very human nature. For our nature is transcendent, and surpasses all other things of creation. "By its liberty, the human person transcends the stars and all the world of nature" (Jacques Maritain). In this important way, among all creatures the human person is most like God. In his essay *Common Sense*, Thomas Paine appeals to this reality in his argument for revolution:

> The cause of America is in a great measure the cause of all mankind. Where, say some, is the king of America? I'll tell you, friend, He reigns above ... The Almighty implanted in us these inextinguishable feelings for good and wise purposes. They are the guardians of His image in our heart. They distinguish us from the herd of common animals.

Our nature is to be conscious, and on the basis of that experience, to gain insight into the sources of our palpable differences from every other created reality around us. We experience the "light bulb" of new insights (as when we at last see the answer to an algebra problem or catch the point of a joke), we reflect, we judge which insights are true, we decide, we choose whether to act and how. Our ability to choose gives us the power either to make ourselves into the highest developed creatures our consciousness longs for us to become, or to turn aside in a stunted, self-destructive direction. We direct our own future, for good or evil.

Our dignity means that we are responsible for what we make of ourselves, in the circumstances where we find ourselves. In this responsibility, we create who we are becoming. In this creativity, we are (remotely) like God. In this respect, we are made in the image of God, as no other animal in this cosmos is. No other animal has so high a responsibility.

BACKGROUND BELIEFS

In order to grasp the vision of the universe in which our philosophy of natural rights was born, and gain a working idea of own human nature as our founders knew it, which fitted us for development into full human persons, we need to become clear about several intellectual preconditions.

First, there is the belief that humans are created by an Intelligence of infinite power and understanding. Everything that exists in the universe springs from one unified Understanding, who grasps and has total insight into every creature it has made. In other words, there is one Logos, one Understanding, in whom and by whom and through whom everything that is has been formed.

In turn, everything that we encounter in the universe, whether by sense, or imagination, or insight, or judgment based upon compelling evidence, is infused with one luminous intelligence. In that luminosity, truth and evidence are decisive.

In that luminosity, civilization is possible. For we humans, who do not see all the truth about everything, and who see any evidence only partially, can nonetheless reason together with our fellows about the many parts of the truth each of us does not yet understand. Those who do grasp a little more can present portions of the evidence that others do not yet share. Through such mutually instructive conversations, civilization advances. More and more minds are bathed in the light of evidence-based knowledge.

Only if this light is operating in the world is reasoned conversation possible. Civilization is constituted by such conversation. Civilized persons reason together. Barbarians club one another into submission.

Here an important note: "Evidence" is not supplied by sense experience alone. Beyond this bare data, we learn how to distinguish civilized discourse from barbaric communication by three steps. First, we learn rules of inquiry, insight, and evidence, although often these rules just come naturally. Second, experience teaches us the checks upon each of these rules that correct and guide the process of reaching true understanding. For example, we are not in the best position, or we do not have enough requisite experience, or we are not now taking account of some factor that distorts sense experience – for example, the bending of an oar in water. We learn through a kind of self-knowledge, indirect and, as it were, self-reflective and self-aware – a knowledge which helps us to avoid frequently encountered sources of error. And this self-knowledge is experienced by the self as more than sense experience. Our modes of intellectual perception and understanding are not reducible only to sense experience, for they depend upon reflection and self-correction.

In other words, although it appears that all knowledge *begins* in our senses, it seems equally evident that it depends on other inputs, too. It depends, for instance, on the self-awareness that assures us that we are in the proper frame of mind for making dispassionate and disinterested judgments, faithful solely to evidence as it is, not as we might wish it to be. This awareness requires more than sense experience; it requires, for instance, honest self-knowledge and common sense (that is, reflective awareness corrected by much experience).

John Adams, our second president, wrote that the world is more indebted to the Hebrews than to any other people for the possibility of civilized discourse. The Hebrews introduced the insight that all created things are in principle understandable by humans who seek truth in the light of evidence, not merely in the shape of their own desires. For all created things are infused with intelligibility insofar as they have been created by One who understands what He created. All of creation, in all its details, is luminous to the Creator's understanding. They all have intelligibility infused into them.

And to humans it is permissible – no, it is commanded – that they use the best efforts of their minds to come to understand the whole world around them and within them. Out of the human impulse to grasp intelligible reality comes the notion of the pursuit and progress of human understanding, the pursuit of science, and even growth in common sense and more acute human sensitivities in interpersonal relations.

Thus, it is no accident that the pursuit of science as a good in itself, for its own sake, became so cherished a vocation in all the peoples instructed by Judaism and Christianity. In this pursuit of science, many women and men chose for themselves a life of discipline and asceticism, denying themselves many creature comforts in order to pursue their rigorous inquiries and to invent new investigative techniques. All were assured that the truth about things was worth pursuing, because it had first inflamed the mind of the Creator of all things. (In more recent times, of course, many have thought they can do all this without reference to a Creator. But, then, more recent secularists were not the founding fathers, who thought differently.)

More than that, according to the Jewish and Christian meta-narrative, the Creator not only thoroughly understood all the things He has made, but also found his Creation "good," and loved it. The Creator is not finally hostile to his creatures or his creation. In fact, to humans in particular, made in his likeness with self-awareness, inquiry, insight, and judgment, this God offered his friendship. But he offered freely, leaving humans to decide for themselves whether to accept his friendship or not. For friendship must be free; it cannot be coerced, for then it is not friendship but a form of slavery. *If friendship, then liberty*, as William Penn of Pennsylvania put it.

Civilization, in the Jewish and Christian meta-narrative, has as its preconditions the twin founding habits of rational inquiry and desiring will, of reflection and choice. A passage from the very first paragraph of *The Federalist* highlights this dynamic: "It has been frequently remarked that it seems to have been reserved to the people of this country, by their conduct and example, to decide the important question, whether societies of men are really capable or not of establishing good government from reflection and choice."

The destiny for which humans have been formed by the Creator since the beginning of time took a large (but not final) step forward in the founding of a system of republican government: a government formed through reflection and choice, and best likely to survive through the same. Unchecked desire, submission, and accordingly another relapse into serfdom and dependency are sure ways to destroy a republic, and with it, its habits of personal responsibility and independence.

THE FRAGILITY OF LIBERTY

For a whole people to cherish responsibility for their own self-governance, and over a long time is a rare occurrence in the history of the world until now. Not enough time has elapsed since 1776 to prove that our form of government can long survive the hazards and dangers of historical trial. That is why the American founders spoke of their republic as an experiment, the testing of a proposition. Even four score and seven years after the Declaration of Independence, Lincoln described this nation at Gettysburg (1863) as still "testing whether this nation, or any nation so conceived and so dedicated, can long endure."

An experiment based upon the strength of the human commitment to personal responsibility is the most fragile of all ventures. If but one generation gives up the struggle for self-mastery because of its arduous demands, turn out the lights.

The testimony of great human thinkers to the fragility of liberty draws its perennial force from clear-eyed observation: *Everywhere people say they want liberty – give it to them. Out of terror at its rigors, in fifteen minutes they start giving it back* (paraphrase of a passage in Dostoevsky). Try this in class: Tell a class they are responsible for writing their own exam. Almost immediately they will want to know what the instructor is testing them on, what the requirements of passing the test are, how they should study. Most persons follow guides. Few self-direct and lead.

The terrors of liberty are quite frightening – at least to those who know their own weaknesses. Yet religious liberty also brings to bear important supports for the mind and will of free persons, supports valid also in dark times.

FIVE STRENGTHS RELIGIOUS LIBERTY ADDS TO A REPUBLIC

As an experiment in liberty, a republic is in a far better position to survive and to flourish if it is the beneficiary of certain advantages exclusively communicated by the free exercise of religion, a number of which were cataloged by Alexis de Tocqueville in 1835.

First, faith corrects morals and manners. As an ill-fated bill in the Virginia Assembly put it in 1784, "The general diffusion of Christian knowledge hath a tendency to correct the morals of men, restraining their vices, and preserve the peace of society." Although Americans are bold and enterprising in making their fortunes, Tocqueville wrote:

> American revolutionaries are obliged ostensibly to profess a certain respect for Christian morality and equity; and that does not allow them easily to break the laws when those are opposed to the executions of their designs; nor would they find it easy to surmount the scruples of their partisans even if they were able to get over their own. Up till now no one in the United States has dared to profess the maxim that everything is allowed in the interests of society, an impious maxim apparently invented ... to legitimatize every future tyrant.[1]

Thus, while in a free society "the law allows the American people to do everything, there are things which religion prevents them from imagining and forbids men to dare" – such as breaking the laws. When consciences are active, policemen needn't be numerous. Citizens are law-abiding willingly. Colonial Americans had already experienced long periods of decline in religion, accompanied by a steady moral decline. They had also seen religious awakenings lead to tangible social peace. That was why they all believed that religion "is necessary for the maintenance of republican institutions. That is not the view of one class or party among the citizens, but of the whole nation; it is found in all ranks."

Second, Tocqueville noted: "Fixed ideas about God and human nature are indispensable to men for the conduct of daily life, and it is daily life that prevents them from acquiring them." Since daily life keeps most people so busy, these "fixed ideas" are difficult for most to reach. Even great philosophers stumble in trying to come to them. But biblical faith provides to reason practical fixed ideas that only a very few philosophers – and they only uncertainly – can reach for themselves. Thus, sound religion, tested in long experience, gives a culture an immense advantage. For men cannot act without living out general ideas. Clarity of soul prevents enervation and the dissipation of energies. Some ideas, Tocqueville wrote, are a particular boon to free men: ideas rooted in the unity of humankind, duties to neighbor, truth, and honesty, and love for the law of reason. Regarding these essential ideas, the answers that biblical religion gives are "clear, precise, intelligible to the crowd, and very durable."[2]

Third, religion adds to reason indispensable support for the view that every human being is not simply a bundle of pleasures and pains. A human

[1] Tocqueville, *Democracy in America*, Vol. I, Chapter XVII: Principal Causes Maintaining The Democratic Republic—Part II.

[2] Tocqueville, *Democracy in America*, Vol II, Section 1, Chapter V: Of The Manner In Which Religion In The United States Avails Itself Of Democratic Tendencies.

being is not just a higher kind of cow or kitten or other contented domestic animal. Alas, however, "[d]emocracy favors the taste for physical pleasures," Tocqueville wrote. "This taste, if it becomes excessive, soon disposes men to believe that nothing but matter exists. Materialism, in its turn, spurs them on to such delights with mad impetuosity. Such is the vicious circle into which democratic nations are driven. It is good that they see the danger and draw back."

The principle of equality that animates democracies, pulling men downward by the law of entropy, what Lincoln called "the silent artillery of time," will slowly destroy their nobility of soul. It is religion that checks and reverses this process and, more than that, spurs greatness – or so Tocqueville thought. Faith sows its good effects in art and manners as well as in the arena of practical action. Belief in immortality prods humans to aspire upward and in this way grounds their awareness of their own special dignity and natural rights.

Fourth, faith adds to a morality of mere reason an acute sense of acting in the presence of a personal and undeceivable Judge, who sees and knows even actions performed in secret, even willful acts committed solely in one's heart.

Thus, faith adds motives for maintaining high standards and for seeking to do things perfectly even when no one is looking. Faith gives us reasons to paint the bottom of the chair and to clean the unseen corners of a room: godliness entails attention to details that no one but God sees. Whereas morality construed within the bounds of reason alone is, at best, a matter of utilitarian calculation or deontological rules, faith sees moral behavior in terms of relations between two persons – ourselves and the God whose friendship we enjoy, if we choose.

In this vein, Benjamin Franklin chastised his colleagues at the Constitutional Convention for their ingratitude to their beneficent Friend who had assisted them when they were in need:

> In this situation of this Assembly groping as it were in the dark to find political truth, and scarce able to distinguish it when presented to us, how has it happened, Sir, that we have not hitherto once thought of humbly applying to the Father of lights to illuminate our understandings? In the beginning of the contest with G. Britain, when we were sensible of danger we had daily prayer in this room for due divine protection. – Our prayers, Sir, were heard, and they were graciously answered. All of us who were engaged in the struggle must have observed frequent instances of superintending providence in our favor. To that kind providence we owe this happy opportunity of consulting in peace on the means of establishing our future national felicity. And have we now forgotten that powerful friend? Or do we imagine that we no longer need his assistance? I have lived, Sir, a long time, and the longer I live, the more convincing proofs I see of this truth – that God governs in the affairs of men.[3]

Fifth, in America, Tocqueville wrote, religion "reigns supreme in the souls of women, and it is women who shape mores." Faith in America has had a

[3] Benjamin Franklin, Constitutional Convention Address on Prayer, delivered Thursday, June 28, 1787, Philadelphia, PA; accessed at http://www.americanrhetoric.com/speeches/benfranklin.htm.

dramatic effect on mores, especially in the home. "Certainly, of all the countries in the world, America is the one in which the marriage tie is most respected and where the highest and truest conception of conjugal happiness has been conceived." Tocqueville had no doubt that the "great severity of mores which one notices in the United States has its primary origin in beliefs." The comparative laxity of morals in Europe bred mistrust even in the home, and broader ripples of mistrust in the public sphere beyond the home.

> In Europe almost all the disorders of society are born around the domestic hearth and not far from the nuptial bed. It is there that men come to feel scorn for natural ties and legitimate pleasures and develop a taste for disorder, restlessness of spirit, and instability of desires. Shaken by the tumultuous passions which have often troubled his own house, the European finds it hard to submit to the authority of the state's legislators.[4]

When there is no trust in the home, trust in public life is highly improbable. Where there is a lack of self-government at home, self-government in the public sphere has little probability of success. Even if one denies that "[i]n the United States religion influences the laws or political opinions in detail," Tocqueville continued, "it does direct mores, and by regulating domestic life it helps to regulate the state."

In sum, to say nothing of otherworldly benefits, Tocqueville argued that faith adds to reason five worldly strengths: restraint of vice and gains in social peace; fixed, stable, and general ideas about the dynamics of life; a check on the downward bias of the principle of equality and the materialism toward which it gravitates; a new conception of morality as a personal relation with our Creator, and thus a motive for acting well even when no one is looking; and the quiet regulation of mores in marriage and in the home through the high honor paid to the marriage bond. For such things, religious liberty is indispensable.

Reason left to itself can be a pretty poor thing. Indeed, if Jewish and Christian faith did not rank it so high in the order of creation, as the jewel in the Creator's crown, it is doubtful whether reason would enjoy the prestige it has long had in our civilization. Hobbes, Machiavelli, and Hume did not put much confidence in it.

The question is not whether Jewish and Christian faith may be reconciled with reason. The beauty, rather, is this: Jewish and Christian faith tout reason as the human vocation par excellence, and have greatly facilitated its work by nourishing such virtues as honest inquiry, careful deliberation, sound judgment, and social responsibility, which are the preconditions of reason's good functioning. Without the libraries, museums, schools, universities, and schools of dialectic nourished by the synagogue and the church down the ages – without the long, patient work of monks and rabbis, manuscript copiers, inventors, librarians, logicians, and dialecticians – reason in the West today would be only

[4] Tocqueville *Democracy in America*, Volume II, Chapter XVII: Principal Causes Maintaining The Democratic Republic—Part II.

a shadow of itself. And without the vision of radical freedom at the heart of the human project and the powerful claim that the human project is in some way at the heart of the mysteries of the universe, modern science would have lacked the confidence it has had that it can be a progressive, liberating, and ultimately an immense gift to humankind. It might, after all, have become a Frankensteinian monster and source of human destruction.

The human mind has reasons for pride, and Judaism and Christianity have praised it mightily, encouraged its practice, nourished its necessary virtues, warned of false turns it may take. Most scientists today seldom think about how much they owe to the religious devotees who cleared the way for them and imbued our culture with confidence in reason – far beyond what it had then earned on its own merits. Even most ordinary decent people, with good solid moral views, do not always recognize how deeply those fixed principles by which they live and breathe were implanted in our culture by faith. Since our generation is in the process of uprooting and destroying as many of those fixed principles as possible, we (or our children) may yet have reason to learn whether a republic without faith, reduced to internally conflicted reason alone, can long remain free.

THE SPIRIT OF RELIGION AND THE SPIRIT OF LIBERTY

One of Tocqueville's most penetrating passages has touched me deeply ever since I was a young man. This is his passage on the historically novel combination of the spirit of religion and the spirit of freedom. The passage deserves to be read in its entirety but I here content myself with an excerpt:

> I have already said enough to put Anglo-American civilization in its true light. It is the product of two perfectly distinct elements which elsewhere have often been at war with one another but which in America it was somehow possible to incorporate into each other, forming a marvelous combination. I mean the spirit of religion and the spirit of freedom ... Far from harming each other, these two apparently opposed tendencies work in harmony and seem to lend [each other] mutual support.
>
> Religion regards civil liberty as a noble exercise of men's faculties, the world of politics being a sphere intended by the Creator for the free play of intelligence. Religion, being free and powerful within its own sphere and content with the position reserved for it, realized that its sway is all the better established because it relies only on its own powers and rules men's hearts without external support.
>
> Freedom sees religion as the companion of its struggles and triumphs, the cradle of its infancy, and the divine source of its tights. Religion is considered as the guardian of mores, and mores are regarded as the guarantee of the laws and pledge for the maintenance of freedom itself.

What are the implications of these Tocquevillian insights today? Granted, Jewish and Christian faiths did put in place three crucial preconditions of democracy: truth, freedom, and dignity. It is not at all certain that, for most people, secular philosophy supports these preconditions other than pragmatically; nor is it clear that other world religions support these preconditions with equivalent vigor and intellectual clarity.

Enunciated in a little more detail, these three ideas are, first: a strong idea of truth, the idea that is helpfully conceived of as a regulative ideal of our minds, driving our inquiries to weed out all that is bogus, false, and unworthy of reasoned assent. The second idea is a moral conception of human freedom, a morality based on personal responsibility for one's choices in life. Third is the idea human beings are called to a special dignity and nobility among all other animals, and indeed all other creatures, a dignity and nobility that extend both to body and to spirit. (And here we mean by spirit above all the spirited inquiring mind, and the spirited zest to act creatively, bravely, and with full responsibility for how one uses one's own liberty.) These are the three background beliefs that make intelligible both the conception of human rights and the spiritual primacy of human liberty.

Without the regulative ideal of truth, the practice of liberty lapses into license, and self-government decays into self-indulgence. Where truth is no criterion, into its vacuum the self asserts: "What the heart desires, the heart desires." In 1992, the US Supreme Court came very close to endorsing such lawlessness as a fundamental axiom in the *Planned Parenthood* v. *Casey* decision: "At the heart of liberty is the right to define one's own concept of existence, of meaning, of the universe, and of the mystery of human life." That proposition unleashes the destructive logic that right and wrong are whatever we desire them to be. That is a logic which strips the powerless of any defense to hold up against the powerful – not even truth, not even justice. That is a logic of human woe.

From Tocqueville's point of view, the spirit of religion is indispensable to the spirit of liberty; and also the reverse. That was, he noted, without exception the view of the early Americans.

In short, pre-existing duties to our Creator not only undergird the American understanding of inalienable natural rights. These same duties strengthen our motives for carrying out moral duties in daily life. These duties to the Creator undergird not only our natural rights but also our practical, everyday habits of daily living. What has virtually never been explored, however, is how these inviolable duties ground the *inalienable* part of all such rights. That is why I have concentrated my energy on this point. I have tried to lift it from the background, and bring it into the foreground.

CONCLUSION

One more point I want to underline. I believe I am correct in unfolding carefully the underlying argument offered by the founders for the existence and inalienability of human rights, *natural* rights. But it does not follow from that unfolding that all who today accept the existence and inalienability of natural rights must also accept as true the natural theology of Judaism and Christianity. For it is the beauty of the traditional Jewish and Christian conception of the Creator that it recognizes the freedom of every human being to reject it, if so they choose.

At a minimum, though, in intellectual honesty, it does seem to be incumbent upon unbelievers at least to recognize their historical debt to Jewish and Christian culture for bringing full accounts of individual conscience, religious liberty, and the ground of all natural rights to light. One does not have to be a Christian or a Jew to accept the American conclusions about the inalienability of human rights. But one must in intellectual honesty at least recognize the historical matrix in which the necessary ideas came to be born, and the daily practices and supportive institutions that made them operative.

It may be possible to develop other theories of inalienable natural rights. I have not yet met any that I find as adequate and convincing – certainly not those of Hobbes and Locke. The American view rests on realities *prior to* civil society; theirs do not. But all this is a subject for further discussion. Mine today has already run too long.

Index

Lightning Source UK Ltd.
Milton Keynes UK
UKOW02n1029260117
292933UK00001B/4/P